Praise for From Tidewater to the
Shenandoah Valley

From Justin Verlander to Ray Dandridge and Deacon
Phillippe, David Driver and Lacy Lusk have captured the
rich history of baseball in Virginia. A must addition to any
baseball fan's library.

Thom Loverro, Award-winning columnist of The
Washington Times and author of several sports books

It dives into Virginia's rich baseball history from professionals to amateurs. Local fans might find sections on the
Valley Baseball League and the Rockingham County Baseball League — Harrisonburg area staples for decades — of
particular interest.

Shawn Mettlen, Daily News-Record, Harrisonburg

The 360-page paperback, written by David Driver and Lacy
Lusk, wanders all over Virginia for vignettes, profiles, and
nuggets presenting baseball at the high school, college,
summer league, minors, and majors

John O'Connor, Richmond Times-Dispatch

What a great idea. The book is a detailed list of so many snapshots from Virginia's rich and impactful baseball history, with color photos on the front and back covers and inside, as well. There are several chapters on past and present Washington Nationals and Baltimore Orioles, who have ties to Virginia, plus info about high schools and colleges in the metro area .

Dave Facinoli, insidenova.com/Sun Gazette

Driver said he and Lusk interviewed about 200 people for the book, which consists of both original stories and updated stories that they wrote for other publications and then received permission to republish.

Eric Gorton, The Harrisonburg Citizen

Focusing exclusively on the major league talent Virginia has produced also would preclude a broader look at some of the people who have shaped the commonwealth's various minor league and summer collegiate teams and circuits, including the Rockingham County Baseball League, which was founded in 1924.

Scott Allen, The Washington Post

FROM TIDEWATER TO THE SHENANDOAH

Snapshots from Virginia's Rich Baseball Legacy

DAVID DRIVER

LACY LUSK

Copyright © 2022 by David Driver

All rights reserved.

No part of this book may be reproduced in any form or by any electronic or mechanical means, including information storage and retrieval systems, without written permission from the author, except for the use of brief quotations in a book review.

ISBN: 978-1-7333036-2-0 (print)

9780107333036-3-7 (eBook)

Published in conjunction with the Walker Press, Harrisonburg, VA

Cover images, clockwise from top right: Justin Verlander; Ryan Zimmerman (right) and Sean Doolittle; Willie Horton; Ray Heatwole; Julie Croteau

Cover photo credits: Houston Astros, Washington Nationals, Courtesy of Willie Horton, JMU, St. Mary's College of Maryland

Some of the stories were reprinted by permission of The Washington Times, the Richmond alumni magazine, and Daily News-Record, though all of those were revised and updated through July 7, 2022.

 Created with Vellum

(From David)
*To my mother Marilyn, who encouraged me to take a typing class in high school;
to my late father Dan, who made sure his three sons had the opportunity to play
Little League Baseball; to Katie and Dani, who found that their sport is
volleyball--and there is nothing wrong with that.*

(From Lacy)
To Abi, Levi, Mom, and Dad.

Contents

Part VI
Northern Virginia and Back to Richmond

Foreword

It was a pitcher from a tiny town in Southwest Virginia whose name might never be guessed in a trivia showdown who won the first World Series game ever—and against the winningest pitcher in baseball history, Cy Young, no less.

Young won 511 games in his career, but that Thursday afternoon in October 1903 at the long-since-gone Huntington Avenue Baseball Grounds, pitching for the host Boston Americans, he surrendered four runs to Pittsburgh in the first inning of a game the Pirates would win 7-3. The winning pitcher was Deacon Phillippe, who was born in Rural Retreat in 1872, then a town of fewer than 1,000 residents (and even today only about 1,400) off of what is now Interstate 81 about halfway between Roanoke and the Tennessee line and best known for ties to Dr. Charles Pepper, the namesake of the soft drink.

Phillippe, who had won 25 games during the 1903 regular season, would win two more games that World Series, but Boston prevailed to win the championship. To that point, Phillippe had won at least 20 games in all five seasons he had pitched in the majors; he would finish his 13-year career with 189 regular-season victories.

Phillippe is an early part of the rich tradition of baseball in the Commonwealth of Virginia, and it has been a joy over the years as a sports reporter to chronicle bits of the more recent chapters of that history.

Much in this Foreword doesn't involve players and games that we personally covered. That's for the rest of the book. But we wanted to whet your appetite by providing an overview of the state's deep connections to the national pastime.

Fast forward from 1903 to the 2021 World Series, and another pitcher from Virginia, Justin Verlander, played a key role, but mostly for his absence from Houston's rotation due to injury as the Astros fell to Atlanta in six games.

Verlander, who won 21 games and the American League Cy Young Award in 2019 before injuring his right elbow on Opening Day 2020 and sitting out most of two seasons, was born near Richmond and pitched at Old Dominion University. He is the only Virginia native among noted author Joe Posnanski's list of the top 100 players of all time.

Virginia natives have played in a host of World Series over the years, from Fredericksburg-born Al Bumbry with the champion Baltimore Orioles in 1983 to Brandon Lowe, born in Suffolk, with Tampa Bay in 2020 to Virginia Beach native Chris Taylor, a former University of Virginia star who helped lead the Los Angeles Dodgers past those Rays.

There was a Virginia connection to the Braves club that prevailed in 2021: the Double-A pitching coach that year for Atlanta was Dan Meyer, a former hurler at James Madison University who saw action in the majors with the Braves, A's, and Marlins.

And it was Lynchburg native Daniel Hudson, who grew up in

the Tidewater region and went to ODU, who was on the mound when the Washington Nationals clinched the World Series win in Game 7 over the Astros in 2019.

"It's pretty cool how well-represented Virginia is as a whole," Verlander told me during that Series.

Verlander, who threw his third no-hitter in 2019 but lost twice to Washington in the World Series, shared a light moment with now-retired Nationals star Ryan Zimmerman, who grew up in the Tidewater region of Virginia and starred for the University of Virginia, during Game 2. The right-hander hit the turf trying to field a dribbler off the bat of Zimmerman.

"Growing up playing against Zim, he gave me a sly little look the other day after I threw the ball off my shin when he was on at first base, which was pretty funny," Verlander said a few days later. "I remember going all the way back to my ODU days, him and I played golf together. From then to now, a lot has happened in both of our lives, but pretty cool to have our lives interconnect like that and to end up on this stage."

A player who perhaps gives Verlander a run as the best recent Virginia native is former New York Mets third baseman David Wright, who was born in Norfolk. Wright, who finished a 14-year career with 242 home runs, hit one in the 2015 World Series during the Mets' five-game loss to the Kansas City Royals. He was inducted into the Virginia Sports Hall of Fame in 2020.

But the history of baseball in Virginia goes beyond the World Series — or even the Major Leagues.

Five natives of the state have been enshrined in the Baseball Hall of Fame — but four of them never played in the majors because they were Black and had careers that ended before the color barrier fell in 1947.

Richmond-born Ray Dandridge, perhaps the best third baseman of the Negro Leagues, was inducted in 1987.

Leon Day, who was born in Alexandria but was very young

when his family moved to Baltimore, was also a star in the Negro Leagues and was inducted to the Hall in 1995.

Negro League stars Pete Hill and Jud Wilson, both of whom were also managers, are also in the Hall of Fame. Hill was born in Culpeper while Wilson is from Remington in Fauquier County and just north of the Culpeper County line.

The other Virginia-born Hall of Famer, pitcher Eppa Rixey, also born in Culpeper, won 266 games, the most for a lefty in the National League until fellow Hall of Famer Warren Spahn came along. Rixey was elected to the Hall in 1963.

Rixey had the most wins of any Virginia-born pitcher as of the end of the 2021 season, followed by Verlander at 226 and Phillippe. The most homers by a Virginia native through 2021 was Willie Horton, who hit 325. He was born in the Southwest Virginia town of Arno and moved to Detroit with his family at an early age. He helped lead the Tigers to a World Series title in 1968 in a difficult year of riots in the Motor City.

The next Virginia native to make the Hall? That could be Billy Wagner, the former star closer who was born in Marion and went to college at Ferrum. He had 422 saves for several teams in the majors. Just over 50 percent of the baseball writers voting on Hall of Fame selections picked him in 2022, below the needed 75 percent level. He has been the baseball coach at The Miller School near Charlottesville for several years, sending several players to college and the minor leagues.

Some of the great moments in baseball history have Virginia ties, though not always positive. Roger Maris broke Babe Ruth's single-season record for homers in 1961, and his 61st shot came off Boston right-hander Tracy Stallard, who grew up in Southwest Virginia.

When Hank Aaron passed Babe Ruth with his 715th homer in Atlanta on April 8, 1974, the Braves used a pinch-hitter later in the game named Johnny Oates, a former star at Virginia Tech and a product of the Valley League who grew up in Prince George. He would go on to manage Baltimore and Texas, taking three Rangers teams to the postseason.

On Sept. 6, 1995, the night Cal Ripken Jr. played in his 2,131st straight game to pass Lou Gehrig, the starting catcher for the Orioles in Baltimore that night was Chris Hoiles. As a college standout in Michigan, Hoiles played in the summer in the Valley Baseball League for the Harrisonburg Turks.

In 2007, when the San Francisco Giants' Barry Bonds broke the career home run mark set by Aaron, the starting third baseman for the opposing team, the Washington Nationals, was Zimmerman.

The state has also produced a number of first-round draft picks since the MLB draft began in 1965. That includes pitcher Jay Franklin, the second overall pick in 1971, taken by the San Diego Padres out of James Madison High School in Vienna in 1971, and outfielder Michael Tucker, who went to Blue Stone High School in Skipwith and was taken 10th overall by the Royals out of then-Division II and now-Division I Longwood University in 1992. Franklin pitched only three games in the Major Leagues, in the year he was drafted, while Tucker amassed 1,047 hits while playing for seven teams over 12 seasons.

Fairfax High and University of Virginia product Brian Buchanan was taken in the first round of the 1994 draft as a first baseman and outfielder by the New York Yankees and two years later, Seth Greisinger, who went to McLean High and UVA, went sixth overall as a pitcher to the Detroit Tigers. Buchanan was a backup player in the Major Leagues for five seasons, and Greisinger lasted four seasons.

Virginia Tech slugger Franklin Stubbs, a native of North Carolina, went 19th overall to the Dodgers in 1982. Stubbs had a couple of 23-homer years in his 10 Major League seasons, and was part of the Los Angeles team that upset the mighty Oakland Athletics in the 1988 World Series.

Speaking of the Hokies—Reggie Harris turned down a chance to play hoops in Blacksburg when he signed with the Red Sox after

Boston took him in the first round out of Waynesboro High in 1987. He broke into the majors in 1990 with the powerhouse Oakland A's.

Virginia also has a rich tradition on the levels below the Major Leagues. There are several towns and cities across the state that have been minor league affiliates, helping begin the careers of young players who can only dream of making The Show.

There are five cities in the state that are home to affiliates of Major League teams: Triple-A Norfolk (Orioles), Double-A Richmond (Giants) and Single-A Salem (Red Sox), Fredericksburg (Nationals), and Lynchburg (Guardians).

The state, early last century, was even far enough South to be used as a Spring Training site.

Norfolk had the Braves, Richmond was home to the Phillies, Charlottesville entertained the Red Sox, and the current Minnesota franchise, which at one point was the Washington Senators, used Phoebus and Charlottesville.

Virginia is also home to the Valley Baseball League, a former minor league circuit that has a rich history as an NCAA-affiliated wood-bat league. The Strasburg Express was champion of the league in 2021, and this year play began on June 2.

David Eckstein, who played for the Harrisonburg Turks, was the most valuable player of the 2006 World Series as his .364 batting average helped lead the St. Louis Cardinals to victory over Detroit.

The Coastal Plain League has three Virginia teams: the Peninsula Pilots in Hampton, the Martinsville Mustangs, and Tri-City in Colonial Heights.

Neighboring the Valley League is the Rockingham County Baseball League, a summer grassroots league for players with a variety of backgrounds, including high school stars, Division I and III players, and former minor and major leaguers. The New Market Shockers won the RCBL title in 2021, and the 2022 regular season was going down to the wire in late July with several teams in contention for the top spot in the standings.

The RCBL began in 1924, making it the second-oldest continuous baseball league in the country after Major League Baseball. I was fortunate to play a few years in the RCBL in the 1980s with the Clover Hill Bucks, who won the title in 1982 despite employing a poor-hitting third baseman—well, OK, yeah, it was me.

At the college level, there are several Division I programs that have sent players to the majors.

The University of Virginia, under Valley League alum Brian O'Connor, has become a national power with a World Series championship in 2015 and a fifth appearance in 2021. According to published accounts, Virginia played its first college game in 1889, against Richmond College (now the University of Richmond).

But it was James Madison University that was the state's first to appear in the College World Series — in 1983.

The Cavaliers and Virginia Tech were ranked nationally throughout most of the 2022 season while the state had two college outfielders who were projected as first-round draft picks in July as this book went to press.

That would be Gavin Cross of the Hokies and Chase DeLauter, a standout at JMU who saw his 2022 season come to an end with a foot injury in April.

The University of Virginia had produced 58 Major Leaguers as of this spring, according to baseball.reference.com. The Cavaliers are followed by Virginia Tech (22 Major Leaguers), Richmond (18), Virginia Commonwealth University (15), ODU (14), JMU and William and Mary (12), Liberty, and Radford (6), the Virginia Military Institute (4), Norfolk State (2), and Longwood (1).

And it was a memorable college season in Virginia in 2022.

Virginia Tech, ranked No. 2 at one point during regular-season play, hosted a regional while the Cavaliers, Liberty and VCU also made the national event.

Shenandoah University of Winchester has made two trips to the Division III College World Series. The Hornets won the Old

Dominion Athletic Conference title in 2022, knocking off Roanoke for the championship and advancing to the national tournament. Also in that field were Lynchburg and Christopher Newport, before getting eliminated.

Shenandoah's long-time coach, Kevin Anderson, in his days leading the Winchester Royals in the Valley League, once added a young George Mason University product to his coaching staff: Dayton Moore, who would eventually become the general manager of the 2015 World Series champion Kansas City Royals and is now that team's president of baseball operations.

Anderson in an interview gave credit to the success of Shenandoah this season to pitching coach Rich Croushore, one of his pitchers when Anderson was a coach at JMU and who played in the Major Leagues for three seasons.

The Apprentice School in Newport News won the USCAA Small College World Series in 2022 with an amazing run. The team won seven games in a row and came back from a 15-2 deficit to beat Miami University Hamilton of Ohio 23-17 in the title game.

Salisbury of Maryland won the Division III World Series in 2021 with two seniors from Virginia on the roster: catcher Matt Padeway from Fairfax and Chantilly High and Joe Doherty, a native of Richmond who went to Midlothian.

The Seahawks advanced again in 2022 to the Division III World Series. So did Catholic of Washington, D.C—for the first time— with a roster that included these Virginia residents: Cole Peverall, Camden Mounts, and Jack Baldridge of Alexandria; Jake Lynes of McLean; Cody Bosak of Woodbridge; and Annandale's Danny Fitzgerald, a pitcher who picked up the win as Catholic University clinched a spot at the national event in Iowa. The Cardinals, whose notable alum is Yankees General Manager Brian Cashman, lost two games and were knocked out of the Division III World Series.

Among current non-Division I schools, Washington and Lee University of Lexington has produced the most big leaguers with 12 as of June 1. But it's been a while. The last Major Leaguer from the school was Rusty Peters, an infielder from Roanoke who played from 1936 to 1947.

Other current non-Division I schools to send students/players to the majors include Ferrum College, Roanoke College, Hampden-Sydney College, and Virginia State University (4 players each); Lynchburg (3); Randolph-Macon College, Virginia Union University, and Emory & Henry College (2); and Eastern Mennonite University, Bridgewater College, The Apprentice School, Shenandoah, and Bluefield College (1).

Those lucky ones? For EMU, it was Erik Kratz, who played for nine Major League teams from 2010 to 2020, and for Bridgewater, it was Ben Huffman, who was from Luray and played for the St. Louis Browns in 1937. Wayne Kirby, from Williamsburg and now a coach for the Mets, is the Newport News Apprentice alum to make it. Hank Hulvey, who was from Mt. Sidney, went to Shenandoah and played one year in the majors, in 1923. Jon Link pitched for the Dodgers is 2010 after starring at Chantilly High and Bluefield.

At the high school level, Turner Ashby of Rockingham County has won seven state titles – the second-most of any public school in the state while Wise has won nine. Among schools to produce the most pro and/or college players is James Madison in Vienna, Great Bridge, Paul VI in Fairfax, Kellam, West Springfield, Greenbriar Christian Academy, First Colonial, Bishop O'Connell, Mills Goodwin, Benedictine, Oakton, Lake Braddock, and Frank W. Cox.

Former Major Leaguer Michael Cuddyer is a product of Great Bridge. In the early part of this century, he was one of four Virginia high school products playing regularly as a third baseman in the majors. The others were Zimmerman, Wright, and Mark Reynolds. Kellam products to make the majors include Zimmerman, Ian Thomas, and Mike Williams. Madison grads to make The Show were Mike Wallace, Jay Franklin, Bob Brower, and Jim McNamara. Cox grads who made the majors: Jason Dubois, a product of VCU, and Taylor, the former Virginia standout.

Greenbriar products who made the big leagues were Josh Rupe,

B.J. Upton, and Eddie Butler, a Radford product who is featured later in this book.

But it's not just men who have built the Virginia baseball legacy.

Julie Croteau, who went to Osbourn Park High in Manassas, is credited with being the first woman to play college baseball when she suited up with Division III St. Mary's College of Maryland in 1989. According to the book "Women at Play: The Story of Women in Baseball," in which she was featured, Croteau hit .222 that year for St. Mary's.

She also played for the Fredericksburg Giants in the Virginia Baseball League. She later was an assistant coach at the University of Massachusetts, making her the first Division I women's assistant. She appeared in the 1992 film "A League of Their Own," a film starring Madonna and Tom Hanks that highlighted the women's professional baseball league that existed from 1943 to 1954.

Curt Kendall, a long-time athletic director at Bridgewater College, was the Eagles' baseball coach when Croteau was in high school, and he said he still has a copy of the letter he sent her in a recruiting bid.

"I was intrigued by it," Kendall told me in late May.

Kendall wrote back to her and said she was welcome to give BC a shot but pointed out that he had a veteran first baseman hitting in the heart of the lineup that that would be the competition for Croteau.

She ended up at St. Mary's, and Kendall kept track of her career – which included national TV exposure after her first game at St. Mary's.

"What happened is that for some reason I was this hero and everyone accepted it and the media covered it and the media and the school were telling everyone it was a great thing," she said in the book. "When the media went away so did the message." She has spent several years at Stanford as a noted senior communications professional, according to the school website.

Melanie Newman did radio play-by-play for the Single-A Salem Red Sox, of the Carolina League, during the 2019 season. She joined the broadcast team that covers the Baltimore Orioles the next year, and in 2021, she was part of the first all-female team to broadcast a Major League game. Newman was involved in broadcasting Orioles games and also working on national broadcasts early in the 2022 season.

"It really does give this ability to bring people together and put away all of the polarizing topics and the other issues that are going on," Newman said in the Troy alumni magazine of sports and baseball. Whether "you need to come together for a team or your mutual hate for the other team, you can put away so many other things that seem to be dividing."

Samantha Gjormand went to James Madison High in Vienna and graduated from JMU in 2021, serving four years as a manager with the Dukes baseball team. She was a de facto general manager for a team in the prestigious Cape Cod League in 2021 and then began a job in baseball operations at the College of Charleston. Her story is included in the pages that follow.

The 2022 Major League playoffs will have plenty of Virginia connections.

Seattle catcher Todd Raleigh, who was born in Harrisonburg, hit a walk-off homer on Sept. 30 as the Mariners clinched a wild card spot and a first postseason berth since 2001.

Raleigh is the son of Stephanie and Todd Raleigh, and his father was an assistant coach at JMU in Harrisonburg in 1996. The elder Raleigh was later the head coach at Western Carolina and Tennessee and his son went to high school in North Carolina. Norfolk native Justin Upton played for Seattle for part of the 2022 season before he was let go.

A more historic came on October 4 as Aaron Judge went deep for his 62nd of the year to set an American League record. The homer came against Texas and manager Tony Beasley, a native of Fredericksburg who played in college at Liberty in Lynchburg.

Other Virginia products on playoff teams include Richmond native Jackie Bradley, Jr., who grew up in Prince George's.

Let go by Boston earlier in 2022, Bradley was acquired by Toronto and aided the Blue Jays to secure the second-best record in the tough American League East. The first base coach for the Blue Jays is Mark Budzinski, a former standout at the University of Richmond.

Suffolk native Brandon Lowe, a second baseman for Tampa Bay, hit .221 with eight homers before he went on the Injured List in late September with lower back discomfort. Tampa Bay lefty pitcher Ryan Yarbrough, a product of the Valley Baseball League with Luray in 2012 and ODU, pitched in 20 games with nine starts for the Rays in 2022 before he went on the Injured List on Sept. 23 with a right oblique strain.

The pitching coach for AL Central champs Cleveland is Carl Wills, a native of Danville.

Verlander, who grew up in the Richmond area, had an incredible season on the mound for the Astros as Houston ran away with the title in the American League West.

He was 18-4 with an ERA of 1.75 at the age of 39. Verlander is now 244-133 in his career – that is second to Rixey among wins by a Virginia native.

In the National League, former Franklin W. Cox High and University of Virginia product Chris Taylor helped the Dodgers post the best record in the majors. The director of player development for the Dodgers is Will Rhymes, a former MLB infielder who starred at William & Mary.

A special assistant in player development for the Padres is Steve Finley, who played for the Harrisonburg Turks in the Valley League and had a long MLB career as an outfielder.

Part I

RICHMOND AND THE CAPITAL REGION

Tracy Woodson: From World Series To Return Home

The pull of family and of his hometown have led Tracy Woodson to his job as the baseball coach at the University of Richmond.

"It's where I grew up," Woodson said of Virginia's capital city. "My wife kind of pegged it that at some point we'd be back."

Woodson, who in 2022 was in his ninth season leading the Spiders, was born in Richmond and starred in high school at Benedectine. He went on to become the ACC player of the year with North Carolina State in 1984, when he was drafted in the third round by the Los Angeles Dodgers.

The highlight of Woodson's five-year major league playing career came in 1988, when he was a reserve corner infielder for an L.A. team that won the World Series behind the pitching of Orel Hershiser, a timely home run from a hobbled Kirk Gibson and a bevy of contributions from throughout the roster. The Tommy Lasorda-managed Dodgers, who went 94-67 in the regular season, beat the New York Mets in seven games in the NLCS and the Oakland Athletics in five games in the World Series.

"The run we made, that really stands out," Woodson said. "Everyone says we weren't the best team. The Mets won 100 games, the A's won 104. But we were the best team. We had the best pitcher and we had the best player. Every move Tommy made worked. I was lucky to be in the right place at the right time."

Woodson hit .279 in 506 major league at-bats. The first of his five career home runs came on April 13, 1987 against Houston Astros fireballer Nolan Ryan.

"It was the first pitch I ever saw from him. He threw freaking hard," Woodson said. "I was just looking for a fastball. The next time up, the first pitch was at my head. Alan Ashby (the Astros catcher) kind of caught me. He said, 'If you want to go dancing, we can do that after the game.' "

Woodson played for the Dodgers from 1987-89 and for the St. Louis Cardinals from 1992-93. He was with the Triple-A Richmond Braves in 1991, and the last three years of his career were back in Triple-A through 1996.

By 1998, Woodson was again in the minor leagues as a manager. He started with the Pittsburgh Pirates' short-season Class A New York-Penn League team in Erie, Pa. Woodson managed at several other stops before landing in the Florida Marlins organization. In the Marlins system, he led Double-A Carolina to a Southern League title in 2003 and reached Triple-A Albuquerque in 2004.

In 2003, Jack McKeon became the oldest manager to win the World Series win at 72 he led the Marlins to the title. McKeon continued to manage the Marlins in 2004 and 2005 and eventually returned in 2011.

"I thought I was maybe knocking on the door (of getting a major league managerial job)," Woodson said. "When (Jeff) Torborg got fired by the Marlins, they hired Jack McKeon, and they didn't know how long he wanted to manage. I remember hearing Tim Kurkjian, I guess on ESPN, when we were in Mobile at a hotel. He said they've got a young guy they like in Double-A — Tracy Woodson. But I don't think I had the backing."

Woodson was already at the point where he was ready to focus on family. He had met his wife Lisa on one of his visits to Louisville.

She was an assistant women's basketball coach for the University of Louisville, and he was officiating men's college basketball games in several conferences. Eventually, they moved to Florida and had their first child, Erin, in 2004. Their son, T.J., was born in 2006.

Woodson also has an older son, Michael, who is the men's tennis coach at Baylor.

"I didn't see much of my son because it was all about me when he was growing up," Woodson said. "I just said I'm not doing that anymore."

Eventually, baseball came calling again. Woodson's brother-in-law let him know about the baseball coaching opening at Valparaiso, where Lisa had starred as a basketball player. Tracy took over the Crusaders' program from 2007-13 and led them to two NCAA regional appearances.

Then, the Richmond job opened up and Tracy's wife was proven correct. He has since coached the Spiders to the top half of the Atlantic-10 in five of his seven full seasons. Now construction is underway for improvements to the team's home field on UR's campus. Pitt Field will have new indoor batting cages down the left-field line and a new seating area beyond the right-field fence.

Woodson stopped the basketball refereeing during his first year at Richmond after tearing a meniscus while working in an early-season game at Auburn. But he still has plenty of stories to tell, including one about the time when he gave a technical foul to Chris Mooney, still the men's basketball coach at UR.

The college environment has been good to Woodson, but so was pro ball. He appreciates that he has been able to work in both capacities with a wide variety of players.

"I'm glad I got to do both," Woodson said. "In college, you get to do more of your own thing, which I like. But even when I played, I was almost like a coach. I've always tried to bring guys together."

2

Nick Zona

The Zona family of Mechanicsville is involved in baseball at nearly every level.

Jeff Zona, Jr. is a scout for the Philadelphia Phillies, brother Anthony is on the coaching staff at Division II University of Charleston in West Virginia and younger brother Nick Zona played for JMU for four years as an infielder starting in 2019.

Their father is Jeff Zona, a former minor league player with the Atlanta Braves who has been a scout for the Washington Nationals for several years. Their mother, Aimee, played tennis at VCU and is in the Hall of Fame of her high school.

The elder Zona travels around the country as the Pitching Evaluation and Special Assistant to the President of Baseball Operations and General Manager Mike Rizzo with the Washington Nationals.

When the Nationals beat the Houston Astros in seven games in 2019, Zona earned a World Series ring for his work with the Nationals. The elder Zona, who played at VCU, pitched in Pulaski as a minor-leaguer in the Atlanta system and also played for Idaho Falls in the Pioneer League.

His son, Jeff, was drafted out of Hanover High by the New York Mets in the 38th round but opted to attend JMU.

"I would be interested in him (as a possible draft pick) even if he wasn't my son," the elder Jeff Zona said once of Nick, who hit .282 this past season for the Dukes and also pitched in one game.

In the past, Nick Zona has played for the Harrisonburg Turks of the Valley Baseball League during his time at JMU.

But when the Turks played their first home game of the 2022 season on a Friday night in early June, Zona spent part of the game in the press box at Veterans Memorial Park as an intern for one of the oldest franchises in the league.

Nick Zona told us he put his name in the transfer portal during the 2022 college season and may be looking for a chance to play at a Power 5 conference school as a graduate student.

He noted that Richmond-area product Travis Reifsnider (Collegiate) is transferring from JMU to Virginia for the 2023 baseball season. He hit .303 for the Dukes in 2022.

Reifsnider's father played football at Toledo, his sister, Carter, played lacrosse at JMU, and his brother, Jack, played football at Christopher Newport.

A Public Policy and Administration major at JMU, Zona was using the summer of 2022 to recuperate from some nagging injuries that have bothered him in the past.

His 2020 college season was cut short due to the pandemic and the Dukes also missed out on a few games during the 2021 season due to COVID-19 concerns.

When the 2020 college and pro season was called off, the three sons headed to suburban Richmond.

"All three are in my house," Jeff Zona recalled. "It is kind of interesting; they are all doing their jobs."

Nick Zona took groundballs hit to him by one of his brothers at a field near their house and lifted weights to stay in shape.

Since he was born on July 9, 1999, Nick Zona was eligible for the draft in 2020 but was not chosen. He also was not picked in 2021.

Anthony Zona, a Pitching Coordinator, was in his fourth season as part of the staff at Charleston in 2022.

The pitching staff of the Golden Eagles was third in the nation in WHIP in 2020 and was among the top 25 in ERA at the Division II level.

He played at Patrick Henry Community College before transferring to the University of Charleston, where he graduated in 2018 with a degree in Communications.

As a player for the Golden Eagles, Zona was part of a Mountain East Conference title in 2018 and a runner-up spot in 2017.

Anthony Zona pitched more than 200 innings in college and was part of more than 150 wins. Charleston was 40-18 in 2022 and posted a team ERA of 4.53 while opponents had a mark of 8.99.

Nick Zona was drafted in the 20th round by the Seattle Mariners in July of 2022 and reported to the spring training home of the club in Arizona. "Feels great to be part of the Seattle organization; ready to get to work," he wrote to us.

Zona had one hit in 10 at-bats in his pro debut in the Arizona Complex League.

3

Rich History With The Minors In Richmond

Dennis Pelfrey stood behind the left-field foul pole in Bowie, Maryland, wearing a stylish North Face fleece jacket over his shirt along with some casual pants.

In a few minutes, he would duck into the visiting clubhouse at Prince George's Stadium and begin what minor league coaches and players reverentially refer to as The Grind—that arduous daily schedule that leaves most of them not knowing what day of the week it is.

Pelfrey, a baseball lifer who was born and still lives in Texas, is in his first season as the manager of the Double-A Richmond Flying Squirrels. "Last year we won the High-A championship at Eugene," Pelfrey said. "The next day it was on to the next one. It is a tough business to be in. There are a lot of good players and managers."

Pelfrey lives in the Dallas area in the off-season with his wife and son, age 6. "My wife is an absolute trooper in supporting me," he said. When his son gets out of school, they hope to join him for part of the summer at his apartment in Scott's Addition near the Richmond ballpark.

Richmond has been an affiliate of the San Francisco Giants

since 2010—which just happened to be the first of three years that the Giants won the World Series.

Other titles would follow in 2012 and 2014, but the Richmond baseball tradition of partnering with winners goes way behind this millennium.

The Richmond Braves were the Triple-A affiliate of Atlanta from 1966 to 2008 and during that time won five International League titles.

The list of future Major Leaguers who came through the Virginia capital on the way to Atlanta includes Dusty Baker, Darrell Evans, Ralph Garr, Dale Murphy, and Deion Sanders.

Brian Jordan, a two-sport athlete at the University of Richmond, played in the majors for several teams and in four games with the R-Braves in 2006.

Atlanta won its first World Series in 1995 and some of the former R-Braves who aided that run included Hall of Fame pitchers Tom Glavine and John Smoltz. But the Richmond connection to World Series titles and future All-Stars goes beyond even Atlanta.

The city was the affiliate of the powerhouse New York Yankees from 1956 through 1964. The Yankees won the World Series four times during that run – 1956, 1958, 1961, and 1962. Tom Tresh, for example, was a regular outfielder for Richmond in 1961 then became a starter for the Yankees the following year. He was named an All-Star and won a World Series ring in 1962 as he hit .321 in the Fall Classic in the seven-game series win against the Giants.

PELFREY ADMITS he doesn't know a lot about the history of Richmond baseball – be it with the Giants or other clubs. "I like to have conversations; even with players I don't like to look up guys (bios) a whole lot," he said. "I like to have my own thoughts. I really don't like to dwell in the past."

However, Pelfrey hopes to explore Richmond this summer, though he admits he is prone to staying inside on off days.

What type of roster does Pelfrey have in Richmond?

"It is really the same throughout the Giants' organization," he said. "No matter what team I was managing, every player we have is, one, of most character. And a really good player. All up and own our system we have very good players and prospects. I think it is exciting to be around these guys and see what they can do. I tell them they are artists and entertainers. I want to sit back and let them be the best player they can and show up, and I want to see what they really can do."

In a 22-7 victory on May 29 at The Diamond, the Flying Squirrels set new single-game franchise records for runs (22), hits (24), home runs (7) and RBIs (22). Tyler Fitzgerald and Jacob Heyward each tied the franchise single-game record with five hits in the laugher. The Flying Squirrels still have a challenge as an affiliate 2,900 miles away from the Giants.

"For us, our situation is really unique," Pelfrey said. "You may see some guys get a shot to go to Triple-A Sacramento from high A as opposed to here (in Richmond) just because of the travel."

The goal, of course, is for Richmond to help its Major League boss win a World Series – something the Virginia capital has succeeded at since the 1950s.

4

Olympic Ties For The Spiders

After graduating from Richmond in 2017, Spider pitcher Jonathan de Marte signed to pitch professionally for an independent baseball team in the Frontier League. He was with the team again the following year in Normal, Illinois, when his manager, Billy Horn, approached him about playing in a winter league.

But de Marte, who grew up in a Jewish home in suburban New York, had a larger vision that went beyond his own individual career.

"My immediate response was I wanted to play for Israel," de Marte recalls. "He told me, 'I am friends with Gabe Kapler and will see what I can do.' The next day Kapler got back to me."

Kapler, a former big leaguer and now the manager of the San Francisco Giants, had been a coach with Team Israel in 2012. Soon after, de Marte heard from Eric Holtz, the manager of Team Israel, who contacted him about the possibility of joining the team. Both were from Westchester County near New York City, and de Marte played against the Holtz's oldest son as an amateur.

"I followed his entire career," Holtz said. "I assumed he was Italian with that last name. He wants the ball every time."

That contact put into motion de Marte's role helping the Israel national team qualify for the 2020 Olympics in Japan, though the games were pushed back due to the pandemic. Israel took fifth in 2021.

"I literally started the process the next day. There was a lot of paperwork," said de Marte, who had to become an Israeli citizen to join the team. "In the fall of 2018, I made my first trip to Israel. I went back to Israel to get citizenship, myself and nine other guys (on the team). Some of those guys are still on the team."

He was a member of Team Israel along with Nate Mulberg, an assistant coach and recruiting coordinator for the Spiders under head coach Tracy Woodson.

"I think it was great opportunity for both of them," said Woodson, who as a player won a World Series ring with the Dodgers in 1988.

Mulberg, a former standout at Division III Rochester, was part of the coaching staff for Israel. Mulberg also connected with Holtz to find a spot on Team Israel.

Nate Mulberg

"It is one of those stories of right place at the right time and doing the right thing," Mulberg said. "I really didn't have an ulterior motive or special agenda in my interactions with people other than trying to do the right thing."

Being part of the historic team goes beyond the diamond. While playing for Richmond, de Marte remembers watching Israel in the World Baseball Classic on television while the Spiders were in Texas for games in 2017. He watched the games with his mother and told her he would love to be part of Team Israel.

"A lot of us have similarities from the religion and growing up in a Jewish household," de Marte said. "I have always been proud of being Jewish."

On the mound for Team Israel in the 2019 European Championships in September 2019, the 6-foot-1 de Marte went 1-0 with an ERA of 0.00 in three outings and recorded the win over Germany.

"Beating Germany was incredible," de Marte said. "One of the best games of my life. The last time a team (from Israel) was in Germany was in 1972. Obviously that game meant a lot more than a baseball game. Everyone knows what happened in 1972. That win was like a championship in its own."

A lot of us have similarities from the religion and growing up in a Jewish household. I have always been proud of being Jewish.

Then at the Africa/Europe 2020 Olympic qualifier in Italy later that month, he again did not allow a run over four innings out of the bullpen while recording seven strikeouts with one hit and no walks allowed.

"With every single win we were one step closer to the Olympics," he recalls. "We have the horses to do this. I got the win against Italy. That put us one win from the Olympics. We lost to the Czech Republic and came back and beat South Africa to qualify for the Olympics."

The team became the first Israeli team to qualify for the Olympics since 1972, when a Palestine terrorist group killed 11 members of the Israel Olympic team and a West German police officer during the Munich games.

Woodson said the Spiders followed the games overseas in which de Marte pitched. Some players from the 2019 Richmond squad had been de Marte's teammates.

Both Mulberg and de Marte grew up knowing about Jewish baseball heroes such as Hank Greenberg and Sandy Koufax. Greenberg hit 331 homers in the majors between 1930 and 1947 and was elected to the National Baseball Hall of Fame in 1956. Koufax, the best pitcher of his generation while with the Brooklyn and then the

Los Angeles Dodgers, refused to pitch in the first game of the 1965 World Series since it fell on Yom Kippur. Koufax was elected to the Hall of Fame in 1972 — six years after winning 27 games in his last season in the major leagues.

Despite the legacy of Greenberg and Koufax — and recent Jewish big leaguer Shawn Green and others — Israel has very little history with baseball at the international level. It has been decades since Greenberg and Koufax played, so current Israeli fans may need a primer: The current webpage of the Israel Baseball Association has a link to "What is baseball?"

Mulberg, though, knew that Jewish baseball history.

"I grew up in Cherry Hill, New Jersey. There are a lot of Jewish people in that area," Mulberg said. "I grew up in a conservative household and went to Hebrew school several days a week. My mom and sister keep kosher; I don't. I went to Jewish summer camp. Baseball and Judaism were the two biggest influences growing up."

Mulberg remembers hearing about Ron Blomberg, a Jewish player in the 1970s for the New York Yankees and a member of the National Jewish Sports Hall of Fame.

He told his father about Blomberg, and they had the former big leaguer come to a Jewish book festival in Cherry Hill and were able to spend time with him when Mulberg was a high school freshman in 2006–07.

In high school, Mulberg almost went with a U.S. team to Israel to take part in the Maccabiah Games. Among his teammates was Max Fried, who made his major league debut in 2017 with the Atlanta Braves.

"I got very sick with mono right before we left. I didn't get to go. The team won gold," Mulberg recalls. "My dream was always to play Division I, but it was not in the cards. I did not have the size or speed or ranked in baseball just before he got there. Mulberg was a four-year starter there and after graduating in 2014 knew he wanted to get into coaching.

He was an assistant at Division III Franklin & Marshall in Lancaster, Pennsylvania, and then at Division I Bucknell of the Patriot League in Lewisburg, Pennsylvania.

"There I was introduced to Holtz, whose son had played at Bucknell," Mulberg said.

Holtz was named Team Israel manager in 2018 just after Mulberg had finished the spring season with the Spiders. Holtz wanted to know if Mulberg knew of any players he would suggest for Team Israel — and Mulberg told Holtz about de Marte.

Then Mulberg became part of Team Israel as well. "We had an instant connection there. He identified with my story," Mulberg said of Holtz. "He felt very sad I didn't get to go to Israel. That was a very painful part of when I was in high school, my junior year."

Mulberg has also been involved with Go4theGoal, a nonprofit with a mission to help better the lives of children with cancer.

Woodson said communication is Mulberg's strength as a coach. "He knows how to connect with people. People trust him. That is a great thing to have," said Woodson.

There was more good news for de Marte about two years ago when he signed a minor league contract with the Chicago Cubs and reported to spring training in Arizona.

It was his first contract with an affiliated team after playing in three independent leagues: Frontier, Atlantic, and Canadian-American Association.

During spring training, de Marte worked out with several Cubs with Major League experience, including Kyle Hendricks, Ben Zobrist, and Javier Baez.

"Just seeing the way they carry themselves and go about their business every day, you know they know they are among the best there are," de Marte said.

But then he was also teammates on Team Israel with several big leaguers, including Danny Valencia, who last played in the majors with the Baltimore Orioles in 2018.

Being with the Israeli national team goes beyond baseball, de Marte said. "You feel the connection and the common denominator," he noted. Mulberg was again the staff of Richmond in 2022 while de Marte had yet to pitch in the Cubs' system last season or through May of this year.

5

Ray Dandridge, Hall Of Famer

Ray Dandridge may have been one of the greatest third basemen of all time.

Born in Richmond in 1913, Dandridge played in the Negro Leagues from 1933 to 1942.

He hit .321 but was best known for his fielding.

Monte Irvin, a star in the Negro Leagues and the Major Leagues, told those that would listen that Dandridge was the best-fielding third basemen he saw.

According to Wikipedia, Dandridge was a scout for the San Francisco Giants in the 1950s and got to work with a young Willie Mays.

Dandridge went into the Baseball Hall of Fame in 1987 and died seven years later in Florida.

Other Negro League stars from Virginia who are in the Hall of Fame are Alexandria native Leon Day, Culpeper native Pete Hill and Jud Wilson, who was born in Remington.

In the book "Sunday Coming: Black Baseball In Virginia," written by Darrell Howard and published in 2002, baseball was huge in Black communities.

"From Winchester to Tidewater, Danville to Fairfax, baseball was the most enduring form of entertainment and recreation for black communities in states like Virginia. This story begins in the 1930s, when black baseball was gaining popularity, and goes through to the 1980s," according to that book.

6

Johnny Oates, Part Of History With Aaron

In late June of 1973, my family left Dayton for a summer trip to Georgia. I was in the back seat of a car for several hundred miles but it seemed worth it — the promise of seeing a rare Major League Baseball game in person.

Starting in 1970, with a trip to Baltimore to see the Orioles and Red Sox, my father had started taking me and sometimes my brothers to at least one game per summer.

The trip to Atlanta, looking back, may have been more eye-opening now with the death of Hall of Fame slugger Hank Aaron at the age of 86 in January of 2021.

In a doubleheader on July 1, 1973 — thanks to baseballrefer ence.com — here are some of the players that appeared in the first game for the hosts: Aaron, Ralph Garr, Darrell Evans, Dusty Baker, and Davey Johnson.

I remember a homer by Evans—and now thanks to the baseball website I see cleanup hitter Aaron had two hits while Baker and Johnson hit right back of him. Both Johnson and Baker would later manage the Washington Nationals and I got to hear some of

Baker's stories about Aaron while I was covering the Nationals as a free-lance writer.

Some starters for the Giants in the first game were right fielder Bobby Bonds, first baseman Willie McCovey, and third baseman and Pulaski native Ed Goodson, who had two hits.

Braves pitcher Tom House – who would play a key role the next season – pitched the last two innings as the Giants won 14-6. The last pitcher for the Giants was Randy Moffitt, the brother of tennis legend Billie Jean King.

Aaron was used as a pinch-hitter in the second game as the Braves scored two runs in the last of the ninth to win 8-7 over the Giants, whom the previous year had traded Willie Mays to the Mets.

The starting pitcher in the second game for the Braves was Phil Niekro, a future Hall of Famer. His catcher that day was Johnny Oates, who grew up in Prince George's, starred at Virginia Tech, and is a member of the Valley Baseball League Hall of Fame after playing for Waynesboro. Oates died in Richmond in 2004.

It would be less than a year later after my trip, April 8, 1974, when Aaron would break the all-time home run record held by Babe Ruth with a drive off Al Downing of the Los Angeles Dodgers in that same Atlanta ballpark.

I remember watching that game on national television as Aaron hit the ball into the Atlanta bullpen for the 715th homer of his career. It was House, the lefty reliever, that caught the ball that was hit by Aaron. Johnson started at second and Baker in center for Atlanta in that game and Oates was used as a pinch-hitter.

"Hank Aaron changed my life," House wrote on social media after the death of Aaron. "The greatest moment I ever got to be a part of was catching 715. That moment bonded us forever as friends and teammates. My heart hurts today to learn of his passing. We watched Hank shrug off the weight of the world and just keep swinging."

JOHNNY OATES   VIRGINIA TECH

At a young age, of course, I had no idea about the junk, such as death threats, that African-American Aaron was dealing with as he chased Ruth. Although my mother has German Ruth roots on her side of the family, as a young boy I was a fan of Aaron and pulled for him to break the record.

Let's face it: the issues of racial strife are still with us today.

Hopefully, all of us can learn from the quiet dignity of Aaron – who was much more than one of the greatest players ever. He stayed humble and was able to "just keep swinging," in the words of House.

"One of the best parts of working for the Braves in 2011 was having the honor to cross paths with Hank Aaron from time to time. And then listening to Dusty tell his Hank Aaron stories a few years later. Man. What a legend. What a loss," Kyle Brostowitz, now the director of communications for the Nationals, wrote on social media of Aaron.

Kyle Finnegan, who pitches for the Nationals, was born in Texas in 1991 so he never saw Alabama native Aaron play. But Finnegan told me he has watched the tape of the record home run by Aaron in 1974. "What he had to go through off the field, being from the South" was brutal, Finnegan said.

The record books may say Barry Bonds is the all-time home run leader at 755. But to many of my generation, that record clearly belongs to Aaron. That and many, many other honors as well.

It had been decades since that Braves' game that I had been to Atlanta before my wife and I drove down over the Christmas break a few years ago. We visited the church where Martin Luther King, Jr. was a pastor and also went to the Jimmy Carter Center.

Both men had their flaws, like everyone, and you may not have agreed with their foreign policy (see 1980 Olympics for the former President) or stance on social issues.

Of the three Atlanta legends, only Carter is still alive as this book goes to press. These days, I think we could all learn something from King, Carter, and Aaron.

7

Willie Harris, Has Robinson Ties

Willie Harris hit the first inside-the-park homer at Nationals Park, connecting for Washington in 2010. He also hit a leadoff homer, walk-off homer and grand slam during three seasons with the Nationals.

But the former Nationals outfielder/infielder also has vivid memories of something that happened during batting practice at Nationals Park involving Mark Lerner, now the principal owner of the team.

"He would come down and take flyballs," recalls Harris, who broke into the majors with the Orioles in 2001. "One day he missed a ball and it hit him in the face. The next day he was out there again."

There were plenty of missteps off and on the field in the early day of the Nationals, who lost more than 100 games twice when Harris was with the team.

But Harris understands those growing pains.

"All teams go through struggles when they are in a rebuilding phase," noted Harris, a former manager for Richmond at the Double-A level. "I have a special place in my heart for them."

After his time with the Nationals, Harris played with the New York Mets in 2011 and ended his career with the Cincinnati Reds and manager Dusty Baker in 2012.

Harris has followed in Baker's footsteps and was a first-year skipper in the San Francisco Giants farm system in 2018. "He's awesome," former Richmond lefty pitcher Garrett Williams, now in the St. Louis system, said of Harris in that first year with Richmond. "I feel like he is one of us, with everything he has been through in the game. He is young and understands the grind of minor league baseball."

Harris stays in touch with some of his former Nationals teammates, including current first baseman Ryan Zimmerman.

Harris was drafted by the Orioles in 1999 and made his big-league debut with Baltimore two years later. He also spent part of 2001 with the Bowie Baysox, a team he now manages against in the Eastern League.

He was with the Chicago White Sox from 2002 to 2005, and part of the 2005 team that won the World Series.

Harris, who is black, would like to one day manage in the majors. He was just the second Cairo, Georgia, native to make the majors as a player. The first was Jackie Robinson, who broke the color barrier in 1947 with the Brooklyn Dodgers.

"You look at the great players of the game, be it Latin America or African-American, there are a lot of great ones," he said.

"Not one of them can say they are from the same hometown as Jackie Robinson. It is definitely an honor, not only to play the game but also be a manager."

After managing in Richmond, Harris became the third-base coach for the Cubs in 2021 and is in the same role this season.

8

Tyler Wilson, Hoop Fan

Midlothian High graduate Tyler Wilson made his Major League debut with the Orioles on May 20, 2015.

He was taken in the 35th round by the Reds in 2010 but decided to stay at the University of Virginia.

The right-hander was then selected in the 10th round by the Orioles the next year and worked his way up the minor-league ladder of Baltimore. Wilson split the 2014 season between Double-A Bowie and the Triple-A Norfolk Tides.

"The biggest takeaway from last year is to focus on the moment and stay locked in on my routine," he told us in a 2015 interview. "I just break the season down from one day at a time to one start at a time. It was the most fun I have had playing baseball. It allowed me to develop better relationships."

Wilson was 2-2 with an ERA of 3.50 in nine games with five starts for the Orioles in 2015.

"He locates his fastball, he's got a good delivery, he fields his position, he holds runners, he's athletic, he's smart," former Baltimore manager Buck Showalter said of Wilson when he was in the high minors.

The Midlothian product, who was born in Lynchburg, was 4-6 with an ERA of 5.27 in 24 games with 13 starts in 2016 for the Orioles. He followed that up by going 2-2, 7.04 in nine games with one start in 2017 for Baltimore.

Starting in 2018, he became an everyday starter in the top league in Korea. He won nine games in 2018, 14 the next year, and then 10 games in 2020 for the LG Twins. Wilson didn't pitch at the pro level in 2021 or through the first part of this year.

Wilson remained a big fan of Virginia basketball after leaving Charlottesville. He and his wife bought a house in Charlottesville while he was in the minors.

But Wilson, who turns 33 in September, wasn't the first pitcher from Midlothian to appear in the majors – or even with the Orioles.

Jesse Jefferson was born in Midlothian in 1949, according to baseballreference.com.

He was drafted out of Carver High by the Orioles in the fourth round in 1968 and played in the minors that year in Bluefield in the Appalachian League.

The right-hander spent time with Bluefield and Single-A Miami in 1969 and eventually made it to the majors with the Orioles in 1973.

He went to the White Sox during the 1975 season and later pitched for Toronto and Pittsburgh and ended his career with the Angels in 1981. Jefferson made a career-high 33 starts for the Blue Jays in 1977. He was 39-81 with an ERA of 4.81 in 237 games in the majors with 144 starts.

He died in 2011 and is buried at the First Baptist Church Cemetery in Midlothian, according to baseballreference.com.

9

Jackie Bradley, Jr., MVP, All-Star

Already a two-time College World Series champion, Jackie Bradley Jr., became a World Series champion in 2018 with the Boston Red Sox.

Mickey Roberts, his former coach at Prince George High School, couldn't have been prouder.

"He's one of these guys who works extremely hard," Roberts told the Richmond Times-Dispatch. "He had the work ethic in high school and in college and now in pro baseball. For him to get to this level is great."

Bradley helped send Boston to that 2018 World Series by winning the ALCS MVP honor as he hit two home runs, drove in nine runs, and played his usual stellar defense in center field in a five-game series win over the Astros. He was a Gold Glove winner that season and an all-star in 2016.

With a 1.000 fielding percentage in 2020 and 2021, Bradley lifted his career fielding percentage to .991. He played his first eight seasons for Boston and then one for the Brewers. Boston re-acquired him in a trade on Dec. 1, 2021.

Bradley also had a stellar college career at South Carolina. He was named Most Outstanding Player of the 2010 College World Series as he went 10-for-29 in the final CWS at Rosenblatt Stadium. The next year, he helped the Gamecocks become the sixth program to win back-to-back CWS titles.

The Red Sox took Bradley in the supplemental first round (40th overall) of the 2011 draft. He reached the major leagues on Opening Day of 2013 but played just 37 games and did not make the postseason roster for that Boston team that won a World Series.

Though Bradley had a .230 batting average through 2021, he has had several career offensive highlights. He had a 29-game hitting streak in 2016, the same year in which he hit 26 of his 104 home runs through nine seasons.

Bradley, in his first 150 at-bats this year for Boston, hit .227 with one homer. Bradley was released by the Red Sox in early August of 2022.

Jackie Bradley, Jr. grew up in Prince George and was the Most Outstanding Player of the College World Series with South Carolina.

10

Jim Coates Legacy

It has been more than 50 years since Jim Coates threw a pitch in the Major Leagues.

The native of Farnham passed away in 2019 but his baseball legacy remains through a young pitcher from the same area of the state.

"He taught me how to throw a curve," Matt Kleinfelter said of Coates, who as an All-Star with the New York Yankees in 1960 as that team made it to the World Series.

Kleinfelter is from Lancaster, where Coates died about three years ago. But before his passing, Coates went to the same church as Kleinfelter — who is playing this summer for the Harrisonburg Turks in the Valley Baseball League.

Kleinfelter just finished his redshirt sophomore year at James Madison University after he played the summer of 2021 in the Valley League with the Strasburg Express, which won the title after knocking off Woodstock in the Northern Division playoffs.

After posting an ERA of 9.58 in nine games out of the bullpen this year for JMU, he came on in the first game of the Valley League season in the sixth inning as the Turks beat Charlottesville 4-3 with a walk-off single in the last of the ninth by Casey Smith of JMU.

Jim Coates

Coates went to Lively High and broke in with the Yankees in 1956, according to baseballreference.com. He won a career-high 13 games with three losses in 1960 while posting an ERA of 4.28.

Coates was with the Washington Senators and Reds in 1963

then ended his career with the Angels from 1964-67. He was 43-22 in 247 games with 46 starts in his career.

"Jim was also known as the only pitcher who could sleep with his eyes open and pitch with them closed. Jim's nickname, to his Yankee teammates, was "The Mummy". Following his baseball career, Jim became a high voltage electrician. For three years he worked in the underground Metro in Washington, D.C., and spent 12 years in the shipyards in Newport News. He was inducted into the Virginia Hall of Fame in 1994," according to baseballreference.com.

He was the grandfather of Aaron Pribanic, a former minor league pitcher who was born in Fairfax.

The starting DH for Charlottesville in the game at Harrisonburg on June 3 was Julian Rojas, who just finished his junior year as the top catcher for Division I Radford. Last summer he played in a league in his native Texas. "This is a much more competitive league," Rojas said of the Valley.

That June 3 game came just hours after Radford announced that head baseball coach Karl Kuhn, a former Virginia assistant, had resigned after three years at the helm.

The Roanoke Times had earlier reported of complaints from several players about the aggressive coaching style of Kuhn. When asked about the resignation, Rojas said "no comment."

"COVID-19 has created significant complications for Division 1 athletics. Despite these challenges, Coach Kuhn has upgraded our facilities, added more than 200 donors to the program, secured an endowed baseball scholarship and spent significant time recruiting top players to our program," said Radford athletic director Robert Lineburg in a statement. "We look forward to seeing what these young and talented players are able to accomplish in future seasons and wish the coach well on his future endeavors."

Among the Division III products on the roster to start the Valley year were pitcher Lance Tate, who come out of the bullpen for the Tox Sox on June 3, and Harrisburg outfielder Jaylon Lee, an all-region player at Eastern Mennonite who will transfer to JMU for his final college year. He played for Woodstock in the Valley League in 2021.

Bob Wease is in his 32nd year as the president and general manager of the Turks, and his 20th as the coach. He had a record of 520-338 coming into this season. The second-year pitching coach for the Turks is Larry Erbaugh, a former standout at Turner Ashby High and South Carolina.

Former Turks in the pro ranks as players include pitcher Emilio Pagan, now with the Minnesota Twins; Kyle McCann, who was at Double-A with Oakland this year; and Bryan Arias, who as Double-A with Houston.

Pagan had seven saves and an ERA of 3.00 in games through June 3 of this year; he was not with the Twins for a series in Toronto in early June due to vaccine protocol by the Canadian government, per published reports.

Matt Kleinfelter

Part II

TIDEWATER

Tim Naughton, Rolling With Tides

Tim Naughton, as a young boy, would many times make the trip with his parents from North Carolina to visit his grandparents in Manassas.

"They have probably lived in the Manassas area for 30 years," Naughton notes. "My grandfather used to work at the Pentagon; he recently retired and stayed in the area."

Several times that summer excursion included a drive of a few extra miles to see a minor league baseball game in Woodbridge, where his mother went to high school.

"I remember growing up one July 4 there was a game between team USA and Cuba at the old P-Nats stadium," recalls Naughton, now a pitching prospect with the Orioles. "I was 10 years old and it was Team USA, fireworks, and July 4. That was really cool."

Little did Naughton know that about a decade later he would return to Woodbridge – this time as a minor league pitcher in the Baltimore farm system.

A right-hander, he was with Single-A Frederick in 2019 when the Keys played at the Potomac Nationals – who have seen relocated to Fredericksburg.

As the 2022 season began, Naughton once again found himself in the minors in Virginia, but this time Norfolk was a more permanent base as he was part of the pitching staff for the Triple-A Tides, the now farm system in the Oriole's improving system.

He has beaten the odds as a player who was drafted in the 34th round and has advanced to Triple-A this year at Norfolk.

The housing arrangements for minor league players in the Baltimore system are much improved from when Naughton joined the system. This year he is living in a nice apartment a few minutes from Harbor Park.

"I got drafted by the Orioles in 2017 and I went to rookie ball and the housing arrangement there was basically hotels," he said, standing near the Tides' dugout before a day game in late May. "You had two meals provided a day – basically pre-game and post-game and meal money to cover your third meal. After that season I got promoted to short-season which at that time was Aberdeen – I was only there for a week and the housing situation was basically the same – hotels."

"In my first year at Delmarva, which was low A at the time, I had a host family who I still stay in touch with. That was the situation for everybody," he added. "The next season I was at Frederick, which was high A at the time. Host families weren't a requirement but players needed them since it is very expensive. Last year when I got to Double-A Bowie there were not a lot of host families because of COVID (restrictions). The first month of the season the team covered housing; then the second month some of his moved into hotels and shared a room."

"Now with the team covering an apartment, it is like night and day. Everyone appreciates it; I haven't heard a bad word. It has really been a huge boon; I really wish they had done this earlier. Now a majority of organizations are covering housing and if they are not they definitely should. The Orioles, they have done very well. They did right by us. It is a comfortable feeling," he said.

On the field, Naughton is encouraged by a Baltimore system

that has the top-ranked minor league talent, according to several publications prior to the 2022 season.

"It has been cool to be part of an organization that is turning the tide," he said. "I was around in 2017 and 2018 when they blew up the Major League team and we saw the influx of trades and transactions. We have had so many first-round picks. We are selecting very talented baseball players. And they are my friends so I will say they are good people, too. It is time to win; people want results now. It has been unique to be part of it."

One of his catchers early in the season was Adley Rutschman, who was promoted to Baltimore in late May.

"You won't hear any people that speak badly of Adley," said Naughton, who lived in England for a few years as a young boy with his family. "He is very well-rounded and committed to everything he does."

The top pitching prospect in the system is right-hander Grayson Rodriguez, a native of Texas who started at home for the Tides on May 27. Rodriguez, however, suffered a grade 2 lat strain in early June – postponing his possible rapid rise to Baltimore.

"I have been with Grayson since the year he got drafted," Naughton said. "He was already very good; to see him three years later he is even better. The sky is the limit for him."

Naughton, a reliever, held opponents to an average of .146 in his first 10 outings this year. He had an ERA of 3.38 in his first 13 appearances before landing on the 7-day Injured List.

When Norfolk hosted the Gwinnett Braves, the top farm team of Atlanta, in late May a key hitter for the visitors was infielder Phil Gosselin.

He was drafted in the fifth round out of the University of Virginia by the Braves in 2010 and since then had played for seven Major League teams through the 2021 season – Atlanta, Arizona, Pittsburgh, Texas, Cincinnati, Philadelphia, and the Angels.

Harbor Park in Norfolk has a long and rich history.

Norfolk won the Governors Cup title in 1972, 1973, 1982, 1983, and 1985.

That 1983 team – the Tidewater Tides – was the top affiliate of the New York Mets and included outfielder Darryl Strawberry, the overall No. 1 pick three years earlier out of a Los Angeles high school.

Other players to come through Tidewater that season included infielder Wally Backman and pitcher Ron Darling, a star at Yale.

That title team was managed by Davey Johnson, the former second baseman for the Orioles.

Three years later, Johnson led the Mets to the World Series title over the Boston Red Sox and among the key players for that team was Strawberry. Johnson later managed the Orioles and Nationals.

Perhaps the most vital person in Tidewater baseball history was Dave Rosenfield, the long-time general manager who died in 2017 at the age of 87.

He won several national awards during his long tenure with the team, including the Gil Hodges award from the Mets in 1983.

As you walk into Harbor Park back of home plate, there are plaques for those in the Hampton Roads Hall of Fame.

Among those baseball players honored are outfielder D.J. Dozier, who played at Norfolk State and in the majors; Wayne Gomes, a standout at ODU and the majors; slugger Michael Cuddyer, who won a batting title in the majors; former ODU coach Bud Metheny; and Marty Brennaman, the long-time voice of the Reds who got his start in Virginia. (This reporter recalls seeing Brennaman calling a basketball game at Madison College, now JMU, in the 1970s).

According to the Virginian-Pilot, "Organized baseball in Norfolk dates back to 1896, when the Norfolk Tars made their debut in the Virginia League. They later played in the Piedmont League as a farm team of the New York Yankees."

Naughton was let go by the Orioles in July and then signed with the Gastonia Honey Bears of North Carolina on August 5, 2022.

12

Justin Verlander, Top 100

Justin Verlander pitched in just one game for Houston in 2020 and didn't see action the next year due to injury.

But the Richmond-area native and former ODU standout certainly made a strong return to The Show this year.

In his first 10 starts this season for the Astros and manager Dusty Baker had posted an ERA of 2.23 with a WHIP well below 1.00.

Perhaps that should not be surprising for the veteran right-hander, who was named the 75th-best player in MLB history in a book published by Joe Posnanski in 2021.

He was the ALCS MVP in 2017 and that year helped the Astros win the Fall Classic.

Verlander was back in the World Series in 2019 and pitched against the Nationals, who won all four road games to take the series in seven games.

That Fall Classic included Washington's Ryan Zimmerman, a former University of Virginia product, and Lynchburg native Daniel Hudson, a reliever who also pitched at ODU.

Hudson was traded by the Nationals to the San Diego Padres in

July of 2021 and is now with the Dodgers; he was on the mound for the last out when the Nationals beat the Astros in Game 7 of the 2019 World Series.

Verlander was drafted out of ODU in the first round in 2004 by the Detroit Tigers while Hudson was taken in the fifth round by the Chicago White Sox four years later.

"Yeah, pretty cool," Verlander said during the 2019 World Series. "I actually haven't had time to speak to (Hudson). Go figure, World Series, we're pretty busy doing other stuff."

Verlander also has history with Zimmerman, who played at Kellam High in Virginia Beach and was drafted by Washington out of the University of Virginia in 2005.

"It's pretty cool how well-represented Virginia is as a whole," said Verlander, who played at Goochland High before becoming an all-conference pitcher at ODU.

Verlander shared a light moment with Zimmerman, who retired after the 2021 season, during Game 2 of the World Series in Houston. The right-hander tried to field a dribbler off the bat of Zimmermann but fell down while trying to make the play on the infield single.

"Growing up playing against Zim, he gave me a sly little look the other day after I threw the ball off my shin when he was at first base, which was pretty funny," Verlander said. "I remember going all the way back to my ODU days, him and I played golf together. From then to now, a lot has happened in both of our lives, but pretty cool to have our lives interconnect like that and to end up on this stage."

Hudson was born in Lynchburg and moved to the Tidewater region with his family at a young age. He played at Princess Anne High School in Virginia Beach before heading to ODU. He and his wife, Sara, met as freshmen in college and were married in 2011.

While Verlander broke spring training with Houston, Hudson was looking for a job when he was released on March 22 by the Los Angeles Angels in 2019. Three days later he was signed as a free agent by the Toronto Blue Jays, and he was 6-3 with an ERA of 3.00 in 45 games with the team before he was traded to the Nationals in late July.

The first game Hudson suited up in Washington with the Nationals just happened to be ODU Night at Nationals Park.

"It is a big coincidence," Hudson told this reporter that night. "I had a couple of people text me this morning and tell me they were going to be here. I didn't even know it was ODU Night. It is pretty cool."

The hard-throwing right-hander ended regular-season play with a 3-0 record and an ERA of 1.44 with six saves in 14 outings for the Nationals.

He then stepped up his game in the playoffs, as Hudson got the save in the wild-card game win over the Milwaukee Brewers in a stirring comeback win at Nationals Park on October 1. In the loud and joyous clubhouse after the game, Hudson filmed the celebration for his family, as his wife was back in Arizona waiting for the birth of their third child.

Hudson helped the Nationals beat the Los Angeles Dodgers in five games in the National League Division Series, then he missed Game 1 of the National League Championship Series against the St. Louis Cardinals to be with his wife as she had their third daughter.

He returned to the club for Game 2 and then got another save at home on October 15 in Game 4 against the Cardinals as the Nationals swept the National League Championship Series at Nationals Park.

Verlander was 18-4 in regular-season play in 2022 to give him 244 career wins – 22 back of Virginia native and Hall of Famer Eppa Rixey. At the age of 39, Verlander posted his first World Series win in Game 5 over the Phillies on November 3 and two days later he was a world champion once again as the Astros downed Philadelphia to win the series in six games.

13

Lorenzo Bundy, Veteran Manager

As a minor leaguer, Lorenzo Bundy played for teams in North Carolina, Virginia, Hawaii, New Hampshire, and Canada.

Bundy, as a manager in the minors, guided teams in Florida, South Carolina, Georgia, Iowa, and Nevada — plus 26 years in the Mexican winter leagues. For good measure, the former James Madison slugger was part of coaching staffs in the Major Leagues with Colorado, Arizona, Los Angeles, and Miami.

But until last year, his career had never taken him to a certain town in upstate New York: Binghamton, with about 50,000 people and once known as the Valley of Opportunity for its defense contracts during the Cold War. The Baseball Hall of Fame in Cooperstown is about 80 miles northeast of Binghamton.

"Ironically, in my 40 years of professional baseball, between playing, managing, and all that stuff, I've never been to Binghamton," said Bundy, a former MVP in the Valley Baseball League with New Market and in the Rockingham County Baseball League with Shenandoah.

Bundy, after being let go by the Marlins after the 2017 season, was set to be the manager of Double-A Binghamton in the New York Mets' system for the 2020 season.

He was in Florida in spring training with Mets' prospects when pro baseball shut down in March 2020 due to the pandemic. Bundy eventually made his way home to Arizona, where he has lived for many years with his wife and their daughter.

And while in Arizona, he waited ... and waited.

He managed again in the Mexican League prior to the 2021 season, then headed to Port St. Lucie to get ready for this season.

"Last year, unfortunately, we were not able to get here," he said of Binghamton. "Now we are here and it's time to play baseball. As bad as it was for me, who has been in this game a long time, I felt for my players, I felt for the players who didn't get a chance to play. It was put on hold last year. This is the most important thing: these guys are back on the baseball field and they are going to get a chance to continue with their development and hopefully on their way to the Major Leagues."

"Obviously, it's a special time," added Bundy. "It only took me 16 or 17 months to get here."

Bundy was on the move again this season as he joined the Chicago White Sox system to be the manager of high Single-A Winston-Salem in North Carolina.

That gives the White Sox another Virginia connection.

Gavin Sheets, the son of Staunton native and former big leaguer Larry Sheets, played for Winston-Salem on his way up the ladder with the White Sox.

The younger Sheets made his Major League debut in 2021 and has seen time back in the majors with the White Sox this year.

Bundy says he was grateful to land with the White Sox system after he parted ways with the Mets.

Winston-Salem, under Bundy, was 27-41 in the second half of the 2022 season in the Single-A South Division of the South Atlantic League.

14

Ryan Zimmerman Retires

Jeff Garber was a standout shortstop at JMU in the 1980s but never reached the majors as player, going as high as Triple-A in the Kansas City system.

But the native of Pennsylvania has been able to work with several All-Star big leaguers over the past decade with a focus on infielders in his work in player development with the Washington Nationals.

When Ryan Zimmerman announced his retirement on Feb. 15 of this year, Garber was quick with a compliment.

"What a great honor to watch and get to know Ryan! He set the standard for all Nationals!" Garber wrote.

"It was truly an honor to manage and share a clubhouse with Ryan Zimmerman," Washington manager Dave Martinez said in a statement. "Like many around Major League Baseball, I had a lot of respect for Ryan from watching the way he played and competed as an opponent. It wasn't until I came to Washington that I learned of his true impact on this organization, the fans and the community. He was a fierce competitor but also a calming presence when we needed it most. Ryan's numbers and accomplishments speak for themselves, but the way he led by example and was respected not only in our clubhouse but around the game—that is what I will remember most about his career. Not only was he a player I enjoyed managing, but he's also become a great friend. Congrats, Ryan. I wish you, Heather, and the kids nothing but the best."

When my family returned to the Washington area in the summer of 2004, after spending the academic year in Hungary, I picked up a print copy of Baseball America and was surprised to read that an infielder from the University of Virginia was among the top college prospects for the 2005 draft. He was called up to the majors later that year after less than 100 games in the minors – and Zimmerman was in the Major Leagues the rest of his career.

I grew up in Harrisonburg and followed the Cavaliers' program from a distance but wasn't familiar with the name listed in Baseball America: Zimmerman, who ended his career as the all-time leader on the Nationals in several categories, including home runs with 284. He won a Gold Glove at third base before making the switch to first.

Baseball America, as is usually the case, was right. Zimmerman had a strong year in 2005 for Virginia and was drafted in the first round by the Nationals that year. And you probably know the rest of the story.

Early in his career, if my memory has not failed me, Zimmerman told me at one point he planned to play baseball at JMU.

But the stock of Zimmerman grew in high school, Virginia got into the recruiting picture and he was able to face tough pitchers in the ACC while in Charlottesville.

Mark Reynolds and Zimmerman had been teammates at the University of Virginia—and in 2011 Reynolds was in his first season with the Orioles.

Zimmerman was a year ahead of Reynolds at Virginia and the two got together for meals when their teams would meet.

They were part of a major league pipeline from the Tidewater region which included David Wright, B.J. and Justin Upton, and Mike Cuddyer, among others. Zimmerman was born in North Carolina and went to Kellam High in Virginia Beach while Reynolds was born in Kentucky and went to First Colonial High, also in Virginia Beach.

"Funny how that worked out," Zimmerman said. For good measure New York native Brendan Harris, a former Nationals' backup third baseman, played in college at William and Mary and was in spring training with the Orioles as a non-roster invite as well that year.

Zimmerman, like many players, sometimes was hesitant to talk about himself. But when asked to comment on a teammate, Zimmerman would come through with a good quote.

Ryan Zimmerman meets the press on June 18, 2022, the day his No. 11 was retired by the Nationals

Pitcher Sean Doolittle posted this on social media the day Zimmerman retired: "From UVA to DC, Zim had such a huge impact on my career. To the OG Nat Mr. Walkoff -It was a privilege. Congratulations on an amazing career. I can't wait to see what the Ryan Zimmerman statue at Nats Park looks like!"

Mark D. Lerner, Managing Principal Owner of the Washington Nationals, also released a statement in February: "On behalf of my family and the entire Washington Nationals organization, we would like to congratulate Ryan on a tremendous career and thank him for his contributions both on the field and in our community. Ryan will forever be Mr. National. From the walk-off home runs, to carrying the World Series Trophy down Constitution Avenue, to the final day of the 2021 regular season when our fans gave him an ovation that none of us will soon forget, Ryan gave us all 17 years of amazing memories. We wish him, Heather, their four beautiful children and the rest of their family nothing but the best in all of their future endeavors."

Nationals President of Baseball Operations and General Manager Mike Rizzo watched Zimmerman closely for years.

"For 17 seasons, Ryan Zimmerman epitomized what it meant to be the Face of the Franchise. He was an All-Star, Gold Glove, and Silver Slugger winner, Comeback Player of the Year and World Series champion—but those accolades pale in comparison to his impact on our organization and in the community during his career. Ryan always carried himself with class, honor and respect and played the game for the name on the front of the jersey, not the one on the back. I want to personally congratulate Ryan on a fantastic career and wish him and the entire Zimmerman family all the best in retirement," Rizzo said in a statement.

Zimmerman was honored before a game at Virginia earlier this year and his number was retired by the Nationals during a ceremony in June.

15

Chris Marinak, MLB Front Office

Several former University of Virginia baseball players have made it to the Major Leagues.

So has Chris Marinak, though he made it as an executive and not as a pitcher.

The Virginia Beach native is the Executive Vice President, Strategy, Technology/Innovation at MLB, and is involved in nearly every major off-the-field facet that is important to MLB commissioner Rob Manfred.

In the past, he has been heavily involved in putting together the MLB schedule, though now he focuses more on social media and technology.

"We have a pretty complex and extensive software program," Marinak said.

The Marinak family home is normally in Manhattan. He and his, wife, Jennifer have three children.

The former Cavalier reliever has risen better than a high fastball as an executive with MLB.

After he was promoted twice in less than a year, Sports Business

Journal listed him as one of their top 40 in the sports industry under the game of 40 in 2018.

Marinak graduated from the University of Virginia with a Bachelor of Science in Computer Engineering; he also has an MBA from Harvard Business School. He was working with Capital One in Northern Virginia while assisting with the baseball program at James Madison High of Vienna in 2006.

"I decided I wanted to go back to business school. To me that seemed like the perfect fit. I went to business school with the idea of getting back into baseball," he said.

Marinak landed an internship with Major League Baseball in 2007. He joined the Office of the Commissioner in 2008 after graduating from Harvard Business School and has been there ever since.

"Marinak has been called nothing less than an archetypal league executive by his boss, Major League Baseball Commissioner Rob Manfred," Sports Business Journal wrote. "With a background that combines playing baseball at the collegiate level at the University of Virginia, engineering, and business administration, Marinak now has one of the broadest portfolios of responsibility of anybody in the sport outside of Manfred himself.

"Working on league economics, strategy, and initiatives such as MLB's instant replay system for much of the past decade, Marinak was promoted twice last year in the span of just eight months. The first promotion last spring elevated him to executive vice president and added perennially thorny issues such as creating the master league schedule to his plate."

And Marinak has fans in high places.

"If you were going to create a high-potential individual at MLB, it would look a whole lot like Chris," Manfred told Sports Business Journal. "You look at the total breadth and diversity of his background, that checks a lot of boxes for us."

That includes playing at the Division I level in Charlottesville for the Cavaliers — his future was not as a player.

On April 2, 2002, in Harrisonburg, Marinak faced four batters and all of them scored in a 13-4 loss to James Madison. The Virginia Beach product allowed one walk and one hit and did not retire a batter.

"I struggled toward the second half of my senior year; I ended up having some arm problems," Marinak said of his senior 2002 season. "The great thing about playing (against) JMU is you got back to your roots; a lot of friends from high school would come to the game. It was always nice playing JMU."

In his last year at Virginia, he was 2-3 with an ERA of 6.31 in 23 games out of the bullpen in 2002. His teammates that season included slugger Mark Reynolds, a former member of the Baltimore Orioles and Washington Nationals who retired in 2020; and Joe Koshansky, who is from Chantilly and played with the Colorado Rockies in 2007-08.

Chris Marinak

16

Curtis Pride, Gallaudet Coach

Curtis Pride stood in the third-base coaches' box, giving pointers to Gallaudet University baserunner Yebi Areola in the last of the third inning in a college baseball game in northeast Washington.

A few pitches later Areola sprinted home after a teammate hit an infield grounder against Keuka, a New York school. But Areola ran into the catcher, was called out and ejected by home plate umpire Roger Wolfe due to "malicious contact" in the game a few seasons ago.

It's one of the unique challenges for Curtis Pride, the former big-league outfielder who has been the head baseball coach at Division III Gallaudet since 2008. He was a standout baseball and basketball player at William and Mary in Williamsburg.

Pride, who certainly didn't advise such a maneuver on the bases, pointed out that Areola is a freshman who may not have been familiar with the rules. "You can't run over the catcher," Pride said.

Other challenges at Gallaudet, the only university in the country for the deaf and hard of hearing, include fostering communication between infielders and outfielders.

And when it comes to finding athletes, Pride points out there are only so many deaf and hard-of-hearing high school baseball players in the country.

"The biggest challenge is recruiting," said Pride, who was born deaf but reads lips very well. "I probably have the most difficult job of college coaches for recruiting. I recruit deaf or hard-of-hearing players. There are not that many out there. Once I get the player I have to develop the skill to get them up to the college level."

But Gallaudet, while 4-28-1 overall through April 28, has had its share of success under Pride.

Several of his former players appeared in professional independent leagues, and others have played in the Maryland-based Cal Ripken Collegiate League.

And perhaps, more importantly, Pride, who became an ambassador for inclusion with Major League Baseball in 2016, continues to be a role model for many of his student-athletes.

"A lot of kids look up to me," said Pride, sitting in his office. "I want to be able to help them and share my experience with them."

His players look up to former Major Leaguer.

"When I was growing up as a kid I remember seeing coach Pride playing on TV with the Angels," former center fielder Kyle Gumm of Texas wrote in an e-mail. "My father explained to me that coach Pride was deaf. Later on in high school, I found out coach Pride was coaching at Gallaudet and I was thinking about coming here. It has been a great experience that coach Pride has been able to coach me."

Former pitcher/utility man Dylan Hayes welcomed the chance to play for Pride.

"It was tough at times but there were a lot of good lessons to learn," he wrote. "He pushed us to be better players and we developed quicker (maturity wise) because of his coaching. We were also more responsible as students. We stayed focused and learned so much about baseball and life from him. Looking back on the past four years, he was the best coach I have ever had. He made sure we (the team) were good people making the right decisions and doing the right things."

So does Hayes consider Pride a role model?

"Absolutely. One of the main reasons is his own life story. Coming up as deaf he knew the obstacles he had to overcome. So he has instilled in us to believe you can achieve anything," Hayes wrote.

Curtis Pride has been the baseball coach at Gallaudet for more than a decade.

Pride didn't plan to stay at Gallaudet for so long.

He figured he would stay a few years and then get another job in baseball, perhaps as a minor league coach or manager.

But he continues to split his time between the Washington area and his home in Florida, where he lives with his wife Lisa, a son and daughter.

"It's a tough balance," he said of the commuting. "My family is my No. 1 priority. My wife loves Florida."

Pride has a photo in his office of meeting President Obama at the White House, and the Gallaudet coach made several trips there during the Obama administration.

Pride played in the majors from 1993 to 2006, hitting .250 in 421 games.

He is one of the few hearing-impaired players to make the majors. The field at Gallaudet is named for one of them: Dummy Hoy, a native of Ohio who broke into the big leagues with the Washington Nationals in 1888 and stole 596 bases in his career.

Pride has a book about Hoy in his office and would like to see Hoy gain Hall of Fame status. That is one of his many causes, including being a role model for his players.

"I want to help them understand what it means to be a productive member of society," Pride said.

17

Bobby Brown, Bright Lights of NYC

Bobby Brown is one of the few products of Northampton County on the Eastern Shore to play in one of the four sports leagues in North America.

But his journey to the Major Leagues wasn't easy.

Born in Eastville, he was drafted by the Orioles in the 11th round in 1972 and began his pro career in Bluefield that year in the Appalachian League.

Among his teammates in the minors: future Hall of Famer Eddie Murray and pitchers Mike Flanagan and Dennis Martinez. All of them would be key cogs in the 1979 Orioles World Series team.

Brown, however, was released by the Orioles before he made it to Baltimore.

"I got released and came back and worked for a food distributor in Norfolk," Brown, who now lives in Chesapeake, said in a telephone interview in June.

But a former minor league director with the Orioles had been let go and joined the Phillies and suggested Philadelphia sign

Brown.He joined the Phillies' system in 1976 and played in the minors that year for Peninsula in the Single-A Carolina League.

Brown made his Major League debut for Toronto in 1979 going hitless in four at-bats against Kansas City, which started Dennis Leonard on the mound.

The outfielder joined the Yankees later that year and played in the World Series for New York in 1981 against the Los Angeles Dodgers.

The Norfolk native joined Seattle in 1982 and then played for San Diego the next year.

Brown appeared in his second World Series in 1984 as the Padres lost to the Detroit Tigers. He had just one hit 16 at-bats in that series as San Diego was swept by the Tigers.

An outfielder for the Tigers in the series was Richmond native Johnny Grubb.

Brown played his last game in the Majors in 1985 for San Diego; he ended his career with 26 homers and an average of .245 in 502 games.

Brown is a cousin of Charles Fisher, who was a star basketball guard at James Madison University in the 1980s.

18

Jake Cave, Patience

Jake Cave stood in the dugout of the Scranton/Wilkes-Barre RailRiders late Monday afternoon following batting practice a few seasons back, about 90 minutes before game time and 90 minutes after Major League Baseball's non-waiver trade deadline expired.

The former Kecoughtan High star, now at the Triple-A level in the New York Yankees' farm system as an outfielder, realized his season could have turned out much differently had he made the opening-day roster of the Cincinnati Reds.

But the 23-year-old also knows he may be in a good spot as the Yankees appear ready to reshape their roster and make it younger after trades in the past few days of veteran outfielder Carlos Beltran and relievers Andrew Miller and Aroldis Chapman.

Cave was plucked from the Yankees' system by the Reds after the winter meetings early in his career. That meant Cave had to spend the entire season on the Reds' roster or be sent back to the Yankees.

A left-handed hitter with speed, Cave was the last cut by the Reds in spring training and went back to the Yankees. He began the year at Double-A Trenton of the Eastern League before being promoted to Triple-A Scranton of the International League.

"I think if I would have been there (in Cincinnati) until maybe right now, when they traded Jay Bruce, I don't think I was going to play much," Cave said, moments after the Reds traded Bruce to the New York Mets. "Maybe a blessing in disguise. It would have been cool to get a year of service time (in the majors). But I want to play."

Cave was talking on the day that his outfield teammate Ben Gamel was promoted to the Yankees along with pitcher Nick Goody. Both have previous major-league experience.

Cave feels his time will come and he feels his time with the Reds will serve him well.

"It was cool to be able to see a different organization and met different players," he said, standing in the Scranton dugout. "I almost had a chance to be in the bigs. But I am still young. I am 23. I will have a lot of chances to come, hopefully."

Cave started in center field and batted leadoff Monday against the host Lehigh Valley IronPigs, the top farm club of the Philadelphia Phillies. He entered the game hitting .268 with an on-base average of .333 in 62 Triple-A games. He had 231 at-bats, with 12 doubles, six triples, four homers and 28 RBI, with three steals in six tries.

Bruton High graduate Mark Montgomery, a former pitcher at Longwood University, was on a travel team with Cave when the two were in high school. Montgomery has been teammates with Cave this season at Scranton/Wilkes-Barre.

"It sounds silly to say, but he is a real good baseball player," Montgomery said of Cave.

In Triple-A, Cave had fanned 55 times but had drawn just 19 walks before the Monday game.

"I started off down in Trenton and started off really well," Cave said. "I got up here (to Triple-A) and started playing pretty good. I have not played as well as late, but that is how the baseball season goes. It is like a roller coaster. You have your ups and downs."

"Cave has done a good job for us," Scranton manager Al Pedrique said. "He has been playing all three outfield positions. For the first time he is playing right field. I think he has adjusted to that role really well.

"This is a kid who works very hard. His work ethic is outstanding. He comes to the park wanting to play every day. Offensively, he has been working on timing and hand position. He spends a lot of time in the cage with the hitting coach (Tom Wilson), trying to be consistent with his approach."

Cave has played all three outfield positions on a regular basis this year for the first time in his pro career, which began in 2011 when he was drafted by the Yankees.

"I like him better in left field. But you can put him in center and he does a good job," Pedrique said. "His routes and jumps are much better than last year. I have had him the last three years and I can see improvement in his defense. His arm strength is better this year. He is making the right decisions to throw to the right base. He is a young guy with tools. It is a matter of time for him to put things together. We hope that he will finish up for a solid year."

Cave said he likes center field the best since he played that first. And he certainly takes charge: In the second inning of Monday's game, he drifted well left to catch a routine fly ball off the bat of J.P. Crawford, and Cave shared a laugh with left fielder Jose Rosario.

"I think that was a big advantage to learn center field before the corners," Cave said. "Right field is the one that is not as familiar, but I have played it well and I feel comfortable at all three."

The Yankees acquired top outfield prospect Clint Frazier from the Indians in the deal that sent lefty Miller, a former University of North Carolina standout, to Cleveland.

"Obviously I am a little biased, but I thought we had some good young outfielders in the system, and not just me," Cave said. "I did not know they were going to get him."

But the recent trades may help Cave get a longer look the rest of this season and in spring training in 2017.

"It gives us a little confidence that maybe the Yankees are caring about their young guys now," Cave said. "You have to go out there and play no matter the situation. I just want to get back to consistently hitting the baseball and play the outfield the way I have been playing. I want to finish the year with consistency at the plate. I want to finish the year strong."

The Cave file

Hometown: Hampton.

High school: Kecoughtan.

Born: Dec. 4, 1992.

Bats/throws: Left/left.

Position: Outfield.

Drafted: Sixth round in 2011 out of high school by the Yankees.

Did you know? In high school, he was a travel-club teammate of Mark Montgomery, a former pitcher at Longwood University who is now with Scranton/Wilkes-Barre. ... Cave hit .269 in 125 games with Double-A Trenton in 2015, with 22 doubles and 17 steals in 20 tries, and played in seven games with Triple-A Scranton. ... Cave had several family and friends on hand when Scranton played a series in Norfolk against the Tides in late May.

Update: Cave hit 13 homers as a rookie in 2018 with the Twins, but hit just three while batting .189 in 76 games with Minnesota in 2021. Cave signed a one-year contract for the 2023 season with the Orioles following the 2022 season.

19

Eddie Butler, From The Show To Indy Ball

In his first Major League game, he faced a Dodgers lineup that included Dee Strange-Gordon, Matt Kemp, and Justin Turner in 2014.

In his last outing in The Show, he had the task of facing Seattle hitters such as Robinson Cano and Nelson Cruz four years later.

From the start as a rookie for the Rockies to that last outing out of the bullpen for the Rangers, Chesapeake native Eddie Butler had the challenge of being a starting pitcher at Coors Field in Denver to pitching in the friendly confines of Wrigley Field with the Cubs for part of the 2017-18 seasons.

It was a heady career for Butler, a lightly-recruited pitcher out of Greenbrier Christian in Chesapeake who became one of the few Radford University products to make the majors.

But after 79 appearances in the majors, including 39 starts, the right-hander found himself at the independent league level with the Southern Maryland Blue Crabs when the 2022 season began.

"These guys know what they are doing in the (hitter's) box. They have been around for years," said Butler, 31, standing outside of the Southern Maryland clubhouse behind the left-field wall this past

May. "There are plenty of big-league guys there" in the opposing clubhouse.

In his outing here in May, Butler faced a Gastonia lineup that featured two former big leaguers: Jack Reinheimer, an infielder who played for the Braves and Mets; and outfielder Johnny Davis, who played in eight games for Tampa Bay in 2019.

The DH for Gastonia was Zach Jarrett, who played in the Valley Baseball League with Woodstock in 2014 during his college career at Charlotte. He reached the Triple-A level in the Baltimore system with the Norfolk Tides before he was released before the 2022 campaign.

Gastonia jumped on Butler's fastball early and scored two runs in the top of the first – and threatened for more throughout the six innings Butler was on the mound.

"They make you make adjustments," he said. "I went in with a game plan to attack with hitters and they were ready for it. They hit it around the park a little bit but we were able to find an adjustment and battle through six."

Butler lasted six innings as the Blue Crabs came back to win 4-2 with three runs in the last of the eighth. Alexandria native Mat Latos recorded the last three outs for the save.

Butler doesn't have access to detailed scouting reports in the Atlantic League as he did in the majors.

"We have Trackman; it is a little tougher with the hitters. We see their numbers but we don't have hit charts and stuff like that," he said. "Without having those, you have to go in and attack with your best weapon and make adjustments from there."

Butler grew up in the Tidewater area and around the same as other future big leaguers, including Neil Ramirez, the Upton brothers, Justin Verlander, and Ryan Zimmerman.

"We had a ton of guys I looked up to. We had Josh Richardson, who I played with at Greenbrier Christian," Butler said. "There is a lot of good talent in the area."

Richardson went on to play at Liberty University, was drafted by the Padres in 2013 as a pitcher, and reached the high Single-A level the next year in the California League.

One of the most important coaches for Butler growing up was Gary Lavelle, an All-Star in the majors who made 745 appearances from 1974-87 and had 136 saves with an ERA of 2.93.

Eddie Butler was born in Chesapeake and began the 2022 season pitching for Southern Maryland in the Atlantic League

Butler first crossed paths with Verlander when they were working with Lavelle.

"I first started doing lessons with him when I was 9," Butler said of Lavelle, who was born in Scranton, Pennsylvania and broke in with the Giants in 1974. "He was the head coach when I was at Greenbrier Christian."

Since pitching in the majors, Butler has played in Korea and last year was with Triple-A Omaha in the Kansas City system.

"I have struggled in the past with walking guys; I need to attack hitters, I need to put them away. I need to go out there and show them I am healthy and try to get a job" with a Major League organization.

Having made plenty of money in The Show, Butler wouldn't have to be riding buses in the Atlantic League and making a penance of what he made with the Cubs, Rockies, and Rangers.

"We are all kids, we all love the game," Butler said. "If we didn't love the game we wouldn't be here. It is a good league and all that. But you have to love the game to be out here playing every day."

Other pitchers on the Southern Maryland roster this spring included three more Virginia natives: former Major Leaguer Latos, who grew up in Florida; Nick Wells, who was also born in Alexandria, went to Battlefield High and was in the minors with Washington before he was released in March; and Patrick Baker, a native of Fairfax who reached the Single-A level in the Orioles' system.

Baker didn't allow a run in his first 11 outings this year, Butler had an ERA of 5.68 in his first seven starts, Latos had 11 saves as of early June and Wells posted an ERA of 1.98 in his first 13 games with the Blue Crabs.

"He has been good; his stuff is electric," Butler said of Wells, who was drafted by the Blue Jays out of Battlefield. "He has a lot of deception, a lot of moving parts."

Southern Maryland lost 10-2 in Game 5 to Lancaster on Sept. 25, 2022 as the season ended for the Blue Crabs.

Butler was 12-6 with an ERA of 4.94 in 26 starts for Southern Maryland in 2022.

Part III
CENTRAL VIRGINIA AND SOUTHSIDE

20

Brian O'Connor, Powerhouse

Brian O'Connor had never been to Virginia when he started driving from his native Nebraska to Harrisonburg in the spring of 1990 to play for the Turks in the Valley Baseball League.

"I drove out here with two of my teammates that I played with at Creighton," recalls O'Connor, then a college pitcher at the Omaha school.

Little did he know that more than 30 years later his name would be part of the baseball landscape in Virginia as the coach of the college power Cavaliers.

That 1990 Turks team also included catchers Tom Walter and Kevin O'Sullivan. Both are also current Division I head coaches—Walter at Wake Forest and O'Sullivan, who played at Virginia, at Florida. While one of the goals of the VBL is to help send players to the pro ranks, this Harrisonburg team paved the way for top-flight college coaches.

"That is pretty amazing there are three Division I coaches" from that team, O'Connor said.

The 1990 season was the first as an owner for Bob Wease with the Turks.

"They were all three pretty good players," said Wease, also the long-time Harrisonburg manager. "I am really proud of those guys. It is an honor to watch these guys play and then go on with their lives, either as players or coaches."

The most prominent in these parts is O'Connor, who in 2015 led the University of Virginia to the College World Series title in his hometown of Omaha. Six years earlier the Cavaliers made their first showing at the CWS—and the first for a Virginia school since James Madison made a trip in 1983 under Brad Babcock.

Virginia Coach Brian O'Connor (left) led the Cavs to the College World Series title in 2015. He is shown here with Mike Cubbage,(right) a former star at Virginia

O'Sullivan led Florida to the national title in 2017.

"Two of those guys have won a national title. I am hoping to complete the trifecta," Walter said, with a laugh.

That 1990 Turks team also included JMU products Mike Hubbard, Larry Mitchell, and Doug Harris. Lynchburg native Hubbard, a catcher, and Charlottesville High graduate and pitcher Mitchell made it to the majors as players. Harris peaked at Triple-A as a pitcher and was an assistant general manager last year for the world champion Washington Nationals.

Hubbard began the 1990 summer season playing with the Harrisonburg Chicks in the Rockingham County Baseball League before Wease, who was overseeing both clubs, called him up to the Turks. The manager for the Turks in 1990 was Curt Kendall, the former coach at Bridgewater College and now the athletic director there.

"I was coming off my freshman year at JMU," Hubbard said. "I do remember Brian O'Connor and other folks."

O'Connor spent the summer of 1990 working for the city of Harrisonburg during the day and playing for the Turks at night.

"I needed to make money. I got up early in the morning and worked for the city on the paint crew, and painted street lines," said O'Connor, who was then 18. "We had this machine on the back of the truck. It taught me discipline. I needed to roll out of bed every morning and work a job. It was a great experience. We all lived together in this old college dorm."

The Turks—in a baseball rarity—had off the night of July 4, 1990, according to O'Connor. So he headed to the nation's capital for the first time in his life and took in the anniversary celebrations on the National Mall, along with some VBL teammates.

That summer of 1990, Walter also had a day job.

"I worked on the back of a trash truck," he said. "It was the greatest summer job of all time. You worked your route until you were done. You would get paid for eight hours. We would start at 7 a.m. and there was never a day we were not done by 11 a.m."

After that summer, Walter went back to Georgetown for his senior season. Once his college career was over, he got into coaching as an assistant at George Washington.

He was later the manager for the New Market Rebels as they won the VBL title in 1994. One of his pitchers was lefty Mike Venafro, a JMU product who would play in the majors from 1999 to 2006.

Another future Major Leaguer with the Turks in 1990, according to Wease was pitcher Sean Maloney, a Georgetown product who broke in with Milwaukee in 1997 and pitched for the Dodgers the following season.

As for O'Connor, he doesn't remember his statistics from his season with the Turks in 1990. "I got to start some games on the mound. The competition was very good," he said.

O'Connor, after a summer in Harrisonburg, spent 1991 playing in the Alaskan League. After college and one summer of Rookie ball he got into coaching and took over the Cavaliers before the 2004 season after working as an assistant at Creighton and Notre Dame.

He learned to win in Harrisonburg three decades ago, though the Turks lost in the playoffs in 1990.

"Bob had a fire in his belly," O'Connor said. "Bob Wease wanted to win. He did not like losing; I liked that. You want to win all of the time. He was very, very competitive."

Virginia advanced to the College World Series again in 2021 but had the 2022 season come to an end in the Greenville Regional.

On July 7, 2022, former University of Virginia pitcher Andrew Abbott was named to the roster of the National League for The Futures Game to be held in Los Angeles at Dodgers Stadium on July 16. Born in Lynchburg and a product of Halifax County High, Abbott is a promising prospect with the Reds. He was at Double-A in early July after being drafted in the second round by Cincinnati in 2021 out of Virginia.

21

Mike Cubbage, A Baseball Lifer

Charlottesville native Mike Cubbage, a former University of Virginia baseball standout, hit .264 in his first full season as an infielder for the Minnesota Twins in 1977.

That same season teammate Rod Carew, a future Hall of Famer, flirted with the magical .400 mark before settling at .388 by season's end.

"He just had a phenomenal year," recalls Cubbage, a member of the Valley Baseball League Hall of Fame after playing for Charlottesville and Staunton as an amateur.

"The next spring, I think, he offered to make a bet with me. He said, 'I will bet you a hundred dollars I will out-hit you by 100 points.' You have to take that bet. You are not much of a man if you don't take that bet. So I took that bet."

In 1978, the lefty-hitting Carew 'slipped' to an average of .333 while Cubbage had the best of his eight seasons in the majors with an average of .282.

"So in 1978 he lost that bet but he never paid up," recalls Cubbage, a graduate of Lane High in Charlottesville. "But when you are dealing with someone like Carew it is not a sure thing. If he hit .388 again I was going to have to hit .288."

"I had a really good first half that year," Cubbage recalls of 1978 with the Twins. "At the All-Star break, I think I was third in the league in hitting. Of course, Carew was leading and then Fred Lynn (of Boston) and then Mike Cubbage. It was the best half I had. It seemed like I never put a full season together."

Mike Cubbage

THAT IS JUST one of the Major League memories for Cubbage, who retired about two years ago after a long career in pro baseball as a player, big-league manager, minor-league manager, and scout.

After six years as a professional scout for the Nationals, Cubbage retired at the end of October, 2020 after assisting Washington in its World Series run in 2019.

"To me, he is a very humble guy," Bobby Myrick, a long-time amateur scout for the Nationals based out of Colonial Heights, said. "He is very, very intelligent. He is a quality, quality baseball man. He did everything" in the game.

Cubbage, who also played football for the Cavaliers, was drafted out of Virginia in the second round by the Washington Senators in 1971. In addition to playing for the Rangers, Twins and Mets from 1974-81, he was an interim manager for the Boston Red Sox and Mets before becoming a scout for several teams.

He hit a homer in his last at-bat, in October 1981 for the Mets against reliever Jeff Reardon of Montreal. Cubbage never appeared in a postseason game as a player but was a coach third-base coach for the Red Sox in the 2003 playoffs.

Cubbage, a lefty hitter, broke into the majors with Texas.

"I first made the Rangers in 1974 out of Double-A baseball under (manager) Billy Martin," Cubbage said.

"Billy kept three rookies that year. The other two were Jim Sundberg, a catcher who had a nice long career, and Mike Hargrove, who was the rookie of the year. They were starters. I really was just pinch-hitting and riding the bench. I was bouncing between Spokane in the Pacific Coat League" and Texas.

"I came back in 1975 and Billy put me in the lineup and I had a chance to play," Cubbage said. "Billy has a special place in my heart. He was the manager that told me I had made the club" at the end of spring training in 1974.

"Billy played me a lot. I had some 70 some at-bats that spring. Dave Nelson was the starting second baseman and he would lead off and get two or three at-bats. I would get three or four at-bats in a game I ended up making the club," said Cubbage, a second cousin to former Orioles' catcher Larry Haney of Orange County.

Cubbage also played in the majors for manager Gene Mauch with the Twins from 1976-80.

"Gene Mauch, to me, in all my years in baseball was the smartest guy I have ever known in uniform," Cubbage said. "It is not even a close contest. He was brilliant. He was a master psychologist and a serious competitor. I loved playing for Gene. He made me feel better about myself than any manager I played for."

Cubbage said that Hall of Fame manager Tony La Russa, now with the Chicago White Sox, was a big fan of Mauch — who died in California in 2005.

"He modeled his style after Gene Mauch," Cubbage says of La Russa. "If they had a clinic how to manage a Major League team, Mauch would be the model. He had the respect. He had those heart-wrenching defeats with the Phillies (in 1964) and the Angels against the Red Sox in the 1986 playoffs."

"That was the cross he bore and took to his grave. I learned so much baseball from Gene Mauch," Cubbage added. "The fundamentals of the game. I learned a lot of sports psychology from Gene Mauch that I used for my entire career."

As a manager in the Mets' minor-league system, Cubbage guided Lynchburg in the Single-A Carolina League for two years. The second year his pitching coach was Jim Bibby, who played for the Pirates in the 1979 World Series against the Baltimore Orioles. Cubbage also managed Norfolk in the Mets' system.

Cubbage managed the Mets in 1991 for just a few games at the end of the season after Bud Harrelson was fired as manager. "It was not a very good team. It got Bud Harrelson fired," Cubbage said.

Frank Cashen, a former Orioles' general manager, was the Mets' executive that asked Cubbage to take over. "He was a big fan of mine," Cubbage said of Cashen, who retired after the 1991 season.

Jeff Torborg became the manager of the Mets in 1992 and Cubbage stayed on as a member of the coaching staff. The Mets were playing Montreal late in the season when a fan hollered at Cubbage, who was on the field during a break in play.

"It could be worse. You could be managing this team," said the fan, according to Cubbage. "Those were bad teams."

The Mets' roster that year included two pitchers who went to high school in Northern Virginia: Pete Schourek and Rich Sauveur. In his last game as Mets' manager, Cubbage watched as ace New York pitcher David Cone fanned 19 batters in Philadelphia for a team that was 77-84.

Cubbage, as a scout for the Nationals, followed the Milwaukee Brewers at the end of the 2019 season. He turned in a report on the Brewers and lefty reliever Josh Hader, who had been drafted out of high school by the Orioles.

It was Juan Soto of Washington that got a hit with the bases loaded against Hader in the eighth inning of the Wild-Card game that gave the host Nationals a win en route to their first World Series crown.

Cubbage was still in high school when he first played in the Valley League with his hometown Charlottesville club. He was still eligible to play another year of American Legion ball, but instead, he got to face pitchers with pro experience at a time the Valley League allowed former minor-league standouts to play.

"I was 17 and my first game was at Waynesboro. My first two at-bats I struck out against some really good curveballs. My third at-bat I hit a home run," said Cubbage, who played briefly for the Staunton Braves before turning pro the next year.

And from there, the Charlottesville native took off for a pro career that lasted more than five decades. Now he spends time with his extended family and is a member of the Virginia Sports Hall of Fame located in the Tidewater region.

22

Tanner Morris, Hitting Machine

Tanner Morris has gone from playing in the Rockingham County Baseball League in 2020 to reaching the Double-A level in the Toronto system this year with New Hampshire.

And the former University of Virginia infielder has also gone a long way in terms of geography – he was in Vancouver, British Columbia last year at the Single-A level in the Toronto farm system.

He hit .285 last season and was hitting .324 with an OPS of .941 in early June of this year with the Fisher Cats of New Hampshire.

Morris, from Crozet, was drafted out of Virginia by the Blue Jays in 2019 in the fifth round. With no minor league season in 2020, he played for Stuarts Draft in the RCBL.

He has worked out in the past at Next Level Athletic Development in Harrisonburg under the guidance of owner Mike Martin.

"He is a very smart and well read guy, including research related to hitting and performance, so he wanted to know the, 'why,' behind a lot of the stuff we did because it needed to resonate with him. I appreciated that about him because not only did it force me to stay on my toes, it also allowed us to build a pretty quick base of trust in terms of the training design," Martin notes.

"The other thing about Tanner is he does a great job filtering out noise. Meaning, he's pretty single-minded when it comes to his career, eliminates distractions and is very process-oriented in terms of his development. He drove about an hour each way, every day from Crozet to train here which clearly speaks to that," added Martin, a graduate of Eastern Mennonite University. "From a physical standpoint, he knew he needed to continue to build a solid movement and strength foundation last off-season in order to put himself in a position to make a big jump physically this upcoming off-season with the end goal being to drive the ball more and improve his power numbers at the plate. In sum, he's able to see the big picture and then break that into individual steps he needs to reach in order to obtain the end goal."

Will Wagner, the son of former Major League closer Billy Wagner, made his pro debut on Aug. 4, 2021, for Single-A Fayetteville of North Carolina in the Houston farm system.

He went 1-for-3 in his first game against Fredericksburg, a farm team of the Nationals.

Wagner played for Montezuma in 2020 in the RCBL and was drafted the next year by the Astros in the 18th round. He hit .299 last year in the minors and was batting .272 in early June of this year with Single-A Asheville.

He played at The Miller School of Albemarle for his father—who spent time with Houston during his career—and then in college at Liberty in Lynchburg. Billy Wagner was drafted out of Ferrum in the first round by Houston in 1993 and broke into the majors two years later with the Astros. The lefty ended up with 422 career saves in the majors.

Former Clemson catcher Adam Hackenberg, who played for Montezuma in 2020 in the RCBL, made his pro debut on Aug. 3, 2021, for Single-A Kannapolis of North Carolina in the Chicago White Sox system.

Hackenberg, from the Charlottesville area, was drafted by the White Sox earlier this year in the 18th round. He hit .320 in the minors in 2021 and was batting .266 in early June for Winston-Salem and manager Lorenzo Bundy, a former standout at JMU, the Valley Baseball League, and in the RCBL with Shenandoah.

Another White Sox prospect with ties to the RCBL is Gavin Sheets, whose father Larry played for Shenandoah while in college at Eastern Mennonite.

The younger Sheets split time between the White Sox and Triple-A Charlotte last year. He hit a homer at Baltimore last season with his father, a former Orioles' slugger, in the stands.

Gavin Sheets was hitting .208 with four homers in early June with the White Sox this season.

Roanoke native Nick Robertson, a former JMU standout, was back with Double-A Tulsa in the Dodgers' system this year as a reliever.

He had an ERA of 3.53 last year and that was was up to 5.23 in his first 15 outings out of the bullpen this year.

Robertson was drafted by the Dodgers in the seventh round in 2019 by the Dodgers.

He did not play in 2020 since there was no minor league season, but he was in Instructional League last fall in Arizona and then in spring training with the big club earlier this year.

The last pitcher —and player—to appear in a Major League game from the JMU program was Ryan Reid, who grew up in Maine.

His last appearance came on July 4, 2013, for the Pittsburgh Pirates against the Phillies. The last hitter he faced was John Mayberry, who grounded out as Phils won 6-4.

Reid pitched in seven games that season for the Pirates.

Other Double-A pitchers from the JMU program this year included Shelton Perkins, with Bowie in the Baltimore system, and Kevin Kelly, also at that level before he was promoted to Triple-A.

23

Larry Haney, Orioles Glory Days

Larry Haney was a baseball and football star at Orange County High and appeared headed to Virginia Tech to play football as a quarterback.

. But in 1961, at the age of 18, he decided to sign with the Baltimore Orioles at the urging of legendary scout Walter Youse.

"It was probably the best decision I ever made," he told us in a phone interview this year.

Not only did Haney go on to play in the Major Leagues from 1966 to 1978, but the resident of Barboursville may have faced a tough challenge in football for the Hokies.

Haney most likely would have to battle with Richmond native and Midlothian High graduate Bob Schweickert, who would be drafted by San Francisco of the NFL and New York of the AFL and played for the Jets in 1965 and was a backup to Hall of Fame quarterback Joe Namath with the Jets two years later.

As for Haney, he began his minor league career in 1961 in the Appalachian League in Bluefield. He eventually made the transition from infielder to catcher, a position he had played sparingly in high school.

By 1966 he had reached Triple-A Rochester for the first time and was playing for a manager named Earl Weaver.

"Earl called me into his office and said you are going to the big leagues," recalls Haney, who turns 80 in November.

It was late July of 1966 and Andy Etchebarren, the regular catcher for the Orioles, had been injured when he took a foul tip off his hand.

Haney, after getting the word from Weaver, flew to Baltimore the next day and headed to Memorial Stadium on 33rd Street in Baltimore.

The Charlottesville native didn't know he would be in the starting lineup for manager Hank Bauer on July 27.

The Orioles' lineup that night against Cleveland included several All-Stars and three future Hall of Famers: Frank and Brooks Robinson and Luis Aparicio.

The batting order was Luis Aparicio at short, Boog Powell at first, Frank Robinson in left, Brooks Robinson at third, Sam Bowen in right, Davey Johnson at second, Paul Blair in center, Haney at catcher and Dave McNally on the mound.

Haney was retired on a grounder in his first Major League at-bat, in the last of the third.

The Orioles won 7-1 as McNally allowed just one run on seven hits.

Baltimore won the World Series that year though Haney didn't play in the Fall Classic. He was part of the Oakland team that won the World Series in 1974.

Among the Hall of Fame pitchers that he caught included Jim Palmer of the Orioles and Jim Hunter and Rollie Fingers of the A's.

Haney's son, Chris, went to Orange High and played in college at Charlotte. Chris Haney pitched in the majors from 1991 through 2002, ending his career with the Red Sox.

24

Michael Tucker, The
Longwood Basher

There was a bevy of scouts hanging around Farmville in the spring of 1992.

That is because outfielder Michael Tucker of Longwood – then a Division II program that is now Division I – was tearing up the baseball for the Lancers.

Tucker wound up going as the 10th overall pick in the draft to the Kansas City Royals.

The Bluestone High (Skipwith) graduate began his minor league career in 1992 with Single-A Wilmington in Delaware in the Carolina League.

Tucker also played that year for Double-A Memphis and made it to the Royals in 1995.

He went to Atlanta before the 1997 season then joined the Reds for the 1999 campaign.

The lefty slugger hit at least 10 homers in six straight seasons, through 2001.

Tucker hit a career-high 15 homers for the Reds in 2000; he was back with the Royals in 2002 then played for the Giants and Phillies before ending his career with the Mets in 2006 at the

Major League level, then played Triple-A in the Boston system in 2007.

He ended his Major League career with 114 steals and 125 homers.

Tucker is the only Longwood product, through 2021, to make the majors.

Former Longwood pitcher Mark Montgomery, who is from Williamsburg and went to Bruton High, reached the Triple-A level with the Yankees, Cardinals and Tigers.

Kyri Washington, an outfielder from Longwood, was drafted in the 23rd round by the Red Sox in 2015 after starring for the Lancers. He played for Single-A Lowell in 2018.

Maceo Campbell, a pitcher, played for Longwood and was doing well with the Single-A Salem Red Sox out of the bullpen earlier this season. After posting an ERA of 5.30 in 24 games for Salem, Campbell was promoted to the high Single-A Greenville Driver in South Carolina on August 4, 2022. In eight games there, he posted an ERA of 9.82 with two holds.

25

J.C. Martin, World Series Controversy

Born in the tiny town of Axton, just north of the North Carolina border, J.C. Martin was involved in one of the most controversial plays in World Series history.

Playing for the New York Mets in 1969, he laid down a bunt against pitcher Pete Richert and the favorite Baltimore Orioles in Game 4 of the Fall Classic.

While Martin was running to first base, the ball hit him on the throw to first by Richert as a Mets' teammate scored the winning run. The underdog Mets won that game and took Game 5 as well over the Orioles to win the World Series.

"You try to do everything you possibly can," Martin told the Society of American Baseball Research (SABR). "You know from experience that if you run close to the first-base line, the throwing angle is very narrow, particularly if the pitcher is left-handed (as Pete Richert was) and has to turn to make the throw. So you run as close as you can. I wasn't thinking about getting hit or anything. I was just looking to shield the ball from the man covering first. As it turned out, the ball happened to hit me on the left wrist. But there was no argument at the time. All the controversy was in the media the next day."

Martin went to Drewry Mason High in Ridgeway, according to baseballreference.com.

He made his Major League debut with the White Sox in 1959, played for the Mets in 1968-69, and ended his career with the Cubs in 1972.

Martin played in 908 games and never hit more than five homers in a season with an average of .222. He was an infielder early in his minor league career but switched to catcher.

Martin was far from a superstar (a career .222 hitter), but he cherished his time in the major leagues.

"I wouldn't trade it for anything," he told SABR. "I spent 14 years in the big leagues seeing the best players ever, guys like Bob Gibson, Willie Mays and Carl Yastrzemski. Guys like that just aren't around anymore. Baseball was better back then. … they didn't have the DH, which has killed all the suspense in the American League, and the ballparks were fair. You didn't have this emphasis on hitting home runs all the time. It was great." Martin caught five Hall-of-Fame pitchers: Early Wynn, Hoyt Wilhelm, Tom Seaver, Nolan Ryan and Ferguson Jenkins.

Martin was teammates with fellow catcher with the Cubs from 1970-72 to veteran Randy Hundley, a native of Martinsville.

Another top player to come out of Martinsville was Lou Whitaker, who was born in Brooklyn but went to Martinsville High. He broke into the majors with the Tigers in 1977 as a second baseman and formed a record-breaking double play tandem with shortstop Alan Trammell. Sweet Lou played through 1995 and had 244 homers, 143 steals with 2369 hits. He won three Gold Gloves, four Silver Sluggers and was chosen to five All-Star games.

26

Al Worthington, Keeping The Faith

Al Worthington, who turned 93 in February, was a pitcher of modest success when he left the Chicago White Sox in the middle of the season because he could not take part in the stealing of opponents' signs due to his Christian beliefs, according to his autobiography.

Worthington, who later became the first baseball coach at what is now Liberty University in Lynchburg, was also not willing to use a spitball since it was considered an illegal pitch.

The year was 1960 and now years later Major League Baseball is still dealing with the stealing of signs. But now technology is at the core of the controversy — back in the 1960s a runner on second base would try to relay information to his teammate in the batter's box.

"We didn't have the technology," said Turner Ashby High graduate Alan Knicely, who played in the majors from 1979-86 — with most of that time at catcher.

About two years ago, Major League Baseball suspended Houston general manager Jeff Luhnow and manager AJ Hinch for their role in stealing signs, starting in 2017. The Astros had a camera in center field and that information was relayed to their batters through some banging noise (off-speed pitch) or no noise (fastball) coming from the team's dugout.

"That is a little bit over the top," TA graduate Brian Bocock, who played in the majors in 2008 and 2010, said of using audio signals. "As far as I know there was no outside technology being used" during his MLB stint.

The Astros eventually fired Luhnow and Hinch and the next day the Red Sox let go of manager Alex Cora, who was a bench coach for the Astros in 2017 and was also named in the report by MLB.

"Major League Baseball showed they were in control," said Knicely, who broke in with the Astros and now lives in McGaheysville. "It sent a clear message. It is definitely going to discourage teams" from stealing signs.

There were rumblings in the majors about what the Astros were doing and the Nationals were prepared for that in the 2019 World Series. When the teams met in the World Series, the Nationals had five sets of signs for each pitcher, according to published reports.

"It's the worst feeling in the world stepping on that mound and having an idea that the hitter knows what's coming," former Nationals pitching coach Paul Menhart told The Washington Post. "It's one of the most unnerving feelings. You feel helpless. You just get ticked off to the point where you lose total focus and confidence. So we had to make sure our pitchers didn't think about it. We had to eliminate the possibility."

Bocock played infield for the Giants in 2008 and for the Phillies in 2010. "Sign stealing has been part of baseball for a long, long time," he said. But he noted that was relegated to trying to mostly read signals from the third-base coach.

Lynchburg native Mike Hubbard, a former JMU catcher, played in the majors from 1995 to 2001. "As a catcher you are constantly aware; you are on the alert" of possible sign stealers, he said. "It has been going on for decades."

Worthington, the White Sox pitcher in 1960, won 75 games in the majors from 1953-69. He was the baseball coach at Liberty from 1974-86 and was the school's athletic director from 1983-89. Worthington is a member of the Alabama Sports Hall of Fame.

The baseball field at Liberty was named in his honor last year.

"The White Sox let him go when he confronted management about the (sign) stealing," according to David Schauer, who pitched against JMU for Liberty in Harrisonburg under Worthington in the 1980s. "He's always been a man of strong principles and a sense of right or wrong."

Former Liberty baseball coach Al Worthington with David Schauer, who pitched at Liberty in the 1980s, and Krista, David's wife.

27

Quade Tomlin, Following Father's Footsteps

Quade Tomlin isn't focusing on his batting average from his first pro season.

"I am not too worried about the stats," the infield prospect of the Nationals said earlier this year. "I didn't have an injury; my swing felt good all year. It was definitely a learning experience for me, a humbling one at that."

The son of former Major League pitcher Randy Tomlin, the younger Tomlin signed with Washington out of high school in 2020.

He made his pro debut in the Florida Complex League last year and hit .100 in 60 at-bats for FCL Nationals' manager Jake Lowery, the Richmond native who was promoted to manage at Single-A Fredericksburg this year.

"I love Jake; I actually played for his dad" in travel baseball, Tomlin said. "Jake is young, so he relates to guys really well. He knows how to be cool around the games. He is easy to talk to. He is especially good at relating to guys; he had 10 years under his belt" as a player in the minors.

"He has upper baseball knowledge," Tomlin added. "I am sure he will have a great coaching career."

Quade Tomlin, who turned 20 on Feb. 11, played shortstop in high school in Lynchburg but saw a lot of action at second base and third base in Florida as a rookie pro.

"It was a good experience, for sure. I made a lot of life-long friends that I got to spend the year with, so that was great," he said. "Baseball-wise, it was definitely a learning experience for me. Personally, seeing the velo all year round was kind of an adjustment going from a local, smaller area. But it went well; I learned a lot. Once again, God was good."

He spent a lot of time with hitting coach Mark Harris, a native of southwest Virginia.

"He is great and our relationship blossomed from there," Tomlin said of the former minor league player. "I have been in contact with him all off-season. He has been helping me and that has been awesome."

"The first year was definitely a learning year. A lot of the guys usually say that," he added.

Tomlin also picked up tips from pro veterans such as outfielder Alec Keller and pitcher Aaron Barrett, both of who spent time on rehab in the Florida Complex League in 2021.

Keller was born in Richmond, played in college at Princeton and for several years in the minors for Washington while Barrett made his Major League debut out of the bullpen with the Nationals in 2014.

"It was very cool learning from those guys," Tomlin said. "The biggest difference for me was the speed of the game."

Tomlin was impressed with fellow infielder Brady House, the first-round pick of the Nationals out of a Georgia high school in 2021. House had an OPS of .970 as a shortstop for the Florida Complex League team in 2021 then jumped up to Single-A Fredericksburg this season.

"I kind of knew Brady because of travel ball. You want to talk about a God-given, raw talent. Obviously, he is going to have a great career," Tomlin said.

Tomlin has worked out in the past with former high school teammate and catcher Wes Clarke, who is now in the Milwaukee farm system after he was drafted out of the University of South Carolina in 2021.

Tomlin also got married in November to Ally, his high school sweetheart.

He played in high school for his father at Lynchburg Christian Academy. The younger Tomlin was one of the top high school players in the state in 2019 and 2020.

The younger Tomlin didn't make a full-season minor league roster coming out of spring training this year with the Nationals.

Clarke, with Single-A Wisconsin in the Brewers system, was hitting just .181 in early June but had 30 RBI in his first 42 games this season. Clarke was promoted to Double-A Biloxi in the Milwaukee system on August 30, 2022 and in 16 games he hit .254 with that club.

Tomlin ended the year with an average of .176 in 32 games in Florida.

Tony Beasley, another former Liberty standout, was named the interim manager of the Texas Rangers on August 15 after Chris Woodward was fired. A native of Fredericksburg, Beasley grew up in Bowling Green and was drafted in the 19th round by the Orioles out of Liberty. He played in the minors with the Baltimore and Pittsburgh systems.

"After spending over a majority of his coaching career in the Pittsburgh and Washington organizations, Beasley joined the Texas Rangers major league staff in 2015, mainly serving as their third base coach. In early 2016, he was diagnosed with cancer forcing him to miss all of the season. After being diagnosed cancer-free, he returned to the Rangers in 2017," according to the Liberty website.

Beasley was on the coaching staff with the Nationals under the late Frank Robinson, a Hall of Famer who helped the Orioles win the World Series in 1966 and 1970. At Liberty, Beasley played for former Major League pitcher Al Worthington.

28

Zach Peek, Another Strong O's Arm

One of them went to college in Harrisonburg for several years through 2019 while the other pitcher was a newcomer to the city a few winters ago.

Despite differences in what brought them to the Shenandoah Valley, Shelton Perkins and Zach Peek have now moved on to Maryland with a lofty goal in mind — climbing the minor league baseball ladder of the Orioles and making it to Camden Yards and The Show.

Both right-handed pitchers were raised in North Carolina: Peek in Pineville, before graduating from high school in Forest, near Lynchburg, while Perkins is from Wilmington, North Carolina, and began his college career at East Carolina before joining the Dukes in Harrisonburg.

"I knew Peek's name because he and Christian Bourne went to high school together," said Perkins, who was teammates with fellow pitcher Bourne at JMU.

Jefferson Forest High product Bourne was named director of baseball operations and player development at Georgia Southern in 2021.

Perkins and Peek were teammates with high Single-A Aberdeen in the Baltimore system in 2021, after both began the season at low Single-A Delmarva in Salisbury, Maryland. And they both moved up to the Double-A level this year with the Bowie Baysox, a farm team just a few miles southeast of downtown Baltimore.

In his first six starts this season for Bowie, Peek was 0-2 with an ERA of 3.97 while Perkins, as of early June, was 0-2, 4.11 in 12 games out of the bullpen with his firsts save at the Double-A level.

Peek was drafted by the Angles out of Winthrop in the sixth round in 2019 then traded to the Orioles on Dec. 4, 2019, in a deal that sent veteran pitcher Dylan Bundy to the Angels.

After coming to the Orioles, Peek met Turner Ashby graduate Brenan Hanifee — a fourth-round pick of Baltimore in 2016. Hanifee told Peek about Next Level Athletic Development in Park View, where the Rockingham County resident has trained for several years.

With his girlfriend from high school finishing up her senior year at James Madison, Peek felt it would be a good fit for him to train as well with Mike Martin and pitching specialist Spencer Davis last winter before heading to spring training in Florida last year.

"I knew Perkins was there [at JMU] and he put me in touch with Hanifee," said Peek. "I had met Brenan at spring training. It was nice to have a relationship with him there."

"We really focused on the analytics and really focused on pitch crafting and predominantly re-training some different [athletic] movements. Just some nitpicking things that Mike was able to pick out; working with him and Spencer, who was over there, was fantastic. It was just a good [group] of minds so it works well together," Peek added about Next Level.

Davis, a 2013 Fort Defiance graduate, pitched in high school and at Division III Marymount University in Arlington. He said that Peek has a balanced approach with an analytical side to pitching as well.

"When they first come in, I just let them decide how much they want to do," said Davis. "His pitches were really good. We spent a lot of time on his change. His spins the ball really well."

Peek was at Next Level before heading to Sarasota, Florida, last year.

"It is very nice to know the depth we have here," Peek said of the minors. "It is nice to have very good arms right beside you [with teammates]. You can learn from that as well. It has been a joy — it has been so much fun after last year, being able to come out here and compete. It's nice to really put a lot of work in and find success."

"I would just like to think I am using my brain a little bit more," Peek added last year. "I worked a lot on my off-speed crafting this off-season; I wanted to be able to go to all of my pitches whenever I needed to and I feel like I have been able to do that pretty consistently. I can throw different pitches earlier in the count then throw harder pitchers later in the count."

The pandemic called off the minors in 2020, which hurt the development of Peek and Perkins.

Drafted by the Orioles in the 16th round, Perkins was used as a closer in both Salisbury and Aberdeen.

"I would say I have had a decent season. I have made some mistakes, more so here than I did at Delmarva," he said. "There are things you can get away with there that you can't get away with here."

Perkins was about 10 when he saw his first Orioles game at Camden Yards.

The mother of a good friend in North Carolina was from Baltimore, and she brought the boys to the city to see a game against the New York Mets.

"Jose Reyes of the Mets hit a home run," recalls Perkins, who said he later lost his glove at Camden Yards.

Other Virginia products who have played for Bowie this year include Roanoke native and first baseman J.D. Mundy, who played at Radford and Virginia Tech and for Covington in the Valley Baseball League; pitcher Garrett Stallings, who is from Chesapeake and like Peek came to the Orioles from the Angels; and pitcher Ryan Watson, who was with Front Royal of the VBL in 2017. Stallings threw the first six innings of a combined no-hitter by the Baysox at home earlier this season. Watson was drafted out of Auburn by the Dodgers.

Hanifee, after Tommy John surgery in 2021, returned to the minors with an outing on June 24, 2022, in Florida. The third outing of the year for the TA graduate came July 8, 2022, when he went 2.2 innings for Single-A Aberdeen and allowed one run in a game at Brooklyn.

Peek went on the Injured List on July 10, 2022, after he made 11 starts with Double-A Bowie and posted an ERA of 3.57. He had Tommy John surgery in early August of 2022 while Hanifee made his fourth start for Double-A Bowie on August 5, 2022, at Harrisburg - a farm team of the Nationals. Another TA grad, right-hander Justin Showalter, made his pro debut on August 7, 2022, as he had a scoreless outing for the Washington Wild Things in Washington, Pa.

Peek fires to home for the Double-A Bowie Baysox in 2022.

Hillcats Manager Made Debut With O's

Omir Santos was with Triple-A Norfolk as a catcher in early September of 2008 when he was called into the office of then-manager Gary Allenson, a long-time catcher in the majors.

Allenson informed Santos that the native of Puerto Rico would not be playing the next day.

"Do I have the day off?" Santos asked Allenson.

"No, you are going to be traveling to Baltimore," replied the former skipper of the Tides.

Allenson then congratulated on Santos on his first promotion to The Show.

"I went outside (at Harbor Park) and she didn't believe me," Santos recalled, after a game in late April at the home of the Lynchburg Hillcats. "I said I am serious. We are going to Baltimore tomorrow."

Santos made his Major League debut on Sept. 5, 2008, for the Orioles at Camden Yards in Baltimore against the Oakland A's.

"A lot of things were going through my mind," he said. "I was telling my wife, 'I can't believe it.' It was six years in the minors, almost seven. Then I saw my uniform with the logo on it. That is when I felt like I am here."

He entered the game as a reserve for starting catcher Ramon Hernandez and was retired in his only trip to the plate.

One day earlier on Sept. 4, 2008, Luke Montz made his big league debut – also as a catcher but for the Washington Nationals.

Montz is the manager of the Salem Red Sox and his team played a series in Lynchburg in late April of this season.

Both of the former catchers played their last game in the majors in the spring of 2013, before beginning a coaching career that landed them in Virginia for this season.

Santos got his first Major League hit on Sept. 23 of that year against James Shields of Tampa Bay.

"But I was thrown out at second base" going for a double, Santos said.

Now he is trying to help young players move up the ladder to Cleveland.

"You have to be patient. You are here to help them get to the next level," Santos said of managing at Single-A Lynchburg. "We don't look too much at winning and losing. It is more about development; that is why we are here."

One big change is that now most Major League clubs are paying the cost of apartments for players in the minors.

"Back in the day you had to pay for rent," said Santos, who added he got about $500 a month when playing in the low minors.

Lynchburg – known as the city of Seven Hills – has a rich history in the minor leagues.

"This is my first time in this area," said Santos.

While the central Virginia city has been a farm team of Cleveland since 2015, Lynchburg was an affiliate of the Cardinals from 1943-55; the White Sox from 1963-69; the Twins from 1970-74; the Rangers in 1975; the Mets from 1976-87; the Red Sox from 1988-1994; the Pirates from 1995 to 2009; the Reds in 2010 and the Braves from 2011-14.

It is the connection to the Mets that old-timers still talk about in Lynchburg.

The 1983 Lynchburg Mets won the Carolina League title with ace pitcher Dwight Gooden.

Santos said he met a Lynchburg fan earlier this year that told him about those great Lynchburg Mets squads from the 1980s.

That year the right-hander was 19-4 with an ERA of 2.50 while striking out 300 batters in just 191 innings.

The next year, 1984, Gooden would be named the Rookie of the Year in the National League and the next year he won the Cy Young Award.

Gooden helped the Mets win the World Series in 1986 and another key part of that team was center fielder Lenny Dykstra, who was teammates with Gooden in Lynchburg in 1983.

Another key to the World Series champ was slugger Darryl Strawberry, the No. 1 overall pick by the Mets in 1980 who played in Lynchburg in 1981 and was the National League Rookie of the Year in 1983.

Other future Major Leaguers to play in Lynchburg included outfielder Don Buford and catcher Andy Etchebarren, both of whom would aid the Orioles' 1970 World Series title squad.

Virginia native J.C. Martin, a catcher, played in Lynchburg as part of the White Sox system in 1962. One of his teammates was Dave DeBusschere, who would have a long run in the National Basketball Association.

Reid Johnston, a pitcher for the Hillcats this season, was drafted out of North Carolina State by Cleveland in 2021. He had an ERA below 3.00 in early June in nine outings for Lynchburg, with two starts.

"The last four years I was in college and I always had the dream of playing professional baseball," Johnston said.

He said as a freshman for the Wolfpack he pitched in a game at Virginia Tech and then he appeared in a game as a junior at the University of Virginia.

"They are both well-coached," he said of the Hokies and Cavs.

Of the Cavs, he said: "They were one of our biggest opponents when I was at N.C. State." But this season it was the Hokies who advanced to the Super Regionals, hosting Oklahoma in early June.

Santos notes there are new rules now in the minors, such as a clock that allows a pitcher limited time between offerings.

"Baseball has changed a lot," Santos said. "Some people like it, some people don't like it. We just have to adjust. It is going to be tough for the first year but everybody has to get used to it."

Lynchburg Hillcats manager Omir Santos

30

Eppa Rixey, Hall of Famer

The state of Virginia has produced eight U.S. presidents, a ton of tobacco, and is home to thousands of Federal workers and installations.

And the Old Dominion finally had its first Baseball Hall of Famer when Culpeper native and one-time Charlottesville resident Eppa Rixey was elected to Cooperstown in 1963 – a few weeks before his death.

He was the first player to pass away between the time of his election to the Hall of Fame and the actual ceremony. The same tragedy happened to Alexandria native Leon Day, a Negro League star, in 1995.

Rixey won 266 games from 1912-33 with the Phillies and Reds and that was the most by a lefty in the National League until Warren Spahn came along.

He was born in Culpeper and then his family moved to Charlottesville, where Rixey played for the University of Virginia before turning pro with the Phillies.

The Virginian, who was traded to the Reds prior to the 1921

season, was an intense competitor who hated to lose, according to one of his former catchers.

"He was one of a kind. He would break chairs in the clubhouse after he lost, and you wouldn't see him for a few days," Clyde Suke-forth, who played with Rixey on the Reds from 1926-31, told us several years ago from his home in Maine.

Sukeforth, who died in 2000, helped bring Jackie Robinson to the Brooklyn Dodgers and managed that team for two games in 1947.

"He had a good assortment of pitches," said Sukeforth of Rixey. "Like all good pitchers, he had good control."

Despite his penchant for outbursts, Rixey was well-liked on the team and mingled well on the train during road trips, said Suke-forth. "He was Virginia thoroughbred," said the former catcher. "He had been around a lot, so he had lost most of his (southern) accent" by late in his career.

In 1909, at the age of 18, Rixey entered the University of Virginia in Charlottesville, about 45 miles south of Culpeper.

Eppa Rixey birthplace in Culpeper

His family had moved there from Culpeper when he was 10. By his third year at UVa, 1911-12, the school yearbook listed his feats: member of the baseball and basketball teams and the singles champion in tennis. Of course, he pitched for the baseball team. Rixey received a B.S. in 1912, and a M.A, in chemistry in 1914. In college the big (6-foot-5, 210-pound) pitcher played for Charles (Cy) Rigler, who was a National League umpire.

After Rigler helped Rixey get signed by the Phils for $2,000, the National League prohibited umpires from serving as liaisons for other teams. Rixey began his big league career with the Phillies and teammate Grover Cleveland Alexander in 1912, going 10-10, 2.50 in 20 starts and three relief outings for a team that placed fifth.

The next year Alexander went 22-8, then 27-15 in 1914 and 31-10 in 1915. Rixey went 9-5 in 1913 and slumped to 2-11 in 1914. After placing sixth in 1914, the Phils fired manager Red Dooin. He was replaced by Pat Moran, who became a supporter of Rixey on and off the mound.

The Phillies won the league title in 1915, which would give Rixey (11-12 that year with 22 starts and a 2.39 ERA) his only World Series appearance in 21 big league seasons. In game five against the Boston Red Sox in Philadelphia on Oct. 13, with his team one loss away from elimination, Rixey came on in the third inning in relief of starter Erskine Mayer, who had won 21 games in the regular season. The Phils went ahead 4-2 with two runs in the bottom of the fourth, and Rixey kept the Red Sox scoreless in the fourth, fifth, six and seventh.

But Boston outfielder Duffy Lewis hit a two-run homer off Rixey in the top of the eighth to tie the game at 4. Lewis had hit just two homers in 557 at-bats that year. In the top of the ninth, Red Sox outfielder Harry Hooper hit his second homer of the game, which like his first bounced into the center-field stands (there was no ground-rule double at the time). Boston starter Rube Foster held the Phils in the bottom of the ninth for a 5-4 win and the Series title. Rixey was the loser in his only Series showing.

The 266 wins by Rixey remains the most by a native of Virginia. Justin Verlander entered this season with 226 victories. According to published reports, Rixey taught Latin at a school in Alexandria in the off-season. He wrote poetry, took advanced classes in several fields and was a fine golfer.

31

Tony Womack, World Series Champ

Tony Womack is among the Virginia natives who has won a World Series ring.

Born in Danville, Womack hit .250 with three RBIs and three doubles as an infielder as Arizona beat the New York Yankees in seven games in the 2001 Fall Classic.

Womack went to Gretna High and then crossed the border to play in college for Guilford in North Carolina.

He was drafted by the Pittsburgh Pirates in the seventh round of the 1991 draft and made his Major League debut two years later.

The speedy Womack was an All-Star with the Pirates in 1997 as he led the league in steals with 60. It was the first of three straight years he led the league in stolen bases.

In 1999, in his first season with Arizona, he had a career-high 72 steals.

He had a league-high 14 triples for the D-backs in 2000.

Womack ended his career with the Cubs in 2006.

He had 363 steals in his career – the most of any Virginia native going into the 2022 season.

Another Virginia native to win a World Series ring was J.C. Martin, who played for the New York Mets in 1969.

Florida native David Eckstein, who played for the Harrisonburg Turks in the Valley Baseball League, was the World Series MVP with the St. Louis Cardinals in 2006.

Pitcher Vic Raschi, who was born in West Springfield, Mass., and was a star at William & Mary, won six World Series rings while playing for the Yankees from 1947-53.

Jackie Bradley, Jr., a native of Richmond who went to Prince George's High, won a World Series ring as an outfielder for the Boston Red Sox in 2018.

Ryan Zimmerman, who went to high school and college in Virginia, helped the Nationals capture the World Series title in 2019 over Justin Verlander and the Astros.

Those are just some of the players with Virginia ties to win a ring.

32

Jeremy Jeffress, First Round Pick

Jeremy Jeffress is one of the few Virginia natives to be a first-round draft pick out of high school and make it to the majors.

Born in South Boston in 1987, he was taken out of Halifax High in South Boston by the Brewers in 2006.

He worked his way up the minor-league ladder of Milwaukee and made his first Major League appearance on September 1, 2010.

In that game against the Reds, he came on in the eighth inning with the Brewers trailing 6-1.

Jeffress, a right-hander, allowed a single to Miguel Cairo then got a double-play ball off the bat of Paul Janish. He then retired Ryan Hanigan, a native of Washington, D.C., for the third out in his one inning of work.

The product of South Boston was 1-0 with an ERA of 2.70 in 10 outings that season out of the bullpen for the Brewers.

He had a career-high 27 saves in 2016 as he split time with the Brewers and the Texas Rangers.

Jeffress was an All-Star two years later as he went 8-1 with an ERA of 1.29 with 15 saves as he was back with the Brewers. He made a career-high 73 appearances that year with Milwaukee.

One of his teammates in his second stint with the Brewers in 2018 was catcher Erik Kratz, who played for Waynesboro and Harrisonburg in the Valley Baseball League while in college at Eastern Mennonite.

Jeffress pitched in 22 games with the Cubs in 2020.

He was signed in spring training by the Nationals in 2021 and then let go a few days later. The Washington Post reported he was let go "due to personal reasons." He was suspended for "drugs of abuse," during his career, according to The Washington Post and other publications.

In 414 games in the majors, the reliever has a stellar ERA of 3.08 with a record of 32-12 while finishing 144 games and recording 52 saves.

Part IV

SOUTHWEST VIRGINIA

33

Kevin Barker, From Bristol To The Brewers

Kevin Barker went from Bristol to Blacksburg to the Brewers.

Born in Bristol in 1975, Barker played at Virginia High, then took his left-handed bat to Virginia Tech.

The slugger was drafted in the third round in 1996 out of the Hokies' program by Milwaukee.

In his first Major League game in August of 1999, he had two hits in five trips to the plate against Houston.

He flew out in his first Major League at-bat against Chris Holt, who became a pitching coach for the Orioles after his career.

Barker hit three homers in 38 games for the Brewers in 1999.

After playing in 40 games with Milwaukee in 2000, he spent the next season in the minors at Double-A and Triple-A in the Brewers' system.

He played in seven games with the Padres in 2001, in 12 games with Toronto in 2006, and in 29 games with the Reds in 2009 – his last Major League season.

Barker played in 126 games in The Show and had six homers. His last pro appearance was in the Mexican League in 2011.

34

Memories Of The Appy League

Jeff Leatherman had just graduated from Auburn University in 1991 when he flew to Toronto to begin his professional baseball career.

"The first couple of nights I nearly froze to death," recalls the Harrisonburg High graduate, whose minor-league stint began in Welland, Ontario after getting a ride from the airport. "I called my parents and told them to bring my car and some warm clothes."

A standout infielder for the Blue Streaks and Auburn, Leatherman began his short pro sojourn in the New York-Penn League as a minor leaguer in the Pittsburgh Pirates' system. He hit .271 in 55 games in his first season in the pros.

"We played in Batavia (New York) one night and when we got done we drove all the way to Pittsfield (Massachusetts) and got to the hotel at 7 a.m. and played" that night, recalls Leatherman, who today is a physical therapist and lives in Alabama.

Two years ago, the Appalachian League and the New York-Penn League became wooden-bat circuits for college players.

Gone are the days when many Virginia high school products would begin a pro career in the low minors in the Appy.

Bristol is among the Virginia towns that lost a Major League affiliate.

"I think they were vital to the economy of these towns," Leatherman said of pro ball in the rookie leagues. "It is just a pity that these teams are going away. It breaks my heart."

Former Turner Ashby, VMI and Virginia Tech pitcher Ian Ostlund played for Oneonta, N.Y. in 2001 when he was in the Detroit Tigers' farm system. Oneonta was a farm team of the New York Yankees before the Tigers came to town.

"Oneonta was a really neat experience for me," Ostlund said. "It kind of harkened back to the golden age of baseball. It just an air of aura to it. I was told the batting cage we used had been used at Yankee Stadium."

His pitching coach was the late Bill Monbouquette, a teammate with hitting legend and Hall of Famer Ted Williams with the Boston Red Sox. "He would tell us Ted Williams' stories. He would eat a sausage and onion sandwich every day and it would spill out into the dugout," Ostlund recalled. "He was old-school."

Ostlund said once Monbouquette was teaching him how to improve his curveball and told the TA product he wasn't bending his back enough. With no warning, the coach hit Ostlund in the gut – and the pitcher bent his back. "Just like that," noted Monbouquette.

Tom Bocock, another TA product, was an infielder in the St. Louis Cardinals' farm system when he played for Johnson City, Tennessee in 1982 after he was drafted out of JMU. He usually hit second back of leadoff man Vince Coleman, who would go on to steal 752 bases in the majors.

Both were promoted in 1983 to Macon, Georgia and that season Coleman set a minor-league record with 145 steals, again with Bocock batting back of him a lot in the lineup. Coleman gave Bocock a signed bat and wrote Bocock was the best No. 2 hitter around.

Another teammate with Bocock in Johnson City was Terry

Pendleton, who would play 15 years in the majors and won an NL MVP award. "He could always hit but he made himself into a good defender," said Bocock, who hit .249 for Johnson City in 66 games.

Some of the lessons that Bocock learned he passed on to his son Brian, a TA graduate who was drafted out of college at Stetson by the Giants 2006 and played in the short-season Class A Northwest League that summer.

"I told him there were going to be a lot of good players. You have to take advantage of your opportunity and he did," the elder Bocock said of Brian, who played in majors with the Giants and Phillies.

Johnson City had been in the Appy off and on since 1911 and had been a farm team of the Cardinals since 1975.

The Virginia towns that were to be part of the 2020 season in the Appalachian League, before the pandemic called off the schedule, were Bristol, Danville and Pulaski. The park in Bluefield, West Virginia sits near the state line with Virginia and had been home to a Blue Jays' farm team.

EMU graduate Larry Sheets played in Bluefield in 1978-79 on his way to the majors with the Orioles in 1984. The Staunton native played basketball for the Royals of Park View during his time in the minors and was the Orioles MVP in 1987.

Another Staunton native, the late Jerry May, began his pro career in the Appy with Kingsport, Tenn., in 1961 and broke in with the Pirates as a catcher in 1964. He died in a farm accident in Augusta County in 1996.

Two state products who played in both the Appalachian League and New York-Penn leagues were Spotswood's Austin Nicely and Larry Mitchell, a Charlottesville High graduate who also pitched for JMU.

Nicley played in the New York-Penn League with Tri-Cities and in the Appalachian League with Greenville, both in the farm system of the Houston Astros. The pitcher was 2-6 with an ERA of 3.88 in

2014 in the Appy League and 5-4, 6.80 in 14 games with seven starts in 2016 with Tri-Cities.

Nicely saw the economic importance of minor league teams in the two leagues.

"I think both leagues … they are positioned in some towns where that is the only team they have to support," said Nicely. "I felt like everyone loved their home team. It was unique and fun to play in. Every team had great fan support, for the most part."

"The Appy League is like that first taste of pro ball to get your feet wet," Nicely added. "The New York-Penn League, that is where a lot of higher draft picks start their careers."

Tri-Cities was based in Troy, New York, not far from capital Albany.

"It was a great ballpark and great fan support," said Nicely, who has played in the Atlantic League with York, Pa. the past two seasons. "There were a lot of sellout games."

He said the longest bus trips in the New York-Penn League were about six or seven hours, including trips to Lowell, Massachusetts – north of Boston and the home of a Red Sox farm team.

Nicely lived in an old apartment in downtown Troy with other players. In the Appalachian League, he played in Greeneville, Tennessee and stayed in a motel.

"Some of those towns really relied on the team as a point of interest," he said of the Appy league. "Pulaski, that was one of my favorite places to play. For one, it was closer to home" in Grottoes.

Rick Croushore was a non-drafted free agent out of JMU when he headed to Glens Falls, New York, in the Cardinals' farm system in 1993. He eventually made the majors and pitched for St. Louis in the game that Mark McGwire hit a record-setting 62nd homer in 1998 against the Cubs.

"They let me do my thing," Croushore said of pitching in the New York-Penn League. "They did not have anything invested in me."

Now the pitching coach at Division III Shenandoah in

Winchester, Croushore was roommates on road trips with Glens Falls teammate Alan Benes – a first-round pick who would pitch in 115 big league games. On off days, players with Glens Falls would head to Lake George in upstate New York.

But the New York-Penn League is more than those memories that to the former JMU pitcher. "That is where I became a prospect," said Croushore, who threw in 31 of 77 games out of the bullpen for Glen Falls then headed to the Instructional League in Florida later in 1993. A few years later he was in the majors.

Leatherman, Ostlund and Croushore said they each made $850 per month in rookie ball.

Ostlund said he received a signing bonus of just $1,000 by the Tigers when he signed out of Virginia Tech. Despite some struggles in the New York-Penn League, he made it all the way to Triple-A in 2007 with the Tigers.

And the living arrangements were not very luxurious in the low minors.

"They put us up at the Oneonta" hotel, Ostlund noted. "The first night there was orange shag carpeting and I had fleas all over the place."

Later, he and some teammates piled into an old house to live – only to have a racoon and pigeons fall through the ceiling.

The ballparks were not so great either – and those spartan conditions, according to MLB, is one reason some of the small cities lost their affiliation with a big-league club.

"There was chicken wire around the backstop in Oneonta," Ostlund said.

Starting in the rookie leagues was a family affair for the Knicelys.

Alan Knicely began his career in the Appalachian League with Covington soon after graduating from TA in 1974. He eventually made it to the majors with the Astros in 1979 and lasted until 1986 in The Show.

His son, Jeremy, a Spotswood graduate, played in the New York-

Penn League with Auburn in 2003 while in the minors with the Blue Jays. Another player with Auburn in 2003 was EMU graduate Erik Kratz, who reached the majors in 2010.

Even for local products who didn't make the majors, the low minors was a chance to be teammates with future stars.

Leatherman, the HHS product, was teammates in the New York-Penn League with Tony Womack, a Danville native who help Arizona win the 2001 World Series over the New York Yankees.

Bill Leatherman, the father of Jeff, is a former basketball coach at Bridgewater and JMU who took his family on summer trips to see Major League games and has written books about baseball.

But the pro career of Jeff Leatherman ended far from the bright lights and huge salaries of the majors. After playing in Ontario, he was promoted to Augusta, Georgia in the low Single-A South Atlantic League in 1993 and hit just .179 before being released a few months later.

"I wouldn't trade it for anything," Leatherman said of his two years in the minors.

Shenandoah University pitching coach Rick Croushore played in the minors in the New York-Penn League, which like the Appalachian League is no longer an entry point for many first-year pros.

35

Willie Horton, Hometown Hero In Detroit

Willie Horton was born into a large family in the coal mining town of Arno in southwest Virginia in 1942 and he grew up in Stonega.

"When the mines closed, it was 1951 when we came north to Detroit," Horton told us in a phone interview on June 22, 2022. "Even though I left real young, I can drive around (southwest Virginia) with no problem. I thank the good Lord for giving me a great memory. I never forgot home."

He went to Northwestern High School in Detroit then began his pro baseball career with the hometown Tigers as a minor leaguer in 1962.

The right-handed hitting slugger was in the majors the next year and in 1968 he helped the Tigers win the World Series over the St. Louis Cardinals, just months after riots had rocked Detroit and other U.S. cities.

Horton hit a career-high 36 homers that season.

"I don't have the words for the joy of life; that is something that is part of your life," he reflects. "As long as you live, it is something they can't take away from you. It was good for the city and the state of Michigan after the riots. I always say that God put us here to help heal the city."

Horton played for the Tigers until he was traded to Texas during the 1977 season. He ended his career with 325 homers, the most by a Virginia native as of June 22, 2022.

"I didn't know that," said Horton, who also had 1993 hits and an average of .273.

Norfolk native Justin Upton, who joined the Mariners on June 17, 2022, had 324 homers in late June of 2022 to rank second back of Horton.

Horton still has relatives in southwest Virginia and Tennessee and has made return trips over the years. He took his grandson a few years ago to the region "to show him where I came from, up in the mountain part," Horton notes. "I used to go fishing in Appalachia" in Wise County. A daughter of his late uncle lives in Big Stone Gap. His mother was born in Gate City.

The only other sibling who is alive is a sister of Horton. "She is 96; she motivates me," he said.

A few years ago, Horton visited Shenandoah to help out with a weekend baseball youth clinic put on by Page County High graduate Wayne Comer.

Horton and Comer were teammates on the World Series team with the Tigers in 1968. "I really enjoyed it down there in Shenandoah," Horton noted.

These days, Horton is a Special Assistant to the General Manager of the Tigers.

When he first went to Lakeland, Florida, for Spring Training with Detroit in the early 1960s, he had to walk several miles from downtown to the team complex since taxi drivers would not service

Black riders. He hopes to be in Lakeland for Spring Training in 2023 – he has been there more than 60 times since his pro career began.

Horton will enter 2023 tied for Upton for most homers by a native of Virginia at 325. Upton hit one homer in the majors in 2022 – with Seattle. The last homer in the career of Horton came in 1980 – also with the Mariners.

Seattle made the playoffs in 2022 as catcher Cal Raleigh, a native of Harrisonburg, hit a walk-off homer to clinch a postseason spot for the Mariners. Raleigh was born in Harrisonburg in 1996 when his father, Todd, was an assistant baseball coach at JMU. The elder Raleigh was later the head coach at Western Carolina and Tennessee.

Horton will enter 2023 tied for Upton for most homers by a native of Virginia at 325. Upton hit one homer in the majors in 2022 – with Seattle. The last homer in the career of Horton came in 1980 – also with the Mariners. Seattle made the playoffs in 2022 as catcher Cal Raleigh, a native of Harrisonburg, hit a walk-off homer to clinch a postseason spot for the Mariners. Raleigh was born in Harrisonburg in 1996 when his father, Todd, was an assistant baseball coach at JMU. The elder Raleigh was later the head coach at Western Carolina and Tennessee

36

Billy Wagner, Hall Of Fame Closer?

Before Billy Wagner became one of the most dominant closers in major league history, he blew away Division III hitters at Ferrum College.

MLB scouts flocked to see the 5-foot-10 lefthander, who struck out a Division III-record 19.1 batters per nine innings in 1992. In the next year's draft, the Houston Astros took him 12th overall.

"I didn't see myself with a lot of ability," Wagner told the Virginian-Pilot in 2012, the year he was enshrined in the Virginia Sports Hall of Fame. "My coaches and team saw more than I did."

Wagner's coaches and teammates were right about his ability and dedication. He went on to save 422 games (sixth all-time) in a 16-year major league career with the Astros, Mets, Phillies, Red Sox and Braves. His 11.9 strikeouts per nine innings represent a major league record for pitchers with at least 800 career innings pitched.

A seven-time all-star, Wagner was fourth in the 1999 Cy Young voting with the Astros and sixth in 2006 with the Mets. He won the Rolaids Relief Man Award in 1999.

Wagner remained dominant through his final season with the Braves, when he went 7-2, 1.43 with 37 saves and 13.5 strikeouts per nine innings. He's still a candidate for the Baseball Hall of Fame and received 51 percent of the vote in 2022, the fifth straight year his percentage has risen. He's already in the college baseball and Astros Halls of Fame.

In making Houston's hall in 2021, he said, "I didn't realize it could possibly happen. I don't think the Hall of Fame was ever even spoken about when we were coming up. I think the thing that stands out is when you look up there on the walls and you see the names of Hall of Famers and substantial people like Nolan [Ryan], it's humbling."

Wagner, born in 1971 in Marion, grew up in the Tannersville community in Tazewell County. He went to Tazewell High School before going to Ferrum to play defensive back and pitch. In the process of weightlifting for football, he picked up velocity on his fastball. It went from the mid-80s to the upper-90s, and that was the end of his football career.

A natural righthander, Wagner became a lefthander because of injuries when he was a child. He had plenty of power from the left side, as he regularly hit triple digits on radar guns as a big leaguer.

After Wagner's playing career, he settled in Crozet and started the junior varsity program at the Miller School of Albemarle. He's now the head coach, and his teams have won two state titles. One of his former players, his son Will, was drafted by the Astros in the 18th round in 2021 out of Liberty University. Will Wagner, a second baseman, reached Double-A before the midpoint of the 2022 season. He played in the Rockingham County Baseball League in 2020.

"He's had to fight for everything," Billy Wagner told MLB.com after Will was drafted. "He only had one opportunity to get to college and had to fight for that. He's been a late bloomer. I think the Astros got a sleeper. They got a sneaky pick and they're going to be surprised. A lot of teams that didn't take him, they'll see what [they] missed."

Billy Wagner pitched at Ferrum before beginning a long career in the Major Leagues.

37

Brad Clontz, World Series With Braves

Stuart, a small town in Patrick County, had a population of about 1,400 residents at the 2010 census.

It was named after Confederate leader J.E.B. Stuart, who was from nearby Ararat.

Stuart is the home of Gerald Balilies, the 65th governor of the state, Mary Sue Terry, the first female attorney general in Virginia; and the Wood Brothers racing team.

And Stuart is the birthplace of pitcher Brad Clontz, who was born there in 1971.

After playing at Patrick Henry High, he headed to Blacksburg to play for the Hokies.

Clontz was drafted in the 10th round by the Atlanta Braves in 1992 and he spent part of his first season with Pulaski in the rookie Appalachian League.

The right-hander worked his way up the Atlanta ladder and made his Major League debut in 1995.

Clontz, who also pitched for Richmond in the minors, was 8-1 with an ERA of 3.65 in 59 games for the Braves in 1995.

The next season he led the league with 81 appearances out of the bullpen for Atlanta as a submarine thrower.

Clontz pitched in two games in the 1995 World Series as the Braves beat Cleveland; he pitched in three games in the World Series the next year as the Yankees beat Atlanta.

Clontz played for the Dodgers and Mets in 1998 and was then with the Pirates in 1999 and 2000.

His last appearance in the majors was in April 2000 in a 6-2 loss to the Reds in Pittsburgh. The last batter he faced was Pokey Reese, who hit a triple.

The starting right fielder for the Reds that day was Michael Tucker, a standout at Longwood University who was also drafted out a Virginia college in 1992.

Clontz ended his career with a record of 22-8 with an ERA of 4.34 in 272 games, with eight saves.

He went into the Virginia Tech Hall of Fame in 2011 and in recent years has worked in customer service for the Baha Mar resort.

"You just dream of those things but not coming so early in your career. ... I get chills when people talk to me about it," he told the Society of American Baseball Research. "That ring always attracts people" from the 1995 season.

38

First-Round Misses

An "inexact science" is a term that is used to describe the annual draft, both in baseball and other sports in North America.

That is certainly the case when it comes to several first-round picks from Virginia that never made the Major Leagues.

In 1985, the Phillies drafted catcher Trey McCall out of Abingdon High in southwest Virginia as the 16th pick overall.

He never advanced above Single-A and ended his pro career in 1989.

McCall later became a coach at his high school alma mater and at Emory & Henry. The Wasps were 9-28 this past season under McCall, a graduate of the school who has been the coach in Emory for 18 seasons.

The top hitter for Emory & Henry this season was sophomore infielder Jared Foley, who batted .391 and also led the team in steals with 18.

Among the other first-round picks in the draft with ties to Virginia who didn't make the majors were Mike Sullivan, Tim Grant, Robert Robinson, and Don Collins.

Sullivan, from Woodbridge, was taken as the 22nd pick in the first round by the Reds out of Clemson University.

A pitcher from Alexandria – Atlee Hammaker of East Tennessee State – went right before Sullivan at No. 21 to the Royals.

Hammaker had a long career in the majors while Sullivan never went above Double-A. Sullivan had also been chosen in the first round out of high school at Gar-Field by Oakland in 1976.

Sullivan ended his career at Single-A Tampa in 1982 after reaching Double-A with Waterbury in the Eastern League the previous season. He had a 2.89 ERA in the minors.

Trey McCall

Virginia had two first-round picks in 1968 and neither made the majors.

Grant, from Boykins in southeast Virginia, went 13th overall to the Reds out of Riverview High but never went above Single-A as a pitcher.

Robinson, an outfielder from Thomas Dale in Chester, near Richmond, was the 18th overall pick by the Tigers and reached the Triple-A level, according to Baseball America.

A right-handed pitcher from Newport News, Collins was the 15th overall pick of the first round by the Cardinals in 1980 out of Ferguson High.

He last pitched at the Single-A level for the Brewers in 1983. The starter pitched in 74 games in pro ball and had an ERA of 3.71.

Pitcher Brad DuVall was taken in the first round out of Virginia Tech by the Orioles in 1987 but didn't sign.

He went 23rd overall the next year to the Cardinals but never got above the Single-A level. DuVall, from Maryland, is considered one of the best pitchers in Virginia Tech history.

39

J.D. Mundy, Moving Up

J.D. Mundy said he learned a lot the summer he played in the Valley Baseball League with Covington in 2018, hitting .353 with 14 homers in regular-season play.

"I really learned about the game from an approach-side of the plate," the left-handed slugger said. "We had a really special team."

Now the Roanoke native, who played in college at Virginia Tech and Radford, has taken some of that knowledge to pro baseball after signing as a non-drafted free agent (NDFA) with the Baltimore Orioles in 2020. After playing at the Single-A level last year, Mundy moved up to the Double-A Bowie Baysox in the Baltimore system this year. He was hitting .227 with two homers in early June for the Baysox in a farm system that is rated the best in the majors.

Mundy had a banner first year in the minors in 2021, hitting 15 homers total split between Single-A Delmarva and high Single-A Aberdeen, with home games at the latter stop at Ripken Stadium in Harford County, Maryland, north of Baltimore.

Mundy signed with the Orioles after a solid 2020 season at Radford that was cut short due to COVID-19. "I was very excited," Mundy said at the time.

The only Major League game Mundy has seen in person before turning pro was at Camden Yards his senior year of high school as the Orioles hosted the Yankees. "They were my favorite team growing up," he said of the Orioles. His favorite players were Manny Machado, now with San Diego, Mark Trumbo, and Adam Jones.

After his name was not called in the five-round MLB draft, Mundy heard Sunday from Blacksburg-based scout Rich Morales of the Orioles. Last year Morales signed pitcher Shelton Perkins out of James Madison University and in 2016 he helped land hurler Brenan Hanifee, a fourth-round pick out of Turner Ashby High in 2016. Morales was the Orioles scout of the year in 2018.

Other state connections to the Orioles also include former VBL Hall of Famer and Virginia Tech product Johnny Oates, a former Baltimore manager who died in Richmond in 2004; VBL Hall of Famer Sam Perlozzo, who also managed the Orioles; Staunton native Larry Sheets, a product of EMU basketball who played for the Orioles from 1984-89; and outfielder Steve Finley, who starred for the Harrisonburg Turks and broke in with the Orioles in 1989.

Another Valley League product to sign with the Orioles in 2020 was Auburn pitcher Ryan Watson, who played for the Front Royal Cardinals in 2017. The 6-foot-5 right-hander made five appearances this spring and posted an ERA of 1.23.

Outfielder Aaron Palensky, who played in college at Nebraska, was signed by the Yankees in 2020. He played in the VBL with the Winchester Royals. "A childhood dream came true today and I'm thrilled for what the future holds with the New York Yankees," he told a television station in Nebraska. He was with high Single-A Hudson Valley in early June after seeing time at Double-A late last season.

A first baseman, Mundy played at Northside High. He began his college career at Virginia Tech in 2017 as he made 21 starts at designated hitter. As a sophomore, he made 38 starts split between first base and DH.

Mundy then transferred to Radford, a Division I member of the Big South Conference. He said he made the move mainly due to baseball, figuring he would see more playing time at Radford after a coaching change with the Hokies.

"The transition was pretty easy. Thanks to my teammates for making that transition easier," he said. "I fit in really easy with them."

His uncle, Kelly Dampeer, played at Radford in the 1990s and in the minor leagues with the Cleveland Indians.

Mundy hit .304 for the Highlanders in 2019 and was an all-conference pick — his 13 homers were fourth-best in the Big South. He hit .385 in 17 games and led Radford with four homers and had 19 RBIs before play stopped in 2020. "It was pretty frustrating. We had a pretty good team," he said. "It kind of (stinks) it got cut short."

Before playing in the Valley League, Mundy appeared in the Northwoods League in 2017 for a team in Michigan. Mundy was released by the Orioles on August 8, 2022.

Roanoke native J.D. Mundy hit two homers on June 29, 2022 as the Baysox won at home over Richmond.

40

Magical Season For The Hokies

Franklin Stubbs, who won a World Series ring in the Major Leagues, never got this far.

Neither did Radford native Mike Williams, whose 144 saves in the big leagues is the most for a Virginia native.

Richmond native Chad Pinder, now in his seventh season with the Oakland A's, took part in the NCAA tournament with the Hokies in 2013 but got no further.

Those former Virginia Tech stars – despite individual brilliance – weren't able to experience what the 2022 Hokies did in a magical season here in the New River Valley.

Ranked as high as No. 2 in the nation at one point, a team loaded with Virginia prep talent hosted the Super Regional for the first time in school history.

"A great environment to play in," gushed Oklahoma coach Skip Johnson, after his Sooners held on to win 5-4 in Game 1 of the Super Regional on a glorious Friday afternoon in southwest Virginia in June.

Lefty slugger Gavin Cross, a possible first-round draft pick in July, lined out to right field for the final out for the Hokies.

A sea of orange and maroon-clad fans, many sitting on the grass behind the third-base dugout, left with a bitter feeling in their mouth after some questionable calls by the home-plate umpire.

"We get over things pretty quickly," said outfielder Jack Hurley of the Hokies.

Virginia Tech certainly did, winning the next day 14-8 as third baseman Carson DeMartini of Virginia Beach had three hits in a game started by right-hander Drue Hackenberg of Palmyra.

But a season of firsts ended on a Sunday afternoon before a national televised audience on June 12 as the Oklahoma bats were just took much for the Hokies, who fell 11-2 to the Sooners.

There were five Virginia prep products in the starting lineup for the Hokies in Game 1 of the Super Regional: first baseman Nick Biddison and right fielder Carson Jones of Glen Allen; shortstop Tanner Schobel of Williamsburg; DH Conor Hartigan of Winchester; and DeMartini of Virginia Beach. Jones brought the home fans on their feet in the sixth inning as he crushed a two-run homer.

The Virginia Tech baseball program hosted a Super Regional here for the first time on June 10. The Hokies lost the third and deciding game to the Sooners on June 12.

The Hokies had trailed 5-0 early but mounted a comeback that fell short against an Oklahoma program that is no stranger to the Super Regional and advanced to the College World Series for the 11th time.

The Hokies were bidding to become the third Virginia school to reach the College World Series.

JMU was the first to do so in 1983 with a batboy named Whit Babcock, now the athletic director at Virginia Tech. His father, Brad, who passed away in 2020, was the JMU coach for several years.

The second state program to reach Omaha was Virginia in 2009 and the Cavaliers did so under coach Brian O'Connor, who grew up in Nebraska. Virginia has been four more times since then with one national crown.

The Virginia Tech program also continues to improve under Coach John Szefc, who came to Blacksburg in 2017 from the University of Maryland.

The Hokies have sent 22 players to the majors as of early June, according to baseballreference.com.

Williams was an All-Star with the Pirates in 2002 when he posted a career-best 46 saves.

A native of North Carolina, Stubbs was a first-round draft pick out of Virginia Tech in 1982 by the Dodgers and six years later he won a World Series ring with Los Angeles. He hit 104 homers in the majors.

Those to have appeared this season in The Show as of early June were Pinder, an infielder/outfielder who was hitting .274 in mid-June; Arizona reliever Joe Mantiply, a Danville native (Tunstall High) who had an ERA of 0.41 in his first 25 outings this year; and Packy Naughton, a lefty pitcher with the St. Louis Cardinals.

Another product from the ACC program is right-hander pitcher Zachary Brzykcy, a former Virginia Tech closer who was promoted in early June from Single-A Wilmington to Double-A Harrisburg in the Washington system.

He had an ERA of 0.90 out of the bullpen this year split between the two teams in the first two months. He posted his first win at the Double-A level on June 11 – the same day the Hokies won a Super Regional game for the first time.

Sam Narron, a pitching coach in the Washington system, has been impressed by the fellow North Carolina native.

"He is big, tall, strong kid. Then you watch him throw and it makes it that much more impressive. I first saw a video of him at Virginia Tech and he already had a great arm but the command was lacking," Narron said.

He bounced back from a 5.20 ERA last year in the minors.

"It has been an up and down season," said Brzykcy of his 2021 campaign. "But I'm pretty happy with how things have gone."

That sums up how the program in Blacksburg has progressed over the past few years.

41

Ian Ostlund, Game Saver

Turner Ashby graduate Ian Ostlund collected 26 saves during a pro baseball career that left him on the cusp of making the Major Leagues with the Detroit Tigers.

Now the Rockingham County product is recording more important saves — through a second career with the Department of Game and Inland Fisheries.

After a pro baseball career of nine seasons, Ostlund spent two years as a stay-at-home father before joining the Virginia DGIF in 2011 after six months of academy training.

"I'm a bit of an adrenaline junky; I love adventure, I love being outside," he said. "It was right up my alley."

He was based in Shenandoah and Page counties before taking an assignment based in his native Rockingham — he grew up on a farm in Singers Glen — about four years ago, also as a Conservation Police Officer. About two years ago he became a K9 handler with the DGIF.

"Almost daily, I consider myself to be very fortunate to do something I love to do it and get paid for it," said Ostlund, an avid hunter and fisher. "We also spend a lot of time on waterways."

"He brings that same drive and work ethic" like a pro athlete, said Lt. Rob Ham III, his former supervisor.

Ostlund, who pitched at VMI and Virginia Tech, was working as a Police Conservation Officer in 2013 when he helped rescue a 7-year-old girl and her uncle on the rain-swollen Shenandoah River in Page County after their kayak had capsized.

"That is the most scared I have ever been," he said.

With the guidance of other rescue personnel, Ostlund was able to take their kayak to get close to the two family members who were from out of state.

"I heard the girl scream; her uncle was getting pulled under the water," he recalls. "The girl had a life jacket but the uncle did not. They were maybe 70 feet offshore. They tried to throw lines to them and they were unsuccessful with that."

Eventually, Ostlund was able to get to shore with the girl and her uncle in the kayak.

"It was what needed to be done. It was really pretty amazing no one was injured," Ostlund said. "That was one of my prouder moments. I realized I was entering into a very dangerous situation."

After that, Ostlund was able to spend time with the family. "I got to play catch with the kids. They were big baseball fans," the TA graduate said.

Ostlund has spent a lot of time with Reese — the dog he was assigned to as a K9 handler.

The duties are varied for Ostlund, who is licensed to carry a gun and did six months of training before joining the Virginia DGIF nearly 11 years ago.

"Each K9 team receives specialized training in human tracking, evidence recovery, and wildlife detection," according to a Virginia DGIF blog. "These elite K9 teams assist law enforcement personnel by tracking violators, detecting concealed wildlife and firearms, and conducting area searches for evidence recovery. Additionally, the K9 teams assist other enforcement agencies by tracking fugitives from justice, recovering evidence at crime scenes, and locating missing or lost persons."

Being outdoors — just like he was playing baseball — is just one of the appeals of his job.

"There is no average day as a Conservation Police Officer," he noted. "We don't know exactly what is going to happen. We work such large geographical areas as well."

Ostlund said the COVID-19 pandemic took away some of the personal interactions he has with the public.

Since he and others wore a mask for much of 2020-21, Ostlund said he has to look closely at the eyes of those that he comes in contact with.

"Establishing rapport with the public is very important," he said. "One way I can establish rapport with the citizens is extending my hand and offering a handshake and a smile. Due to social distancing, I (was) not able to shake people's hands. It is very difficult for people to read my facial expression."

Handshakes are a big part of baseball as well, and the big lefty received many post-game greetings during his career.

Ostlund played at TA under former coach Tim Clary and a memorable outing was when the lefty fanned 21 batters in seven innings against Harrisonburg as a senior.

As a sophomore, he was 3-0 with an ERA of 1.08. He went 7-1, 2.26 as a junior and then 10-1, 0.53 as a senior as the Knights advanced to the state quarterfinals in 1997.

After high school, he spent three years in Lexington with the Keydets and was a closer for part of that time.

"He really flourished in that role," said veteran Hampden-Sydney Coach Jeff Kinne, the pitching coach for Ostlund at VMI. "Great work ethic and a great teammate."

After a coaching change, Ostlund pitched as a senior for the Hokies in Blacksburg in 2001. Ostlund, who studied history at Tech, also played for the Harrisonburg Turks of the Valley Baseball League while in college.

He was drafted in the 34th round in 2001 by the Tigers and began his pro career in Oneonta, New York, in the New York-Penn League.

Perhaps his best season was two years later when he was 3-0 with an ERA of 1.59 with with low Single-A Western Michigan in the Midwest League. He finished 40 of the 44 games he pitched out of the bullpen and had a career-high 19 saves while making a post-season All-Star team.

After Tommy John surgery — performed by the notable Dr. James Andrews in 2004 — Ostlund moved up the Tigers' minor-league ladder and reached Triple-A Toledo for the first time in 2007.

He was back at Toledo in 2008 and throwing well out of the bullpen during a stretch when the Tigers needed a lefty reliever in Detroit. But Ostlund didn't get the call, with the promotion going to a pitcher who had been with Double-A Erie.

"That was the first time I felt truly really close" to the majors, he said. "I was being looked at hard by the big club. I knew I was on the shortlist" for a promotion. He would have been the first TA grad to make the majors as a pitcher — Alan Knicely and Brian Bocock made The Show as position players.

After that season, Ostlund signed with St. Louis and was invited to spring training with the Cardinals and manager Tony La Russa in 2009. He still pinches himself that he did fielding drills that spring in Jupiter, Florida with Albert Pujols, the Cardinals' All-Star first baseman at the time. "It almost seemed like a dream," Ostlund said.

He was competing for a lefty spot in the bullpen but didn't make the Opening Day roster.

Ostlund ended his pro career at Triple-A Memphis that year, pitching in 23 games with one start. He ended his minor-league career with a record of 30-23 with an ERA of 3.49 in 325 games, with 11 starts — and those 26 saves.

Now the saves are even more important — like the one on the

Shenandoah River. He worked for the Dayton Police Department before returning to the Virginia DGIF a few years ago.

"He is very dependable in everything he does," said Lt. Ham, a Bridgewater College graduate. "He is very courteous to the public." And sometimes way more than that.

Ian Ostlund with Reese

42

Red Sox Prospects

After the 2008 season, Salem switched its fortunes in the Single-A Carolina League from Houston to Boston.

Those fans in southwest Virginia had no way to know that the Red Sox would win the World Series in 2013 and again in 2018, while the Astros would prevail in the Fall Classic in 2017.

But the minor league team in Salem also had a connection to the 2016 World Series champs – the Chicago Cubs.

That first Red Sox affiliate in Salem back in 2009 had a young first baseman named Anthony Rizzo, who had been drafted in the sixth round by the Red Sox out of his Florida high school in 2006.

Rizzo would hit .295 in 55 games at the tender age of 19 in 2009 for Salem – he made the majors for the first time in 2011 with San Diego, helped the Cubs win that elusive title five years later, and is now with the Yankees.

This season, again a Single-A farm team of Boston, the Salem Red Sox have several high draft picks who could one day find themselves in Boston.

In early June, the roster included infielder Marcelo Mayer, a first-round pick out of a California high school by Boston in 2021; fellow infielder Blaze Jordan, taken in the third round in 2020; and catcher Nathan Hickey, a fifth-round selection last year. Mayer was hitting .326 in his first 89 at-bats this season for Salem.

Some publications have listed Mayer as the top prospect in the Boston system. Jordan and pitcher Wikelman Gonzalez, both on the roster in Salem in June, were among the top 10 prospects with the Red Sox.

"Working with these high prospects is what keeps us busy," Salem manager Luke Montz said in a phone interview in June. "Gonzalez is up there and climbing the ladder."

Montz played in Woodbridge with the Potomac Nationals as part of the Washington system.

Second-year manager for Salem Luke Montz

"I learned a lot in a 13-year playing career from managers, some that cared about you and some that didn't care about you," the

Louisiana native said. "I have tried to build my managerial career from what I have learned. I am here for the guys, I am here for their careers. I give them my full and undivided attention. Our goal is to get these guys to move up the ladder. I want to do that with my full and undivided attention, giving them everything I can. We know that this game is so hard."

Montz is a former Major League catcher who broke into the majors with the Washington Nationals in 2008. He had finished the Triple-A season at Columbus that year and wasn't part of the September 1 call-ups so he drove home to Louisiana from Ohio.

"It wasn't home 20 or 25 minutes that I got in my driveway and general manager Jim Bowden called and said Jesus Flores had got run over at the plate the night before," Montz recalls.

So Montz joined the Nationals in Washington and then a few days later made his Major League debut as he started back of the plate in Atlanta on Sept. 4, 2008.

Montz was drafted by the Montreal Expos and was a teammate in the minors in 2005 in Georgia with Ryan Zimmerman, the first-round pick of the Nationals that year out of the University of Virginia.

"What a great guy and a great teammate," Montz said of Zimmerman.

Another teammate with the Nationals in 2008 was Willie Harris, who was later the manager of Double-A Richmond.

"It was a veteran club," Montz said of the Nats of 2008. "It was tough going since it was a long summer for the guys who were there all summer."

The Salem pitching staff this year has been filled with international free agents from Cuba, the Dominican and Venezuela.

"We are very heavy with international pitching staff; we are young across the board," he said.

Montz lives in Salem during the season with his wife and two young daughters, who are homeschooled.

"We spend a lot of time together," he said. "We will hike some trails, go to museums. Roanoke is a good area; downtown Roanoke has some good restaurants and nice places to eat."

One of the Americans on the staff in June was Maceo Campbell, who was born in Washington, D.C. in 1999.

The right-hander had just one college scholarship offer coming out of Bishop McNamara in Maryland and that was to Division I Longwood University in Farmville.

Campbell saw very little action as a freshman with the Lancers then was academically ineligible his second year at Longwood.

Then he played for the Bethesda (Md.) Big Train in the Cal Ripken League before his junior year and that really helped his development.

"My junior year I became a weekend starter and won all four of the games I started. I also pitched really well at North Carolina State that year and that is where the Red Sox saw me," Campbell said.

He had an ERA of 2.19 in rookie ball in 2021 with the Red Sox.

"I acquired a lot of information last year," said Campbell, who signed with the Red Sox in 2020. "I feel like I learned a lot; I am a significantly better baseball player than any course of my career. The strides I have made are so significant it changes the way I play the game currently."

Pitching out of the bullpen, Campbell had an ERA of 2.95 in early June with one save for Salem.

"He has been great," Montz said of the Longwood product. "He works his tail off, a guy who is trying to get anything he can to have success. He is throwing the ball at 96, 97 miles per hour. It has been impressive; he has bought into what the Red Sox are doing with him. He has turned the corner. He takes his conditioning seriously."

"I have fastball, curve, slider and change. I enjoy that role as a closer; it is a really good role that fits me," Campbell said in June. "One of my main goals is to make the All-Star team; it would be nice to make an All-Star team in my first year in A ball. It is going to be hard as a relief pitcher. My goal for the season is to try and get called up as much as I can."

Campbell is bidding to become the second Major Leaguer from Longwood. The first was outfielder Michael Tucker, a first-round draft pick by the Royals who had a long career in the majors.

Maceo Campbell, a product of Longwood in Farmville, rears back to throw a pitch for the Salem Red Sox.

43

Billy Sample, Salem Legend

Here is our interview with Billy Sample, who was born in Roanoke and went to school in Salem. After playing at JMU, he broke into the majors with Texas in 1978 and ended his career with the Braves in 1986. He was elected to the JMU Athletic Hall of Fame in 1988 and was a notable broadcaster after his playing days.

DD: You were an all-around athlete at Andrew Lewis High, playing three sports. Didn't you catch a touchdown pass in the 1971 high school playoffs and later faced T.C. Williams of "Remember the Titans" movie fame?

Sample: "In that part of the state football reigns. Around the age of 15, I thought if I get a chance to play something professionally it is probably going to be baseball. If I had been three inches taller, I may have tried football. Someone told me after my junior year that Virginia was looking at me (for football). I never heard from them; it might have been a challenge academically. It really turned out for the best.

My football days, I did not start. I was running third-team flanker after the first week of camp my junior year. By the time the season started three weeks later, I had become the starting split end.

We had a real good balance of running and throwing. We won our district and played E.C. Glass of Lynchburg in the regionals. We were losing 14-0 with eight minutes left and we ended up scoring three touchdowns to take the lead. We ended up winning 20-14 and I caught the winning touchdown. I curled behind the linebacker and sat in front of the safety. People in Salem still remember that game. We beat Douglas S. Freeman of Richmond and then lost to T.C. Williams in the state finals; our bubble burst."

DD: You were high school teammates in basketball with Charlie Morgan, who coached new JMU basketball coach Mark Byington at Salem High. What do you remember about Morgan and games Andrew Lewis played in basketball in Harrisonburg?

Sample: "I was the point guard and he was the two guard. He got to shoot all of the time; what a good player. I averaged five points per game as a senior. If I drove to the lane and you fouled me, you only helped to improve my shot. We played in a tournament between Robert E. Lee of Staunton, Harrisonburg High, and Turner Ashby. Preston Green (HHS) played in that tournament. I could handle the rock; I was good at that. Jack Arbogast of TA just abused me. I fouled out and didn't score. He would just isolate ... It was just he and me. I didn't get enough help" on defense.

DD: What colleges did you look at besides JMU and how did you end up in Harrisonburg after being drafted by the Rangers out of high school?

Sample: "I had nothing (else); there was talk about maybe Virginia Tech. Notre Dame sent me a questionnaire for football. But I had nothing going. I was drafted by the Rangers in the 28th round by scout Joe Branzell. I don't think Joe had envisioned me signing anyway. He told me 23 other teams passed over me 27 times. So, I went to JMU and played in the Valley League two summers. I was not on scholarship per se but I didn't have to pay for anything. I told my dad, 'Make us sound even poorer.' "

DD: How did playing for the Harrisonburg Turks in the Valley Baseball League help your development?

Sample: "That really helped me measure up with some of the better players along the Eastern seaboard. I played with (or against) Jim Pankovits and Gene Richards — he had the stolen base record for rookies in the majors before Tim Raines broke it. That was just good competition. I had future Major Leaguers on my team as well. I remember Denny Walling (Waynesboro) was a man among boys. He had a nice career with the Astros, primarily. I saw a good slider for the first time. I had to make some adjustments. I used to hold my bat up high like Cesar Cedeno but I wasn't strong enough to start and then stop my swing on sliders. The second year I played in the Valley I was the MVP."

DD: After the Rangers drafted you out of JMU in 1974 in the 10th round, where did you go next?

Sample: "I went to Sarasota, Florida (for rookie ball). Joe Klein, who just passed away recently (in 2017), was the farm director, but he would go and manage the rookie team to see what talent he had. Steve Comer, a right-handed change-up artist out of the University of Minnesota was there. He made it to the majors. And Brian Allard, with the Rangers and Mariners. That was it; those two and me" made the majors.

DD: What are your memories of your first MLB game with the Rangers on Sept. 2, 1978, in Milwaukee as you hit leadoff for Texas? How did you find out you were being called up from Triple-A to the majors with a few others?

Sample: "Rich Donnelly was our Triple-A manager. He was the third-base coach with Jim Leyland in the majors for several years with the Pirates and Marlins. He told me about five days before I was going up. I said, 'Thank you.' My response was kind of matter-of-fact. I figured I did what I needed to do. I went 11 games without a hit in Double-A and went 0-for-37 with Tulsa. That cost me a shot (in 1977). I was hitting .348 before that so you can do the math.

Anyway, we were playing out of Tucson (in 1978). We went to Tucson to Phoenix, Phoenix to Chicago, Chicago to Milwaukee.

By the time I got to old County Stadium and I was a little tired from the jet lag. I looked at the lineup card and it had me leading off. I said, 'Okay.' It also had me playing second base. I had burned my second base glove; I hadn't played second base in a year and a half.

Dock Ellis (Texas pitcher) came up and said, 'Good luck, young man.' I thought it may have been a fake lineup. Before the game (Texas DH) Richie Zisk came up to me and said, 'It's just like Triple-A,' which I thought was a nice thing to do and was his nature. They felt (regular second baseman) Bump Wills, a switch-hitter, was struggling from the right side of the plate. They wanted to give him one less at-bat from that side (so Sample started at second). Jerry Augustine, a lefty was pitching for the Brewers. His first pitch was a sinker low and away. It was almost reflexive, I guess. I hit it to right-center and Sixto Lezcano dove for it and it went off his glove. I am at first base with a Cheshire-cat grin. Then here comes Bump Wills to run for me. Bob Uecker was the broadcaster for the Brewers. I wonder what he thought of all that. Bump and I never talked about it."

DD: What was the biggest adjustment from the minors to the majors?

Sample: "The scouting reports are different. And the pitchers hit their spots better. I think if you can hit Double-A pitchers you can hit Major League pitchers. A lot of pitchers back then went from Double-A to the majors. One of them was Roanoke native Al Holland, who I played American Legion against, went from Double-A to the majors" with the Pirates in 1977.

DD: You were one of the top rookies in 1979 with Texas, hitting .292, and played with the Rangers through 1984. But you never made the playoffs?

Sample: "Perhaps my one regret, from a team standpoint. The 1985 team would have been a wild-card team" had that existed at the time.

DD: In 1985 you are with the New York Yankees. They had

Don Mattingly, Ken Griffey, Sr., Rickey Henderson, Don Baylor, Dave Winfield. What a team that was?

Sample: "It was a potent lineup. It was the last 20-win season for (Ron) Guidry; (Dave) Righetti was closing. As good as that was, Toronto had a young, potent lineup. The Blue Jays won 99 games and we won 97. They had Jimmy Key," who pitched in the Valley Baseball League for Winchester.

DD: That season you got to play for managers Yogi Berra and Billy Martin. Berra was 6-10 and then Martin took over for the rest of the year. What were they like to play for?

Sample: "Yogi was so well-respected. It was nice to be around that kind of baseball heritage. Yogi and wife Carmen, they were just beautiful people. I thought he was a great tactician, Billy Martin." (In 2016, Sample self-published a book "A Year in Pinstripes ... And Then Some" about his season with the Yankees, and his career.)

DD: After that 1985 season you head to the Atlanta Braves and played for them in 1986. They had Ken Griffey, Sr., Dale Murphy, Willie Stargell, and Ted Simmons.

Sample: "We were a game out at the All-Star break and then nothing happened. Chuck Tanner, he was the last of my eight managers in a little over eight years; just a super person."

DD: What happened for you after the 1986 season?

Sample: "The only thing I got was an offer to spring training with the Twins in 1987. It appeared that I had made the team; I was coming off knee surgery. I was on a licensing committee (with MLB players) and a letter was sent to me in the clubhouse in Orlando in spring training. They were in the middle of a collusion (between owners and players). I had signed a three-year contract with Texas and it ran out after the 1986 season. Tom Kelly, the Twins' manager, told me they were going with younger players."

DD: You ended your playing career with a batting average of .272 in 826 games with 46 homers and 98 steals. How did you get into broadcasting?

Sample: "I needed a job; I had a B.S. in psychology. Dan

Patrick (formerly of ESPN) was in Atlanta with CNN and helped me put together a tape, which I appreciate him doing. We sent it to the Braves; I did two years with the Braves, Seattle TV splitting it with Ken Griffey, Sr., Angels radio, and worked for MLB.com for several years." (Sample has also contributed to ESPN, Sports Illustrated, The New York Times, Baseball Weekly, NPR, etc). I covered the World Series in 1987 for a New York outlet and wouldn't you know it, the Twins were in it."

DD: What is your life like today and who is in your family?

Sample: "I have three children. A daughter Stacey attended the University of Rhode Island and threw the javelin. One of my sons, Ian, played college football at Hawaii and caught 10 of Colt Brennan's 53 touchdown passes in 2006. My youngest son, Travis, has been a fitness trainer and speaker. I fight for truth and justice; that is how I roll. I try to educate people on the ways of the world and the ways of the United States."

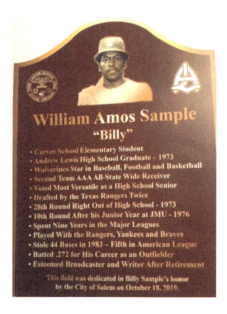

44

Nick Robertson, Dodgers'
Prospect

Soon after he signed with the Dodgers in 2019, Roanoke native and Franklin County product Nick Robertson headed to Arizona and the spring training home of the National League team.

It was there that many prospects met John Shoemaker, 64, a long-time minor-league manager in the Dodgers' system and a colleague of the late Hall of Famer Tommy Lasorda. The former Dodgers pitcher and manager died in 2021.

"He and Mr. Lasorda were always really good friends so he talked about everything he (Lasorda) had done for the Dodgers' organization," Robertson recalled of that talk by Shoemaker, who managed Single-A Great Lakes in 2019 in the Midwest League.

Robertson is now trying to put himself into the position of one day playing for the Dodgers.

The right-handed reliever advanced to Double-A last season and he was back again in Tulsa to start this year at that level.

In his first 17 games out of the bullpen this year, he was 1-0 with an ERA of 4.91 with two saves.

He had a 3.53 ERA in 39 games with one start and a record of 2-4 in 2021 with Tulsa.

Robertson, a seventh-round pick of the Dodgers in 2019, was in Instructional League with the Dodgers in the fall of 2021 and was able to watch the clinching game of the World Series win by the Dodgers over Tampa Bay on television with other Los Angeles prospects.

One of the key players for the Dodgers in that series was Chris Taylor, the former University of Virginia standout and Frank Cox High star. Taylor had five homers in early June with the Dodgers this season.

Robertson was one of four JMU pitchers drafted in 2019. He gives a lot of credit to Coach Marlin Ikenberry and Jimmy Jackson, the associate head coach who works with pitchers.

"I just think the way he is able to relate to the pitchers once you get on campus. As soon as I got up there, I felt comfortable with him, and the other coaches, too, since he was my position coach," Robertson said of Jackson.

Robertson has worked out in the winters at his alma mater, Franklin High School.

His high school coach was Roanoke native Barry Shelton, who was drafted out of West Virginia State by the Chicago White Sox in the 21st round in 1995 as an infielder/outfielder.

Nick Robertson began this season in the bullpen with Double-A Tulsa

Part V
SHENANDOAH VALLEY AND BLUE RIDGE

45

Lexington, Reed Garrett, Back In The Show

It took former VMI pitcher Reed Garrett more than three years to get back to the Major Leagues.

And when he did, the product of Mills Godwin High was not very far from his Richmond roots.

Garrett made his Major League debut with the Detroit Tigers in 2019 as he appeared in 13 games out of the bullpen.

After that, he pitched in Japan before he was signed by the Washington Nationals prior to the 2022 season.

He began the season at Triple-A Rochester in the Washington system and then was called up to the Nationals.

Pitching at Nationals Park on June 14, he did not allow a run in two innings in a loss to the Atlanta Braves.

It was his first appearance in the majors since May 16, 2019, when he was with the Tigers.

"He is a power guy; he is upward to 97 to 99," Rochester manager Matt LeCroy told us the day after Garrett pitched for the Nationals. "His fastball is the pitch; secondary he has a split and a slider. That is how he attacked people here. I am happy he got a shot to go up. You dangle the carrot in front of these guys. The door is wide open for these guys if they put the work in for that moment."

Garrett's coach at VMI was Marlin Ikenberry, who now holds the same job at JMU. The Dukes are moving to the Sun Belt Conference for the 2023 season and Ikenberry signed a two-year contract extension after the 2022 campaign.

Reed Garrett

In 2014, Garrett made 13 starts for VMI and was 6-6 with an ERA of 2.23.

That came after he posted an ERA of 5.56 in 2013 for the Lexington school.

Garrett, as a freshman at VMI, pitched in 25 games with one start and had an ERA of 2.17.

He was drafted by the Texas Rangers in the 16th round in 2014 out of VMI.

"It's definitely a tough decision (to play abroad), because this is the pinnacle of the sport," he told Mid-Atlantic Sports Network of being back in the majors. "This is where you want to be. Japan has really good baseball, and this was an opportunity for myself to prove myself a little bit more and take a little financial stress off, make a little bit of money. It made things easier if I was to play in the minor leagues again."

Garrett's brother played baseball at Lynchburg College and his father played semipro ball.

The other school in Lexington is Washington and Lee, a Division III member of the Old Dominion Athletic Conference.

Zach Perkins hit .348 in 2021 and then batted .339 in 2022 as a junior outfielder for the Generals.

Perkins played at James Madison High in Vienna and in youth

baseball with James Triantos, now a promising infielder in the Cubs farm system.

"He was the best player back then. It is not surprising what he is doing now," Perkins says of Triantos, taken in the second round by the Cubs in 2021 out of Madison.

Perkins has an internship in the summer of 2022 with a consulting firm in Northern Virginia and also hopes to play some in the Northern Virginia Collegiate League as time allows.

Washington and Lee was 20-16 overall and 12-8 in the ODAC in 2022 under Coach Ted White, a former assistant at JMU.

The leading hitter for VMI in 2022 was Suffolk's Zac Morris, who batted .332. The Keydets were 16-40 overall in 2022.

Former VMI pitcher Josh Winder made his Major League debut for the Minnesota Twins on April 12, 2022.

In his first seven games in the majors, the Richmond native had an ERA of 3.68 in seven outings, with three starts. He went to James River High.

The other three VMI products, per baseballreference.com, to appear in the Majors: Buddy Dear, a native of Norfolk who played in 1927 with Washington; Ryan Glynn, a pitcher who appeared from 1999-2005 with Texas, Toronto, and Oakland; and Cory Spangenberg, who played from 2014-19 as infielder/outfielder with San Diego and Milwaukee.

Dear died in Radford in 1989 and is buried in Sunset Cemetery in Christiansburg, according to baseballreference.com.

Winder joined a Minnesota pitching staff that included Emilio Pagan, who pitched in the Valley Baseball League with the Harrisonburg Turks while he was in college.

Pitcher Randy Dobnak, who saw action with the Twins in 2019, 2020 and 2021, pitched for New Market in the Valley Baseball League. He was with Triple-A St. Paul early in the 2022 season.

46

Jerry May, Catcher, Farmer

PARNASSUS - The cemetery here at Union Presbyterian Church is an idyllic, bird-chirping slice of rural Augusta County that sits up a hill a few miles east of Route 42, with a splendid view of the mountains off in the distance towards West Virginia.

There is a row of pine trees at the back end of the cemetery, part of a church that was founded in 1817 and has tombstones that date until at least five decades later — the ravages of time have wiped away the dates of ones that are certainly older.

It is here in a small community a few miles from Churchville that former Major League Baseball catcher and Staunton native Jerry May was laid to rest 26 summers ago after a tragic farm accident that cost him his life at the age of 52 while he was working on a mower.

May was a basketball and baseball star at old North River High in Augusta, scoring 77 points in hoops in a 1960 game. The right-handed slugger played in the Rockingham County Baseball League and in the Valley Baseball League before turning pro.

He began his pro baseball career in the Appalachian League in

Kingsport, Tennessee, in 1961 after he was signed by the legendary Virginia native Syd Thrift, who would later become general manager of the Pirates and Orioles.

May made his Major League debut with Pittsburgh on Sept. 19, 1964, against the San Francisco Giants. A late sub in the game, May had his first at-bat come against future Hall of Famer Juan Marichal — who induced a pop out to third. Other superstars in that game included Roberto Clemente and Willie Stargell of the Pirates and Willie Mays of the Giants.

May, an amateur standout in Augusta County in American Legion as a pitcher, had one of the most memorable games of his MLB career six years later: he was behind the plate as pitcher Dock Ellis of the Pirates threw a no-hitter on June 12, 1970, to beat the Padres 2-0 in San Diego.

Ellis later admitted he was high on LSD for that game, which he was not originally slated to pitch. He was at a friend's house the previous day in Los Angeles and his flight to San Diego got him to the stadium about 90 minutes before the first pitch, according to published reports.

"I started having a crazy idea in the fourth inning that Richard Nixon was the home plate umpire, and once I thought I was pitching a baseball to Jimi Hendrix, who to me was holding a guitar and swinging it over the plate," Ellis claimed in a 1984 interview.

Brougan Sheets, born in 1995 and the only daughter of May, said her father put tape on his fingers so Ellis could see his signals better. May also has an adult son from his first marriage, according to Sheets, who lives with her husband, Travis, a former baseball player at Buffalo Gap, on a dairy farm in Mt. Solon. She was barely a year old when her father died.

It is hard to imagine a battery of men from so different worlds than May and Ellis.

May was White from rural Augusta County while Ellis, who was Black, was born in Los Angeles.

The Society of American Baseball Research (SABR) wrote of Ellis: "Dock attended the predominantly white Gardena (California) High School in hopes of finding a better education but found a good dose of racial prejudice. To avoid suspension when he got caught drinking and smoking marijuana at school, he agreed to go out for baseball. But he found racial resistance there as well. He excelled at basketball, however, as the only black person on the team."

Ellis went to Los Angeles Harbor College in California, but according to SABR ended up in Watts (a mostly Black neighborhood infamous for riots in 1965) playing for Chet Brewer, who had played in the Negro Leagues.

"Brewer scouted for the Pirates and tutored several future major leaguers, including Bob Watson, Bobby Tolan, and Enos Cabell. Fielding several offers, Ellis always wanted to sign with Pittsburgh, as he finally did in 1964, but saw his signing bonus reduced from $60,000 to $2,500 after his arrest for stealing a car," SABR wrote.

May was 0-for-3 in the game that Ellis blanked the Padres. The right-hander would be the starting pitcher for the National League in the All-Star game in 1971. Ellis died in 2009 of liver problems in his native Los Angeles. Another teammate of May's in Pittsburgh, infielder Gene Alley, is a native of Richmond who went to Hermitage High and was with the Pirates from 1963-73.

As a teenager, May was a superb pitcher at North River. "It was like you were playing against a pro," said Ray Heatwole, the former Turner Ashby, Bridgewater and JMU Coach who hit against May in high school while at TA.

A defensive-minded catcher, May was in his first season with the Kansas City Royals when the Pirates made history by fielding a lineup entirely of players of color on Sept. 1, 1971.

Pittsburgh manager Danny Murtaugh was asked after the game about making history.

"When it comes to making out the lineup, I'm colorblind, and my athletes know it. They don't know it because I told them. They know it because they're familiar with how I operate. The best men in our organization are the ones who are here. And the ones who are here all play, depending on when the circumstances present themselves," he told reporters.

A few weeks later, the Pirates beat the Orioles in the World Series. After the 1972 season, Pirates' star Clemente was killed in a plane crash near Puerto Rico while aiding earthquake survivors.

At the time, May was a reserve catcher for the Royals until he was sold to the New York Mets on May 14, 1973.

His last game in The Show was June 3, 1973. He was with the Mets as the starting catcher and drew a walk and was replaced by a pinch-runner in the fourth inning in San Diego — the site of that Ellis no-hitter.

Duffy Dyer, who would later play for the Pirates and catch his own no-hitter in 1976, came in to catch and May never played in another Major League game. The Staunton native played in 556 Major League contests and hit .234 with 15 homers.

"I knew it was over and time for a new career," he told the Daily News-Record in 1974, when he announced his retirement. The new career was farming.

The most dingers he ever hit in a season? That was seven in 1969 with the Pirates. His last homer came at Fenway Park in Boston in 1972 against pitcher John Curtis of the Red Sox.

It was toward the end of May's career that this reporter (Driver) had a chance to see him in person.

When I was a young boy, my mother, Marilyn, taught elementary school at Mount Clinton and one winter May agreed to come and meet the teachers and students one chilly evening during a school function.

While I attended Dayton Elementary, I certainly wasn't going to miss the opportunity — and somewhere there is a photo of May and myself. My aunt, Virginia, taught at North River Elementary in the 1990s and began teaching at Craigsville in 1973 — just weeks after the last Major League game for May.

The fact that someone from this area could grow up on a farm and make it to the Major Leagues left an impression on me.

After his playing career, May returned to his farm in Augusta County. He also had a farm in the Grottoes/Weyers Cave area for a time, his daughter said.

It was a farm accident in Swoope on June 30, 1996, that took his life.

There is another man named May from Augusta County who had a successful career. C.E. May, the uncle of Jerry, grew up in Weyers Cave, studied at Bridgewater College, the University of Virginia, and Columbia, and taught English in Hawaii and the Panama Canal Zone. He was the mayor of Bridgewater from 1958-68 and from 1967-76 was a member of the board of directors of Valley National Bank in Harrisonburg. In 1976 he published "Life Under 4 Flags in the North River Basin of Virginia."

He was also a professor of English and director of information at Bridgewater College from 1946 until his retirement in 1968. C.E. May played baseball in the Valley League, graduated from BC in 1924, was the one who suggested "Eagles" as a nickname for the school and went into the BC athletic Hall of Fame in 1995.

Jerry May, the son of Kit and Norine, is one of a few former Major League players buried in the area. His parents have a grave marker next to his, as his mother died in 1966 and his father 11 years later.

Another former big leaguer buried in the area is Hank Hulvey, a native of Mount Sidney who played one game as a pitcher for Philadelphia in 1923. He died in 1982 and is buried in the Lebanon Church of the Brethren Cemetery in Mount Sidney, according to baseballreference.com.

The final resting spots are serene for two of the select few local natives to make the majors.

The roar of the crowds, from stadiums from Pittsburgh to San

Diego to Boston, are but a distant memory for the family and friends of May. But he achieved two worthy callings that some young boys (and girls) can only dream of or be cut out for: Major Leaguer and farmer.

"He was, and is, my idol," his only daughter, Brougan, wrote on social media last year.

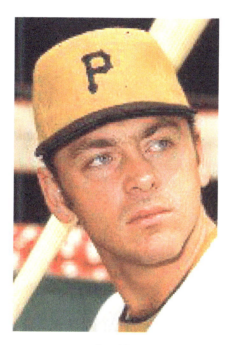

Jerry May

47

Tyler Zombro, Amazing Comeback

When they got the unsettling news, Fonda Morris and Tim Zombro didn't hesitate to react and then act.

Morris and Zombro, the parents of minor league pitcher Tyler Zombro, are no longer married to each other. But when they heard their son had been hit by a line drive while pitching for host Triple-A Durham in the Tampa Bay system against Norfolk, the residents of Augusta County drove that night to North Carolina in early June of last year.

"We went together as soon as it happened," said Tim Zombro, whose son pitched for the Staunton Braves of the Valley Baseball League while in college at George Mason in Fairfax.

They headed to Duke University Hospital, a few miles from the baseball stadium in Durham and where their son was taken after the scary incident.

Zombro was in stable condition in the ICU a few days later. He had brain surgery and continued to progress for the next week and months.

Less than a year after the scary incident, Zombro returned to the mound on April 24 of this year for Durham.

"He was so determined," his mother said in early June. "I knew once they released him from the hospital he would come back."

But his mom didn't think of a comeback right after the scary incident.

"I was so happy he was alive," said Morris, a former volleyball coach who led Wilson Memorial to a state title in 1999.

Zombro pitched again on April 24 of this season for Durham.

His father was on hand for the games in Norfolk while his mother flew to Florida to see him pitch in Spring Training for the Rays earlier this year.

But after those two outings in April, Zombro went on the 60-day Injured List.

"He was having trouble feeling the ball coming out of his hand," his mother said.

The Rays sent him to see a specialist in Texas and Zombro continues to work his way back as this book went to press.

Tim Zombro and Morris were encouraged by the support they have received from the Shenandoah Valley and around the baseball community. What was that been like?

"I mean, as you ask me that, I feel like crying," Morris said. "It (was) overwhelming, honestly. It just speaks volumes for the type of person Tyler is and the people he has touched back in the Valley. We are hearing from there, which is really comforting, and from all over the United States."

Tyler Zombro pitched at what is now Staunton High and for his hometown Braves.

He pitched at Division I George Mason in college in Fairfax then was signed as a non-drafted free agent by Tampa Bay and made his pro debut in 2017 in the minors. He pitched that year for Princeton, West Virginia in the Appalachian League.

Zombro worked his way up to the Triple-A level by 2019 but did not play organized baseball in 2020 since the pandemic called off the minor league season. He worked out in Northern Virginia that winter before moving with his wife to the Charlotte area.

He was a non-roster invitee to spring training last year with the Rays and saw action in three exhibition games with Tampa Bay before he was assigned to Durham, the top farm club of the Rays.

He was pitching in his ninth game this year, all out of the bullpen, when a shot off the bat by Brett Cumberland hit him in the head in the eighth inning last year. The game was suspended and many players on the field began praying for Zombro, according to published reports. Norfolk is the top farm team of the Baltimore Orioles.

In the stands for the game was Moriah, a registered nurse, and good friend Taylor Davis, an assistant baseball coach at Bridgewater College and a former assistant at Eastern Mennonite University. Davis played baseball at Ferrum and is a former coach with the Staunton Braves.

Both of Zombro's parents played sports at Bridgewater College and graduated from the school. Fort Defiance graduate Morris is a long-time educator in Augusta County and former volleyball coach at Wilson Memorial and at Fort.

As for the Staunton Braves this season, Jeffrey Snider of Bridgewater College got off to a fast start at the plate while JMU's Grant Painter was playing for his hometown team in the Valley League.

Pitcher Nathan Knowles, from Arlington and William and Mary, allowed just two hits and no runs in six innings in his first start for the Braves this summer.

Brian Snitker, who played for the Staunton Braves in the 1970s, was the manager that led the Atlanta Braves to the World Series title in 2021. He managed the Triple-A Richmond Braves in 2006; he played in six games for Richmond in 1978 while in the minors with Atlanta.

48

Eric Kratz, Career Delayed

Erik Kratz was in spring training with the New York Yankees catching All-Star pitchers before the pandemic shut down the sport in 2020.

A little bit over a year later the former Eastern Mennonite University backstop is teaching the finer points of baseball to young boys not far from his boyhood home about 40 miles north of Philadelphia.

"It has been different, but has been a really good different. There is always a lot of uncertainty" in pro baseball, said Kratz, who is married with three children. "There are a lot of things that people don't see. There is a lot of packing and stuff, and it is no nice not to be missing it."

After four years of Division III ball at EMU and a pro career that lasted from 2002 to 2020, Kratz was the baseball coach for the middle-school team at Dock Mennonite Academy — which has campuses in Souderton and Lansdale, Pennsylvania in 2021.

"It is really cool; we have kids who have played who are really good to some who have never played baseball before and are learning the game from the grassroots," Kratz said. "It is fun for me."

One of the players on his team is his son Brayden, an eighth-grader who figures to be his shortstop when the team begins games next month.

"He is only 14 so I hope he plays all positions," Kratz said. "On his travel team, he will probably be the shortstop there. He has caught, he has played third, he has played center field."

After Kratz retired in 2020, he spoke with Dock athletic director Tim Ehst about being the varsity baseball coach.

"But I don't have any kids in high school," pointed out Kratz, whose main reason for retiring as a player was to spend more time with his family.

For the same reason, he declined to be a varsity assistant since that would also take him away from his wife, Sarah (Troyer) Kratz, and children.

So Kratz asked Ehst about coaching the middle-school team. "For real? That would be great," said Ehst, according to Kratz.

"We were really excited for him to coach at that level," Ehst, a former EMU basketball player and 1976 graduate, said of Kratz. "He is obviously well over-qualified."

Kratz was drafted out of EMU in the 29th round in 2002 by Toronto. While in college, he played for Waynesboro and Harrison-burg in the Valley Baseball League.

He toiled in the minor leagues before making his Major League debut with Pittsburgh in 2010. Kratz played at least two games in every Major League season for several teams through 2020, with a high of 68 games with his hometown Philadelphia Phillies in 2013.

He ended up playing in 332 Major League games and hitting .209 with 31 homers. Last year, he hit .321 for the Yankees in 28 at-bats over 16 regular-season games.

Kratz was a big part of the Brewers' playoff success in 2018.

"If you're 38 years old and still catching," Brewers manager Craig Counsell told USA Today in 2018 about Kratz, "it's almost assured that you're a very good receiver of the baseball, you have a very good handle on managing a game, you take fast at knowing hitters."

Kratz spent part of 2019 with the Giants. "He has a great way about him," former Giants' manager Bruce Bochy, who grew up in Northern Virginia and won three World Series titles.

The right-handed hitting catcher also played in 1,027 minor-league games, hitting .259 with 134 homers. He was also used for mop-up duty as a pitcher in the majors seven times.

"Baseball is awesome," he said. "It is a lot of fun to play, to be able to do all that. But at the beginning of spring training, there was all of the packing up and settling in. There was the enjoyment of spring training but then it was back to work. With two weeks left in spring training, you are packing up again and uncertain where you are going to go."

Eric Kratz with EMU president Susan Schultz Huxman

Kratz has been watching Major League games on television and stays in touch with some of his former teammates, ribbing them with good-natured texts. "I love watching them," he said. "I don't miss it at all."

So these days, he doesn't have to worry about calling pitches for veteran and rookie pitchers alike. "I never worried about calling pitches. For me, it was hitting them" that was the problem, he said, with a laugh.

Kratz made a change after 2021.

He decided not to coach this year and instead has done some work this season on the radio in Philadelphia covering the Phillies.

Nelson Chittum, Teammates
With Musial, Williams

Harrisonburg native Nelson Chittum was pitching at the Triple-A level in Omaha when he learned he was being called up to the Major Leagues for the first time.

"I was having a good year," Chittum, 89, said in a telephone interview. "On a Wednesday they called me into the office and advised me I was being promoted to the Cardinals. I was to fly to Los Angeles on Saturday and pitch the first game of a doubleheader on a Sunday."

A right-hander in the St. Louis farm system, Chittum faced a challenging MLB debut—against the Dodgers and ace lefty Sandy Koufax.

But the first two Cardinals' hitters smashed homers off Koufax, and Chittum had a 4-0 lead before he even took the mound. Chittum allowed six runs in three innings and didn't figure in the decision as the Cardinals won 12-7 on Aug. 17, 1958.

Later in the season, on Sept. 13, as a reliever, he retired Eddie Mathews, Hank Aaron, and Frank Torre of the Milwaukee Braves in order in an 8-2 loss. In his last outing of the season, on Sept. 28, 1958, he gave up a single to Willie Mays and later a two-run double to Leon Wagner as the Giants beat the Cardinals 7-2 in San Francisco.

"I had the opportunity to pitch against so many guys; probably a lot of them are in the Hall of Fame," Chittum said from his home in Kentucky. "I played with and against some of the best players in the world."

The product of Harrisonburg ended the 1958 season 0-1 with an ERA of 6.44 in 13 games, with two starts, at the MLB level.

Just before the 1959 season, he was traded by St. Louis to the Boston Red Sox for Dean Stone. That meant he went from being teammates with St. Louis outfielder Stan Musial—who had four hits in that first game Chittum pitched—and Red Sox star Ted Williams in back-to-back years.

"They were both great players," Chittum said.

Williams, who died in 2002, was inducted into the Baseball Hall of Fame in 1966, and Musial was enshrined three years later.

"All of the ballplayers loved the guy, especially the ones in Boston," Chittum said of Williams. "Stan, he had a great eye (at the plate). He had the weirdest-looking stance. He was like a corkscrew coming out of the plate. He did not swing at bad pitches. Of course, Ted didn't either."

In 21 appearances out of the bullpen in 1959, Chittum was 3-0 with an ERA of 1.19. "I won three games and didn't lose any. I thought that was pretty good," he said. "That was all I did with the Red Sox was be a reliever."

His first MLB win came on August 28, 1959, at Fenway Park as he went the last three innings out of the bullpen and gave up no runs on two hits to beat the Baltimore Orioles as Dick Gernert hit a two-run homer for a 6-4 victory. "I pitched the eighth, ninth, and 10th and we won it in the 10th," Chittum said.

Williams did not start that day and instead had a pinch-hit for the Red Sox.

Chittum was with the Red Sox early in the 1960 season and

pitched out of the bullpen in games in Washington on April 18 and 22, and in Baltimore on April 27 and 28.

The last appearance of his MLB career came on May 4, 1960, when he retired one batter and gave up a run in Boston in a 5-3 loss to Kansas City.

He finished the year in the minors with Montreal while Williams —the Splendid Splinter—hit a homer in his last MLB at-bat in Boston on Sept. 28, 1960.

Another pitcher with the Red Sox in 1960 was pitcher Tracy Stallard. A graduate of Coeburn High in southwest Virginia, Stallard died in 2017 at the age of 80 and is buried at Powell Valley Memorial Gardens in Big Stone Gap, according to Baseball Reference.

"Tracy was a different animal; he was the goofiest guy I ever saw," Chittum said. "He should have been a lefty. He and I went to spring training in Scottsdale, Arizona in 1960. We roomed together. I will never forget him; he was really goofy. He would walk all over the mound."

Stallard, pitching against the Yankees in 1961, gave up the record 61st homer of the year to Roger Maris—who broke the single-season mark held by Babe Ruth.

Chittum spent 1962 in the minors; he was then signed by the Orioles and spent the 1963 and 1964 seasons in the starting rotation for Rochester, the top farm club of Baltimore.

He was 13-8 with an ERA of 3.18 in 1963 and 11-11, 3.35 the next season. That came after he was 0-9 while pitching for Spokane in the minors in 1962.

Chittum was born in Harrisonburg in 1933 and he recalls going to elementary school downtown.

"We were kissing cousins. I always followed his career," said Barbara Chittum Hutchens. Their fathers were brothers and both grew up in Harrisonburg; Hutchens and her late husband stopped in St. Louis to see her cousin when he was the Cardinals, but he did not pitch while they were there.

The pitcher's family moved to Elizabethtown, Pa., when he was 11. At Elizabethtown Area High, he once threw two perfect games in a span of about a week.

After playing baseball and basketball at Elizabethtown College, where he was inducted in the Athletic Hall of Fame in 2009, he joined the U.S. Army.

His first year of pro ball was in Fresno in the California League as he went 23-7 in 37 games, with 32 starts, for a Cardinals' farm team.

After his baseball career, Chittum worked for several years for the United States Postal Service. He and his wife, Shirley, have a son, Bruce; they lived in Michigan, Indiana, and Tennessee before moving a few years ago to Kentucky. Both of his parents are buried in Mt. Crawford; he was in Harrisonburg in 2010 when his mother died.

Chittum is one of just a few players born in Harrisonburg, according to Baseball Reference, to make the majors. "I had too many experiences to wonder about," Chittum said.

Harrisonburg native Nelson Chittum lives in Kentucky with his wife, Shirley. They have one son, Bruce.

50

Doug Harris, Won World Series Ring

Doug Harris was mowing his yard in 2015 after returning from the Arizona Fall League when he became very tired.

"My lawnmower felt like it weighed 1,000 pounds," recalls Harris, then the Nationals' assistant general manager and vice president, player personnel.

Harris saw his local doctor in Pennsylvania a few days later and learned his "white count was through the roof."

The former minor league pitcher learned he had leukemia.

Despite many challenges since then, Harris won a World Series ring when the Nationals beat the Astros in seven games in the World Series in 2019.

After the 2021 Major League season, the former pitcher at JMU stepped down from his front-office role with the Nationals, citing health reasons.

"Doing my best a day at time," Harris wrote to us in early June from his home in Pennsylvania. "I'm pretty immunocompromised and go to very indoor situations with groups of people. Have advised to be careful. Thankful for where I am and do my best to heed the recommendations."

Harris appeared to beat cancer in 2017. But in 2019, he underwent cutting-edge CAR-T cell therapy at the suggestion of doctors.

"My blood counts are normal, and the therapy has attained the desired molecular response," Harris said at the time.

Harris, who is Catholic, also received support from the church that his wife, Lisa, and their three daughters have attended in the past—Otterbein United Methodist in Carlisle, Pennsylvania. He met his wife when he was playing in the minors in Memphis. Lisa Harris dealt with breast cancer in the past.

Harris grew up in Carlisle and was drafted by the Royals in the fourth round in 1990 out of JMU. He made it as high as Triple-A in the Orioles and Marlins systems.

While in the farm system of the Orioles, he pitched for the Double-A Bowie Baysox in Maryland in 1995 and 1996. Players this year for Bowie with Virginia ties include Shelton Perkins (JMU), Roanoke native J.D. Mundy, Zach Peek of the Lynchburg area; and Garrett Stallings, a native of Chesapeake. Former Turner Ashby High pitcher Jimmy Hamilton, a Ferrum product, was with Bowie in 2000 and 2001.

One of Harris' teammates at James Madison was shortstop Jeff Garber, a longtime minor league instructor in the Nationals system.

"Doug has an incredible ability to bring people together to work for a common goal," Garber said a few years ago. "He makes everyone feel like they are part of a family and he gets them to believe that they can do great things if they do it together."

Garber said Harris has relied on family and friends during his health crisis.

"He has such a great family and I believe they give him great strength and are a huge motivation in his life," Garber said. "He has had unbelievable strength to get through all of this and I believe all his friends tried to help in some way."

After his playing career, Harris was a scout for the Texas Rangers for 13 years and spent one season with the Cleveland Indians.

He joined the Nationals in 2009 as the director of player development and shifted his role after the 2015 season.

While in college, Harris pitched for the Harrisonburg Turks of the Valley Baseball League.

Doug Harrris (center) with wife Lisa (second from right) and their three daughters

51

Travis Harper, Went To JMU Camps

For a four-year period, Harrisonburg native Travis Harper was a durable pitcher for Tampa Bay as he averaged nearly 50 outings per season out of the bullpen.

But those innings finally caught up with the Circleville High (West Virginia) and James Madison University product—he had the first surgery of his career after the 2006 Major League season.

"I went through physical therapy every day and worked out and tried to rehab my shoulder," he recalled. "I actually felt good about where I was at until the spring (of 2007) when I started to dial it up. So we did surgery and there was a lot more damage than (Dr. James Andrews) expected and I expected. We went back to physical therapy for another year. After a year and a half, I didn't have the (arm) strength to return."

Eventually, Harper realized his playing days were over.

"It was the end of the road. My career was going south," noted Harper, who turned 46 in May.

But that wasn't the case for his wife, Tiffany, who was working on her medical studies in Morgantown, West Virginia at the end of Harper's career.

"I became a stay-at-home dad and she took a position at the hospital there," he said. "I got to support her career and got to spend time with my family."

These days he is comfortable playing chauffeur to his two daughters, ages 18 and 14. The family lives in Martinsburg, West Virginia, and Dr. Tiffany Harper—another Circleville grad—works as a Pathologist at WVU Medicine in the Eastern Panhandle.

Both girls have been involved in dance and volleyball.

"I have virtually no involvement in baseball. It requires evenings and weekends. I am still involved in my own daughters and their own sports and my family," Harper said. "If you are going to coach (baseball) in the minors, you have to be all in. That is not something I am interested in."

The thing he misses the most: spring training and being in Clearwater, Florida, in March.

"I miss it some. That is how it played out," he said.

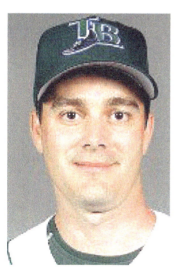
Travis Harper

After starring at Circleville, Harper opted for JMU after also considering West Virginia University and Duke. "I went to JMU (baseball) camps even before high school," he said.

Harper was drafted out of high school by the New York Mets but turned them down to play at JMU.

He played for the Dukes under Coach Kevin Anderson, who now has the same role at Division III Shenandoah in Winchester.

"I got to coach Travis at JMU as an assistant and head coach," Anderson said. "He is just first-class in every sense. He was a quiet, intense competitor. We were really lucky we got him. I got to see him pitch in the big leagues in person."

Harper was drafted out of JMU in the third round in 1997 by the Boston Red Sox. After that season, he became a free agent and signed with Tampa Bay.

The right-hander made his MLB debut in 2000 as he went 1-2 with an ERA of 4.78 in six games, with five starts. His first appearance came that August in Baltimore, as he started and allowed seven runs in less than three innings.

The next year he was 0-2, 7.71 in two starts, and in 2002 Harper was 5-9, 5.46 in 37 games, with six starts.

Tampa Bay made him a full-time reliever in 2003, and he posted a 4-8 mark with an ERA of 3.77 in a career-high 61 games. In 2004, he was 6-2, 3.89 in 52 games, and also saw action in 52 games the next season, going 4-6, 6.75.

Harper was 2-0, 4.93 in 30 games with Tampa Bay in 2006.

His last MLB outing came August 1, 2006, as he allowed home runs to former University of Richmond standout Sean Casey and Brent Clevlen in one inning out of the bullpen in a loss to the Detroit Tigers. For his career, Harper was 22-29 with an ERA of 4.94 in 240 games with 14 starts.

Harper faced some of the best hitters of his era. Alex Rodriguez hit .364 against him with two homers in 22 at-bats, Manny Ramirez batted .471 in 17 at-bats and Jason Giambi hit three homers in only 15 at-bats against Harper.

The JMU product had amazing success against Yankees shortstop Derek Jeter, voted into the Baseball Hall of Fame. In 23 at-bats, Jeter had just four hits (all singles) for an average of .174.

"He never throws the ball straight," Jeter told the Hartford Courant in 2005 about Harper. "He just has nasty stuff, especially when he faces me."

One of Harper's bullpen teammates in Tampa Bay in 2003 was Mike Venafro, another JMU product. Venafro went to Paul VI High in Fairfax, played in the majors from 1999 to 2004, and pitched in 24 games as a lefty reliever in Tampa Bay in his only season with the club.

"That was fun. Mike was a senior when I was a freshman," Harper said of their JMU days. "I got to know him a lot better in the bullpen (in the majors). He is a dynamic person. I really enjoyed my time with him."

Harper's daughter, Leia, was a 6-foot-2 outside hitter for the Georgia Tech volleyball team during the 2022 season.

Steve Nagy, Scout For Cubs

Steve Nagy, a 2020 graduate of JMU, knew early on he wanted to be involved in baseball but not as a player.

And about a decade later he is living the dream as a development scout based in Arizona with the Chicago Cubs. The former high school player from suburban Philadelphia began working in pro scouting on March 1, 2021 — but the roots were laid years ago.

"I wrote a hand-written letter to every Major League team when I was a freshman in high school asking the GMs how to get their job one day, which I look back on and laugh at a little bit since that probably wasn't the best way to go about it," Nagy said.

But it has worked out pretty well for Nagy, who was the director of operations for two years for the Dukes as a junior and senior.

The son of a high school baseball coach, Nagy experienced his first trade deadline last summer as the Cubs dealt away veterans Anthony Rizzo (to the Yankees), Kris Bryant (Giants), and Javier Baez (Mets) for prospects.

Chicago figured it was time to rebuild nearly five years after the World Series victory of 2016.

Nagy scouts many games and his input as relayed to Andrew

Bassett, the director of pro scouting for the Cubs, played a small role in the trades last year. As this book went to press, Nagy and the Cubs were focused on the trade deadline for the 2022 season.

"It was unbelievable, just to have a very, very small part in it," Nagy said of his first year with the Cubs. "I would be lying to myself if I thought I had a big impact on it. It is an exciting time for your team; just to get a taste of it has been an unbelievable experience. I feel like I am living the dream. The night before the deadline I was getting texts from my boss. Things were constantly changing. It was really cool to be part of it in a small way."

Jimmy Jackson, associate head coach/pitching coach for the Dukes, is not surprised at all by the meteoric rise of Nagy.

The JMU graduate had an internship in Arizona with the Brewers after his junior year and appeared to have a job with Milwaukee lined up after graduation before the pandemic hit — causing many Major League clubs to trim from scouting and player development last year.

"He is an incredible guy," Jackson said. "He really knows the game inside and out."

Jackson would not be surprised if Nagy — who played at Great Valley High in Malvern, Penn. — became the general manager of a Major League team one day. He was a business management major at JMU and notes there are other important jobs in pro baseball besides general manager.

"He played at a high level of high school in Pennsylvania," Jackson said. "He is your typical over-achiever."

JMU has a long history with the Cubs.

Of the 12 former Dukes who played in the majors, two of them were drafted by the club: Lynchburg native and former catcher Mike Hubbard, who was selected in 1992 out of JMU and then broke into the majors three years later with Chicago; and pitcher Brian McNichol, a native of Fairfax who was taken in 1995 then pitched in four games with the Cubs in 1999.

The last JMU player to be drafted by the Cubs was pitcher

Adam Wynegar, in the sixth round in 2001. The Centreville High graduate never advanced beyond high Single-A with the organization.

Tom Nagy, the father of Steve, has been an assistant baseball coach for several years at Malvern Prep, his alma mater near Philadelphia. The elder Nagy played in college at Furman and is part of a rich tradition at Malvern Prep — also the alma mater of former Major League catcher Ben Davis, the second overall pick in 1995 out of the school by the San Diego Padres.

"I literally went to practice every day [at Malvern] and loved the game since I was a kid," Steve Nagy said.

That tradition rubbed off on Nagy, who could hardly walk or talk when he saw his first Philadelphia Phillies game in person.

"From an early age, he would sit and watch a nine-inning game with no problem," Tom Nagy said of his son. "I encouraged him to write letters to general managers" while in high school.

The younger Nagy contacted JMU Coach Marlin Ikenberry

before heading to Harrisonburg as a JMU freshman in the fall of 2016.

"For some reason, JMU is a pretty popular school at my high school," Nagy said. "I think 10 students from my graduating class out of 300 went to JMU. I knew right away I was going to get involved with the baseball team and I became a student manager as a freshman."

Jackson said the Dukes found more duties for Nagy to take on after his first year.

And the JMU student has kept in touch with several former players, including the four pitchers drafted out of the program in 2019 — Shelton Perkins (Orioles), Nick Robertson (Dodgers), Kevin Kelly (Indians), and Dan Goggin (Mets) — and others including good friend Kyle Hayes, who began the 2022 season at Single-A in the Kansas City system.

"I tried to make the most of every opportunity and by my junior year was named director of baseball operations. I had a seat in our staff meetings and you start to see there are two sides to absolutely everything and which gave me a unique perspective," Nagy said.

And that perspective is paying off with the Cubs.

53

Emilio Pagan, From Turks To Twins

It was 12 years ago that South Carolina native Emilio Pagan came to Harrisonburg to play for the Turks in the Valley Baseball League.

Now the right-handed pitcher is in his first season with the Minnesota Twins after playing with the San Diego Padres in 2020 and 2021.

"You learn a lot about yourself," recalls Pagan of playing in the Valley League. "That was my first time away from my family for an extended period of time; that is a big deal. You learn a lot about yourself; you have to grow up."

Pagan played with Harrisonburg in 2010 and three years later was drafted by Seattle in the 10th round out of Division II Belmont Abbey in North Carolina. Tampa native Austin Adams played for the Staunton Braves in 2010-11 and was drafted out of South Florida by the Angels in the eighth round in 2012. Adams is back with the Padres this year.

"I got to play with top-notch dudes from some big-time colleges," noted Pagan, who said he was treated very well by Harrisonburg skipper Bob Wease and his family. "It was a fun summer and I enjoyed my time."

Pagan pitched in a career-high 67 games for the Padres last season out of the bullpen and had an ERA of 4.83.

He finished up 10 of those games but didn't have a save.

The bullpens of each Major League team seem to change every year and that was the case for the Padres, who sent Pagan to the Twins in early April of this year in a big trade.

Meanwhile, there were also two Valley alums at Double-A San Antonio in the San Diego system last season.

Pitcher James Reeves played with Staunton in 2013. He is a native of South Carolina, played at The Citadel in Charleston, and was drafted by the Yankees in 2015. He has also spent time at Triple-A last year and posted an ERA of 5.65 with two teams. He became a free agent after last season.

Reeves was able to meet Pagan and Adams in spring training with the Padres.

"Going to Staunton, Virginia was really the first place that I actu-

Emilio Pagan

ally left home for a significant period of time," Reeves said. "It was probably the most fun I have had playing baseball in my entire life. I made some really good friends there. It was just that pure showing up to the stadium and playing."

Reeves stayed with a host family that included the pastor at a Methodist church in Verona. The pitcher went to church with the family one Sunday and was introduced the night after he got the win against Waynesboro.

"Some guy in the back starting clapping," Reeves noted. "The whole church erupted in applause. Man, I realized there is a deep-seated rivalry between Waynesboro and Staunton in this summer league."

Outfielder Michael Curry, a native of North Carolina, was drafted out of the University of Georgia by the Padres in 2018 after playing for Strasburg two years earlier. He retired after last season.

Washington is familiar territory for Adams. Before the 2017 season, he was traded by the Angels with pitcher Kyle McGowin to the Nats for infielder Danny Espinosa.

Adams made his Major League debut with Washington in 2017 and also pitched some with the Nationals in 2018 and 2019 before he was traded on May 4, 2019, to Seattle for pitcher Nick Wells, a native of Alexandria who went to Battlefield High.

In 2020, the Angels traded Adams to the Padres in August.

He was a workhorse for the Padres last year. "He has been great," Pagan said of Adams last year. "He has been electric for us out of the bullpen and we are going to need him to stay that way."

Other Valley League alums in the San Diego system the past two seasons include:

* Pitcher Kyle McGrath went to Louisville and made his MLB debut in 2017; he played for Staunton in 2011. He was let go by the Padres after last season.

* Pitcher Gabe Mosser is a native of Allentown, Penn., and played in college at Shippensburg. Mosser was drafted by the Padres in 2018 and after he played for Waynesboro in 2017. Mosser was at Double-A San Antonio in early June.

* Outfielder Michael Green, a native of Georgia, was signed out of Clemson by the Padres and was on the injured list with Single-A Lake Elsinore in California. Green played for Front Royal in 2018.

Pagan also played infield for the Turks and as a pitcher didn't throw that hard. He never dreamed he would one day make the majors.

Another Valley connection to the Twins is Brea Hinegardner, who is from Woodstock and was a softball standout at Bridgewater College. She is the Senior Manager, Digital Content for the Twins.

54

Amanda Sarver, Inspired By Ng

Harrisonburg High graduate Amanda Sarver was on social media in the fall of 2020 when she heard the ground-breaking news: Kim Ng had been named the general manager of the Miami Marlins of Major League Baseball.

"From that moment on, texts were just flying with women I had worked with and counterparts across the league," said Sarver, who worked in professional baseball for more than a decade with the Orioles. "I was ecstatic. It is about time."

Born in Indianapolis and raised in New York, Ng is the first woman to be the general manager in any of the four North American pro sports leagues.

Ng began working for the Chicago White Sox in 1991, was an assistant GM for the New York Yankees and Los Angeles Dodgers and worked in MLB offices in New York since 2011.

"My family texted me in just the joy of the hiring and what it meant for baseball," Sarver said. "She has 30 years of success in baseball and there have been [other] GMs hired who were [less than] 30 years old."

Sarver now works in Maryland for Maroon PR, headed by John

Maroon – a former Director of Public Relations with the Orioles who has decades of experience in the industry.

In her new job, Sarver was able to recently visit the Baseball Hall of Fame in Cooperstown, New York for the first time.

Another woman with Valley ties who was excited about the Ng news was Woodstock's Brea Hinegardner, a former softball player at Bridgewater College and the current digital content manager for the Minnesota Twins.

She was in a Zoom meeting in the Twin Cities when she heard of the Ng hiring. "My husband texted me and said, 'Did you see who the Marlins hired?' I went straight to Twitter. When I went and looked and saw it was Kim I was so excited," said Hinegardner, who graduated from BC in 2014.

"I was super excited. I think it is going to open up so many doors for women. Her hiring is so overdue since her resume is so impressive," Hinegardner added. "You see that it is being covered by non-sports news people. That wasn't the case for all of the other GMs who were hired this offseason."

Sarver was able to meet Ng about seven years ago in Orlando at a baseball industry event.

"I have followed her career and other women in sports," Sarver said.

Sarver graduated from HHS in 2004 and James Madison University four years later. She worked part-time as a marketing researcher for the Baltimore Orioles in 2009, with the Triple-A Buffalo Bisons in 2009-2010 and then joined the Orioles full-time in 2011.

The Harrisonburg native was hired in public relations by the late Monica Pence Barlow, the former director of public relations for the Orioles who grew up in Port Republic and passed away in 2014 at the age of 36 due to stage IV lung cancer.

Sarver rose to manager of digital marketing before leaving the Orioles about two years ago; she played softball and volleyball in high school.

Sarver was still with the Orioles when Ng was interviewed for the GM job with Baltimore – that eventually went to Alexandria native Mike Elias in 2018.

"I was really excited about the possibility that would happen and I am really glad it finally did," Sarver noted. "I am optimistic and I do think there is a long way to go. There have been 100 years of [Major League] baseball and this is the first time someone thought a woman is just as capable of evaluating talent in the lead role" as men.

"Girls growing up today know they can be a general manager in baseball," said Sarver, adding that young boys will also see that women can make key decisions in the game. "My personal experience is that women in baseball are pioneers and they are breaking barriers."

Sarver knows what it was like to be the only woman in the room.

"I would give presentations annually to our Major League players and minor league players about social media and I would be the only woman in that room," she said. "And that would be 50 or 60 people. I also know what it is like not to be in the room when decisions are made and that can be very frustrating."

She said a lot of times those at the top of the organizational chart with MLB teams are men and mostly White men.

"That speaks to why Kim's hiring matters and why representation matters," noted Sarver, the daughter of former HHS football coach Tim Sarver. "Diversity is important. The players are diverse, the fans are diverse; the front offices should reflect that. Professional sports, with their visibility, have a responsibility to be leaders in diversity. Baseball has the reputation for being the old guard and slower to adapt."

Ng played softball at the University of Chicago and Jessica Mendoza, a baseball announcer, was a standout softball player at Stanford.

Does that matter?

"I think you can bring value from your experience as an athlete.

I don't think it's necessary by any means," Sarver said. "Some of the most respected people never played sports beyond high school."

Who knows, one day Ng may be fired if things don't work out with the Marlins.

"This challenge is one I don't take lightly," Ng told reporters. "When I got into this business, it seemed unlikely a woman would lead a Major League team, but I am dogged in the pursuit of my goals."

Sarver and Hinegardner can certainly relate to that.

Amanda with pitcher Mike Wright, a product of East Carolina University who played with the Orioles.

55

Alan Knicely, Helped Begin
TA Legacy

Turner Ashby High, in the early 1970s, began playing its home baseball games behind John Wayland after years at the old high school in Dayton.

At the time there was no fence at John Wayland, which meant opposing outfielders seemed to disappear near the hill that leads down to the school when right-handed slugger Alan Knicely stepped into the batter's box. He certainly was not a welcome sight for opposing pitchers.

"By golly, he could hit," recalled Ray Heatwole, the former TA head coach and a member of the Virginia School High School League Hall of Fame. "He was very talented. He was big and he was strong."

"He was a man among boys," said former TA teammate Mike Bocock, a longtime coach in the Valley Baseball League who is back this summer guiding Woodstock after the River Bandits reached the North Division title series against eventual champion Strasburg in 2021.

Knicely hit his way from the playing fields of Bridgewater to the Major Leagues. It was a career that began in The Show when he was called up from Double-A to the Houston Astros late in the 1979 season.

He was the first graduate of TA to make the majors.

"When I got called up to the major leagues, that was a big shock," Knicely recalled of a time when players normally had to reach Triple-A before being promoted to the majors. "I was having a heck of a season at Double-A. That was the year they took me from being a pitcher to being a catcher."

Now 67, Knicely lives with his wife, the former Patty Wimer, and Brad, one of their three adult sons, in McGaheysville.

"I am pretty much here around the house," Knicely said. "I am a die-hard deer hunter."

The couple's two other sons both played baseball at Spotswood in Penn Laird: former Longwood University standout Jeremy had one year in the minors in 2003 in the Toronto system with Auburn of the New York-Penn League and Charleston, West Virginia, in the Single-A South Atlantic League.

The No. 11 jersey of their father hangs on a wall near the gymnasium at the "new" TA in Bridgewater, though perhaps an entire generation of students don't realize the impact he had on one of the top prep baseball programs in Virginia.

KNICELY, one of seven brothers or stepbrothers to play baseball at TA, grew up in Bridgewater with Bocock and some his brothers; they would ride bikes together to Little League games.

"We would play pickup games between Bridgewater and Dayton," Knicely said.

Bocock said Knicely, then an eighth-grader, hit a 400-foot home run in an American Legion road game.

Bocock's nephew, Brian, became the second TA product to make the majors when he broke in with the San Francisco Giants in 2008.

A four-year varsity player at TA, Knicely led the Knights to a state title in 1974 as a senior in the clinching game at old Memorial Stadium in Harrisonburg. His ground-rule double in the last of the seventh drove in the winning runs in the comeback victory over Glenvar High of Salem.

Knicely was drafted in the third round that June as a pitcher by the Houston Astros. He played the infield and pitched early on in the minors and eventually made a permanent move to catcher. He hit 33 homers at the Double-A level in 1979 in Columbus, Ga., in the Houston system.

That led to his Major League call-up on Aug. 12, 1979, and he went hitless in his first six at-bats that year.

Knicely kept tearing up the minors but got just eight total at-bats in the majors from 1980-81, with his first two MLB homers coming at end of the 1981 season with Houston in Los Angeles against the Dodgers.

He hit .188 with two homers in 59 games with the Astros in 1982, and in spring training of the following year was traded to Cincinnati.

The right-handed batter had an average of .224 with two homers in 59 games with the Reds in 1983. He got extended playing time back of the plate that summer with Cincinnati as Johnny Bench, a Hall of Fame catcher, was seeing more time at first base late in his career.

"He hustles and is an asset to the team," Russ Nixon, the Reds' manager in 1983, told us that year.

"If I need any help on catching I go to Bench," Knicely said that summer.

At his home today, Knicely has a baseball signed by Bench. "Catch you later," Bench wrote to Knicely on Sept. 25, 1983.

Knicely, in 1984, hit 33 homers with Wichita while also playing in 10 games with Reds. He was named the Minor League Player of the Year by The Sporting News.

He played in 48 games with the Reds in 1985 under player-manager Pete Rose.

That year Knicely hit a three-run homer to help beat the St. Louis Cardinals after starting the season back in the minors. Rose told Knicely in spring training there would not be much playing time for him in the majors.

"When a man like Pete Rose tells you, you believe him," Knicely told reporters then.

The Harrisonburg native was traded to Philadelphia near the end of the 1985 season and finished up his career at the MLB level in 34 games with the St. Louis Cardinals the following year.

His last game came in October of 1986.

He ended his career with an average of .213 and hit 12 homers in 228 Major League games. In the minors he was a terror, batting .295 with 159 homers in 1,102 contests with his last season at that level in 1987 with Texas.

AFTER HIS PLAYING CAREER ENDED, Knicely worked nearly three decades for Coors in Elkton in several roles, including work in the warehouse and with machinery, before retiring about five years ago.

He also played in the Rockingham County Baseball League with the Bridgewater Reds.

"He was a man among boys," according to Bridgewater College athletic director Curt Kendall, a former RCBL teammate. "Our team consisted of Knicelys (5) and Bococks (3) and a few other of us made up the lineup. We had good teams for many years."

Knicely grew up learning the basics of baseball, and generations would follow at TA.

He played as a freshman and sophomore for head coach Jim Upperman on the varsity team at TA. Then as a junior, his new coach was Heatwole, who had played at Bridgewater College.

"We knew the fundamentals. That is what Jim and Ray taught us," Knicely said. Other members of that state title team in 1974 were Harold Knicely, his brother, and Ted Croy, both of whom would also play in the minors.

Heatwole, who was 303-66-2 in 17 years at TA, would eventually help mold several other future major leaguers as an assistant and then head coach at James Madison University from 1986-93.

But as a young coach at TA, Heatwole saw a future big leaguer up close for the first time in Knicely. "I didn't realize how good he was. He could stand out today" as well, Heatwole said.

56

Larry Erbaugh, Memories Of Bobby Richardson

Things went so well last summer that Larry Erbaugh decided to give it another go this year with the Harrisonburg Turks.

A former pitcher at Turner Ashby and the University of South Carolina, Erbaugh returned to baseball in 2021 as he became the pitching coach for the Turks under veteran skipper Bob Wease in the Valley Baseball League.

"It has been about 40 years," said 1968 TA graduate Erbaugh. "I played in the Valley League with the Turks for five years and then I played in the County League for Clover Hill for five years. That would have taken me up to 31 or 32 years of age" when he stopped playing.

After retiring last year from his day job, Erbaugh jumped at the chance to return to the Valley League.

"Bobby called me and asked me if I wanted to be involved. I thought about it a bit; the timing was perfect. I had just retired," said Erbaugh, who spent his career with Rockingham Redi-Mix as a dispatcher.

"Someone who works full-time, there is no way you can do this," he added of the summer gig with the Turks. "I took one night to think about and I thought: 'Why not. I am going to expand my horizons.' I would rather be quiet. But I can make myself be verbal. It is an effort sometimes. I am in a situation here that is a little outside of the box for me. I am enjoying expanding myself a bit. I am enjoying, to tell you the truth, talking to the [players] that want to know how it used to be. I am enjoying letting them know that."

The Turks ended with the third-best team ERA in the league at 4.23 and were 19-21 in regular-season play in 2021.

Harrisonburg had an impressive ERA of 2.73 in the early going this season.

"I am enjoying it a lot more this year," Erbaugh said in early June. "I am feeling more comfortable working with the younger pitchers."

Erbaugh said he doesn't spend a lot of time talking, for instance, about the in-depth details of how to throw a curve with his young staff.

"They know that," said Erbaugh, whose wife, Joyce, is a graduate of Montevideo High. "I could help them a bit with their stuff, but I'm not. But I do know what pitchers want and what they need and the information they need. I think I can organize things a bit."

He admits the obvious: "It's not my generation. Know what I mean? But I am trying, I am trying."

If those young, 20-something pitchers with the Turks want to take a look at the numbers Erbaugh posted down Rt. 42 at TA in Dayton (before the move to Bridgewater) they may be blown away, just like batters trying to hit a Nolan Ryan fastball.

Consider the statistics for Erbaugh as a senior at TA in 1968: he was 7-1 with an ERA of 0.79, and he struck out — get this — 128 batters in 53 innings.

One of the rare losses for Erbaugh at TA was the last setback before the Knights won 40 straight games from April 2, 1968 to May 15, 1970.

Erbaugh threw two no-hitters in 1968: against Page County at Clover Hill and at Luray. He also threw a no-hitter as a junior, beating Broadway 4-1 (TA made three errors) while striking out 13 at home in 1967.

The Knights were 12-1 and won the District 10 title under Coach A.J. Botkin in 1968. For his TA career, Erbaugh had an ERA 1.39 with 253 strikeouts in 140.1 innings.

In 1968, Sam Hess hit .444 in drove in 22 runs in just 45 at-bats; Dwight Eberly batted .455 and drove in 14 runs on 15 hits; and Erbaugh hit .459 and drove in 13 runs in only 37 trips to the plate.

Another star pitcher on the team was Jodie Wampler, who was 4-0 with an ERA of 1.57. As a senior the next year, Wampler was 11-0 and went on to star at Division I George Washington University.

There were no playoffs in 1968, so the first state title for the Knights would have to wait until 1971.

Erbaugh was, however, part of two state-title teams at the American Legion level with a team in Staunton. He played against the American Legion team from Charlottesville — one that featured University of Virginia product Mike Cubbage, who had a long career in the majors as an infielder and recently retired after scouting for the Nationals.

Erbaugh was playing in a Legion tournament in Alabama after his junior year at TA and pitched against a team from North Carolina. The home plate umpire for that game told the coaching staff at South Carolina about the TA product.

Erbaugh is now guiding young pitchers 50 years his junior and many of them have never heard of Bobby Richardson, who played second base for the New York Yankees on seven World Series teams and was the Most Valuable Player of the 1960 Fall Classic — even though the Pirates won in seven games.

Richardson became the head coach at South Carolina when Erbaugh was a sophomore and the relationship went way beyond baseball. Erbaugh pitched some of his freshman year but hurt his hand when he was hit by a line drive during batting practice. "He taught me how to throw a slider," Erbaugh said of Richardson.

A devout Christian, Richardson made the trek to the Shenandoah Valley to give a prayer at the wedding of Erbaugh and his first wife, Dottie, at the Dayton Church of the Brethren in 1974.

"It was a privilege for me to play for" Richardson, said Erbaugh. "It was wonderful playing for him. After I graduated, I was a graduate assistant at USC for one year with him."

Erbaugh, with a degree in math from USC in 1972, never had a sore arm but didn't get any major looks at pro ball. He was in the starting rotation for USC as a junior and senior.

He had two brothers, Don and Doug, who also played baseball at TA. Doug Erbaugh had 255 strikeouts, a career ERA of 1.10 and graduated in 1979 before playing at the University of Virginia. Their brother, Don, also played for the Knights.

Now Larry is imparting some of that wisdom he learned from Richardson and other coaches he had along the way.

"He is doing a great job for us," Wease said of Erbaugh. "I think he is thrilled to be back in the game."

Erbaugh was also part of two state-title teams in American Legion with Staunton in 1967-68 with the event being held in Colonial Heights.

His coach in Staunton was Ted Bosiack, whom Erbaugh said taught him how to throw a curveball. "He was great with teenagers," Erbaugh said of Bosiack, who died in South Carolina in 2000.

Wease announced in early November of 2022 that he was selling the Turks to Gerald Harman, another Valley League veteran. Wease, however, planned to manage the team again in 2023.

57

RCBL Memories

The sun was slowly setting beyond the center-field fence as an annual ritual had begun – waiting for the big orange ball to disappear behind the trees so baseball could be played.

It was a Friday evening this past June in Clover Hill, a small community in western Rockingham County just a few miles from the West Virginia mountains.

With the game time arbitrarily set to begin at 7:30 p.m., Pearce Bucher and Joel Smith of the visiting New Market Shockers warmed up in front of their third-base dugout as a few fans set up their lawn chairs beyond the protective screen down the left-field line. A Tim McGraw country classic blared on the speakers as Bucher and Smith got ready for the game.

Clover Hill manager and Harrisonburg High graduate Kevin Chandler and Nolan Potts, his counterpart with defending champion New Market in the Rockingham County Baseball League, met at home plate to discuss plans for waiting for the sun to set – so it wouldn't be in the eyes of the batter.

Eventually, the first pitch was at 7:54 p.m., which meant the work day would last about 24 minutes longer for Potts, a teacher and coach at a high school in Loudoun County who was a long way from home on this Friday evening.

The RCBL began in 1924, which makes it one of the oldest baseball leagues in the country.

"I think it is the fact the games are in the evening and guys can work a summer job and still play in the evening," said Bucher about the appeal of the RCBL. "It is a really fun atmosphere, and it is good community support."

Infielder/pitcher Tyler Bocock of Clover Hill certainly knows about community support.

Raised in Rockingham County, he played at Turner Ashby High and at Division I Stetson in Florida.

His father, Mike, played at TA and Bridgewater College and is a long-time coach in the Valley Baseball League. His cousin, Brian, also played for the Knights and in the majors for the Giants and Phillies as an infielder.

"The memories begin at Bridgewater Little League, that is where it began," says Tyler Bocock, sitting on the green-painted bleachers behind the home first-base dugout. "I think a lot of guys that go through the TA system or the local baseball system know that Bridgewater Little League is top-notch. That was kind of my first experience in local baseball. I have been on a baseball field every day."

"Baseball is hard. It is hard on your brain, too. There is a lot of adversity. There is a lot of failure, you have to learn to deal with it," he added.

Bocock first played in the RCBL in 2008 when he was a freshman in high school. He has been part of six titles with Clover Hill and two with Bridgewater.

He is now the varsity baseball coach at Sarasota Christian in Florida but comes home in the summer to play for Clover Hill when time allows. He is married and has two children.

"I just like being here at the ballpark at Clover Hill, being around friends. At this point, it is hanging out with friends and the baseball is an extra," he said.

He was an assistant for about 18 months in Florida for legendary Sarasota High coach Clyde Metcalf, who stepped down in May after 950 wins, six Florida state titles, and two national crowns.

"I am trying to take what I learned up here and apply it down there," Bocock said of building his program. "You get to play all of the time in Florida, so that adds another element."

Among his Sarasota High alums to make the majors were former Washington shortstop Ian Desmond and Scooter Gennett, who last played in the majors with the Giants in 2019.

"He is awesome; he brings you in and lets you operate," Bocock said of Metcalf.

Bocock said the tradition of the Sarasota High and TA programs are similar.

"That is a perfect analogy," he said. "But Sarasota has won a national championship."

Josh Eberly, a veteran catcher for the Bucks, came to Clover Hill as a young boy as his father, Charlie, played at TA and grew up on a farm a few miles east of the Clover Dome.

"I would run around and chase balls," said Josh Eberly.

The younger Eberly played football at Broadway High and Virginia Tech and has played for the Bucks for more than a decade.

Another Broadway High grad this season with Clover Hill and skipper Kevin Chandler is outfielder Drew Easter, who is in his 15th season in the RCBL.

He played baseball at Bridgewater College while studying Business Administration. Chandler also played at Bridgewater after starring at Harrisonburg High.

"There is something magical about this place," said Easter, waiting for the sun to set at Clover Hill.

Clover Hill joined the RCBL in 1954 when they moved from Ottobine, according to Randy Atkins, the former commissioner of the league.

The Bucks won their first title the next year and also won one championship in the 1960s (1963) and 1970s (1975) before making up for lost time.

The Bucks have reeled off 14 titles starting in 1982, with an impressive streak of domination between 2007-11.

Clover Hill last won a title in 2019 while New Market won its first in nearly 50 years last season.

"It was a special moment for the town of New Market," Bucher said.

Clover Hill was eliminated from the 2022 playoffs in the semifinals by Bridgewater, which knocked off Stuarts Draft to win the title behind the pitching of Chad Huffman and Derek Shifflett.

The Clover Hill Bucks joined the RCBL in the 1950s, after moving from Ottobine. Buck Bowman Park has been a part of the community fabric in western Rockingham County now for decades.

58

Curt Dudley, Voice Of The Turks

Curt Dudley, early in the college baseball season of 1988, left the sports information and admissions offices at Division III Bridgewater College to work full-time in the sports information office at Division I James Madison University.

His main responsibility was aiding the coverage of JMU baseball, which had advanced to the College World Series five years earlier. Dudley has been a fixture at JMU ever since, and that doesn't figure to change a lot despite a career transition.

A longtime resident of Bridgewater, Dudley retired as of June 1 last year as a full-time member in athletics at JMU. Over the years he has become known as the voice of Dukes, covering nearly every sport in a variety of mediums for radio and television outlets, some in-house. His title is now Director of Broadcast Services Emeritus at the university.

"I am retiring full-time from James Madison University but will continue my broadcasting career, and James Madison will be my primary gig" as a freelancer, Dudley, a 1983 BC grad, said at the time.

But Dudley is still very much a part of the sports scene in the central Shenandoah Valley.

A member of the Valley Baseball League Hall of Fame, he is in his 40th season as the public-address announcer for home games of the Harrisonburg Turks.

The Turks play at the home of JMU at Veterans Memorial Park and Dudley was in the pressbox on June 3 when Harrisonburg had its first home game of this season.

Between innings, Dudley informed the fans of some rule changes this year in the Valley Baseball League, including the international tiebreaker if games go into extra innings.

The Turks got a walk-off win in the last of the ninth against visiting Charlottesville on June 3 and Dudley energetically relayed the result to those fans that stayed around for the ending.

Dudley was part of the broadcast on FloSports for the coverage in 2021 of the Colonial Athletic Association baseball tournament which didn't include JMU – headed to the Sun Belt. That has been a regular event on his calendar for decades in various roles.

"I have thought about it, it does open up the opportunity to do other regional work," Dudley, who grew up in Norfolk, said of his retirement. "I do want to emphasize my primary gig will be James Madison. That will take precedent over all others."

"I was looking at six more years of employment," he added. "When the administration came calling, they said 'You don't have to do this. This is your option, we want to put this on the table and see what the benefits are and if it is financially feasible for you and your family.' They accelerated the process for me. They sped up the process, which is great for everybody."

His family in Bridgewater includes his wife, Maureen, daughter Laura, grandson Oliver, and his mother-in-law, Helen McLaughlin.

For the past few years Dudley has teamed up in the broadcast booth at times with Steve Buckhantz, a 1977 JMU graduate who was dropped – much to the chagrin of many fans – as the veteran television voice of the Washington Wizards of the NBA after the 2018-19 season.

Dudley has been doing Turks' home games since 1983. Dudley received the 2018 JMU Unseen Hero Award, which noted his efforts and dedication outside of the public spotlight, according to the Turks' website.

He has also taught communications classes at JMU and some of his former students or colleagues now work in the media covering pro or college teams or leagues.

Valley Baseball League Hall of Famer and Bridgewater College grad Curt Dudley (left) with Bruce Alger, the former commissioner of the VBL who passed away in the fall of 2021. Dudley is in his 40th season as the voice of the Harrisonburg Turks of the Valley Baseball League.

Many young students and professionals have learned the ropes under Dudley, who got his local start at BC. One of his former students, Kevin Haswell, recently won an Emmy for Outstanding Studio Show as a researcher for SportsCenter on ESPN. Kim Fucci, another former student, won an Emmy for her work with the MLB

Network. She was a former student manager for JMU softball from 2013-16.

Eagles' athletic director Curt Kendall was an assistant baseball coach at Bridgewater when Dudley was a student there. "He had a passion for sports information," Kendall said. "He was pretty good at it; he always had that voice for announcing" as well.

Joe Browning, the senior associate athletic director/athletic communications at North Carolina Wilmington of the Colonial Athletic Association, has worked for years with Dudley and considers him a friend. "The consummate professional," Browning, in his 36th year at the school, said. "He has the voice for the job. He takes a lot of pride in his work."

Ben Trittipoe, a resident of Leesburg, worked in sports information at former CAA school George Mason – a baseball rival of JMU. Trittipoe has been an official scorer in Major League Baseball in Washington for years, and now does Baltimore games as well.

"I have known him since 1992," Trittipoe said of Dudley. "If I knew if I went to JMU [for a game] I would be hosted well. They were there ready to help you out. He is one of the best in the business. He has a distinctive voice; he has made his mark in broadcasting."

Bill Harman, Bridgewater's Only MLB Native

According to baseballreference.com, only one Major League Baseball player was born in Bridgewater: Bill Harman, born on January 2, 1919.

He made his debut in the majors on June 17, 1941, as a pinch-hitter for the Phillies at the St. Louis Cardinals. Harman was retired in his only at-bat of that game against St. Louis pitcher Mort Cooper. One of the outfielders for the Cardinals in that game was Enos "Country" Slaughter, who is now in the Baseball Hall of Fame.

The last game in the majors for Harman came on Sept. 28 of the same season in a loss by the Phillies at Brooklyn. He was once again retired as a pinch-hitter in that game.

The starting second baseman for the Phillies in that game was Danny Murtaugh, who would later manage the Pirates.

Harman, a catcher and a pitcher, hit .071 in 14 at-bats and as a pitcher came out of the bullpen five times in 1941 for the Phillies.

He died in Delaware at the age of 88 in 2007. He is buried at the Lower Brandywine Cemetery in Wilmington, Delaware. Harman attended the University of Virginia.

Chase DeLauter, From Bruins To Cape Cod

There have not many too many players who played in the Rockingham County Baseball League one summer and then in the prestigious Cape Cod League the next.

Chase DeLauter did so – but then again, he is a pretty special player.

And there is no telling where the West Virginia native could end up; as this book went to press, the JMU standout was being projected as a first-round draft pick by a Major League team this July.

He won the Triple Crown with Broadway in 2020 as he batted .545 with 13 homers and 39 RBI then hit .437 in just 24 games this year for JMU with eight homers and 35 RBI.

The stock of the outfielder and left-handed slugger took off once he went to the Cape last year.

"Just for me draft-wise and everything like that, this was a better place for me," he told us. "Of course, I am going to try to take advantage of every opportunity I can get. If I have a chance to play in the best [amateur summer] league in the country I am going to do it."

DeLauter played on the Cape for the Orleans Firebirds and lived with a host family about 10 minutes from the field.

The league has produced more than 1,400 big league players and some of the former standouts for Orleans include Hall of Famer Frank Thomas; ex-Orioles' pitcher Jeff Ballard; William & Mary product and Virginia Beach native Bill Bray, who pitched for the Nationals in 2006; and former Red Sox All-Star shortstop Nomar Garciaparra, who also played for the Cubs, Dodgers and A's.

"The atmosphere up here is like none other," DeLauter said. "We have thousands of fans at every game. It is a great atmosphere to play in front of. From the baseball side of things, I am trying to put good swings on the ball and trying not to get frustrated with anything right now."

The town of Orleans was incorporated in 1797 and was originally known as the South Parish of Eastham, and settled in 1644.

"Honestly, the RCBL was a crazy atmosphere. But up there it was a whole new world. There are 30-plus scouts at every game, some of the best arms in the country. It is about keeping your composure and not worrying too much about results," DeLauter added.

The 6-foot-4 DeLauter has had two fabulous seasons at JMU and then one cut short by injury.

The Martinsburg native hit .382 with one homer and 14 RBIs with an OPS of 1.014 in just 14 games as a freshman at JMU in 2020, as the season was cut short by the pandemic.

With Broadway last summer, he had one of the best offensive seasons in recent memory of the RCBL and as the MVP helped the Bruins win the title.

With JMU in 2021, the slugger hit .386 with six homers, 21 RBIs, and an OPS of 1.231 — a crazy good number — even though the Dukes were last in the South Division of the Colonial Athletic Association.

He hit just .158 in his first six games in the Cape before catching fire.

Before heading north, he spoke to VCU standout Tyler Locklear about what to expect. Locklear was teammates with DeLauter at Orleans, then helped VCU win the Atlantic 10 Conference title this past season as he hit a team-high .402 for the Rams.

DeLauter ended up with nine homers in the Cape Cod League in 2021 and was one of the top prospects in the league.

He was hit by a pitch early this season in a home game at JMU and later ran into the fence – resulting in a concussion.

In April, he broke his foot while playing at the College of Charleston. That forced him to miss the rest of the college season.

DeLauter was drafted in the first round by Cleveland in July of 2022 while Virginia Tech standout Gavin Cross, also an outfielder, went in the first round to the Royals.

DeLauter could make his pro debut in 2023 for Lynchburg, a farm team of Cleveland.

JMU standout Chase DeLauter (right) with Samantha Gjormand (left), who was a student manager for the Dukes and went to Madison High in Vienna.

61

Kirk Messick, RCBL Veteran

Kirk Messick says he plans to play in the Rockingham County Baseball League for either 20 years or until he turns 40.

The 2004 graduate of Broadway High is in his 19th season in the RCBL as a lefty pitcher; he turns 37 this fall. He played for hometown Broadway from 2002-08 then switched to the New Market Shockers, who won the RCBL title last year. "It was pretty special," Messick said this June. "I knew going in we had a pretty good team and if we did what we should do that could happen."

It was the first title in nearly 50 years for New Market, which used to be known as Twin Counties. Messick lives in the Broadway area and the drive to Rebel Field in New Market is something he has done for many years. Messick made his first two starts at home this season for the Shockers; he has been the starting pitcher in at least three All-Star games in the RCBL.

"Make sure you have enough pitching," Messick said. "That is the big thing. When I came into the league, there were not as many pitching restrictions on arms. Since then [a limit] is in youth leagues, and college coaches don't want you blowing out arms in a summer league. There has to be a happy medium where guys are willing, first of all, to come and pitch in an All-Star game instead of having an extra day of rest for themselves."

"I guess the biggest thing is to make sure you have enough pitching. Guys are throwing a decent amount during the regular season then you are asking them to throw one inning in an All-Star game," added the 2010 Bridgewater College graduate.

Another Rockingham County product with All-Star experience is Spotswood graduate Daniel Ouderkirk, who played for Valley League champ Strasburg last year. He saw action in the All-Star game in Harrisonburg; he pitched again this spring for West Virginia University.

"Getting the chance to play at home in the Valley League and be around my friends and family is awesome," Ouderkirk noted last year. "It was an easy decision for me to come play here this summer because it gave me the opportunity to improve by working with Mike Martin and pitching every week before heading back to West Virginia in the fall." Martin is the owner of Next Level Athletic Development in Park View and has to foster a relationship with college coaches on how to best monitor workloads.

Messick played as a freshman at Lynchburg and then transferred to Bridgewater, where he planned to play baseball but opted not to as he focused on academics.

He has been a physical education teacher at Cub Run Elementary School in Penn Laird for more than a decade. Messick was an intern last year for the RCBL as he pursued an advanced degree online from Arkansas State, which he finished in 2021.

Another Spotswood grad with Strasburg last summer was Cam Irvine, who has played at High Point in North Carolina. He was with Grottoes in the RCBL to start this summer season.

Messick was honored with the Spirit Award in the RCBL for the 2022 season. Former Fort Defiance and JMU pitcher Chris Huffman was named the top pitcher in RCBL - he fanned 19 batters on August 8, 2022, for Bridgewater in a deciding game 5 semifinal win at Clover Hill in the playoffs.

62

Daryl Irvine, Finale At Camden Yards

A baseball player never wants their career to end.

But for Daryl Irvine, his Major League finale came in an iconic stadium not that far from his Virginia roots.

The Spotswood High graduate from Grottoes was a pitcher for the Boston Red Sox and his last game came at Camden Yards in Baltimore against the Orioles on Sept. 28, 1992.

He allowed a single to Cal Ripken Jr. and later in the seventh inning a walk to Mike Devereaux — the last batter he faced in the majors.

Camden Yards is known as a hitter's park – even when the Orioles raised the left-field fence prior to this season.

But Irvine knew what that was like as a pitcher for the Red Sox, making his debut in 1990.

"Pitching in Fenway Park, it was almost a hometown feel to it," he said. "I was very comfortable pitching at Fenway. I got more riled up pitching on the road."

The numbers back that up — he had a 3.05 ERA in 23 career outings at cozy Fenway Park and a mark of 10.64 in 18 road games in the majors.

But one of his most memorable games came on the road, in Seattle on Aug. 11, 1990. He entered the game in the last of the 13th inning and was told by manager Joe Morgan he would pitch as long as the game lasted.

Irvine did not allow a hit or run in two innings as Dwight Evans of Boston hit a two-run homer in the top of the 14th. Irvine was credited with his first Major League victory as he retired three straight batters in the last of the 14th, including future Hall of Famer Edgar Martinez of Seattle.

He was traded by Boston to Pittsburgh on April 2, 1993, and pitched in the Pirates system that year in the minors.

After being released by the Pirates, Irvine returned home and played briefly in the Rockingham County Baseball League. He then got a call from the Texas Rangers and pitched in front of former big league lefty Tom House and Mike Scioscia, then coaches with the Rangers, in a tryout session in Florida.

The Rangers wanted to send Irvine to the Double-A level but he was not willing to go that low, so his career was over.

"It was definitely not easy to walk away from it," he said. "It was all I had ever done. It was a very tough decision."

He was pitching in the minor leagues in 1990 when he was summoned to the office of Triple-A manager Ed Nottle.

The Spotswood High graduate then heard the words he had been dreaming of since he played Little League ball in Grottoes — he was headed to the Major Leagues.

"There was a lot of screaming out my window driving up the interstate," recalled Irvine of his 45-minute drive from Pawtucket, Rhode Island, north to Fenway Park in Boston.

After sitting in the bullpen for several games, the right-hander finally made his debut on April 28, 1990, in Boston against the Oakland A's — the World Series winner from the previous fall.

His Red Sox teammates told him to throw fastballs down the middle of the plate since most of the Oakland players had never seen him pitch. So Irvine did just that to the first batter, Walt Weiss, who hit the initial offering for a single off the famed Green Monster in left with the A's down 12-0.

Irvine gave up three runs in one inning in his first Major League outing but bounced back to allow just six earned runs in his next 16.1 innings to finish his rookie season with a ERA of 4.67. After 41 outings in The Show through 1992 and some time back in the minors, he returned to the Shenandoah Valley.

"Baseball has been very good to me, being able to play in the Major Leagues," said Irvine, who graduated from Spotswood in 1983. "I think I am recognized wherever I go. I love the game. I love everything about baseball, including the strategy. I am very fortunate that I played in the big leagues."

For more than 25 years he has worked at Massanutten Resort, where he is now the assistant golf pro. Irvine started working there just before Chad Edwards became the head golf pro. The two had met earlier when Irvine played basketball at open gym at Spotswood.

Daryl Irvine (right) at Fenway Park in Boston with his wife Ricki (far left), daughter Casey, who played basketball at JMU; and son, Cam, an infielder at High Point in 2022.

"He was an all-Valley District basketball player but Daryl had not played a lot of golf; he worked at it," recalled Edwards, now the boys basketball coach at Spotswood. "His body awareness was not like anything I had seen. It was just uncanny. I think his greatest gift is teaching" sports to others.

Irvine didn't play golf as a young boy. "I just picked it up," he said, recalling he once played a round of golf with Red Sox ace Roger Clemens.

Irvine notes many guests to the resort come from the Northeast part of the United States and some are Boston fans.

"People find out I played for the Red Sox. We still have people who come in (from Boston) and remember me," Irvine said.

Irvine, who grew up playing baseball in Grottoes, was a standout at Spotswood and also played for American Legion Post 27 in Harrisonburg for Ray Heatwole, the former Turner Ashby, Bridge-water College, and JMU coach. "He was a really good pitcher and a really good person. We still talk about pitching," Heatwole said.

Irvine, after starring at Spotswood, headed to Ferrum — then a junior college. After his freshman season, he was drafted in the second round by the Toronto Blue Jays in 1984 but he didn't sign and played that summer for the Harrisonburg Turks in the Valley Baseball League.

He returned to Ferrum and then was taken in the first round as the 20th overall pick by the Red Sox in 1985. Irvine was signed by former Red Sox scout Wayne Britton, who lived for many years in Waynesboro. Irvine pitched for Greensboro, North Carolina, in the Single-A South Atlantic League that year and had an ERA of 4.38.

The 6-foot-5 right-hander advanced to low Single-A Winter Haven of the Florida State League in 1986 and appeared in 26 games, with 24 starts.

Irvine made 37 appearances with 16 starts the next year at Double-A New Britain of the Eastern League. He was still at the Double-A level in 1989 when the Red Sox made him a reliever for good — he posted a stellar ERA of 1.28 in 54 games with just one start that season.

The next spring he was in the majors with a Red Sox team that included Clemens, Mike Boddicker, Lee Smith, and Jeff Reardon on the pitching staff. Irvine said Reardon and fellow closer Smith, a future Hall of Famer, helped him as a young reliever.

The Valley native pitched in six games for Boston in 1991 and 21 the following year, posting a record of 3-4 with a 6.11 ERA.

63

Austin Nicely, Independence Day

The saying goes that if you perform well in the Atlantic League there is a chance a Major League organization will sign you.

But that, unfortunately, wasn't the case for pitcher Austin Nicely, who is from Grottoes and played for his hometown Cardinals in 2020 in the Rockingham County Baseball League season.

A former minor-league pitcher for the Astros, Nicely had an ERA of 3.74 in 2021 while pitching for the York (Pa.) Revolution in the independent Atlantic League. He led York with nine wins but that didn't lead to a chance with a Major League system.

He was back at York for the 2022 season and was 1-5 with an ERA of 7.54 in his first eight starts.

Nicely was drafted out of Spotswood in Penn Laird by the Houston Astros in the 10th round in 2013. He reached the Single-A level in 2016, was let go by the Astros after that year then didn't play in 2017 as he recovered from an injury.

"You never take for granted anytime you are able to compete at this level, much less pitch, much less be in the rotation every fifth day," Nicely said. "That is not something a lot of guys get to do so you really can't take it for granted. Really the best part is, after last year and not getting to play [in a pro league] it shows even more that you never know how long you will be able to do this so you enjoy it as much as you can while you are doing it, for sure."

Nicely said it was vital to play for the Grottoes Cardinals during the 2020 pandemic.

"It was huge; it wasn't a walk in the park every night. And it was a lot of fun," he said. "Every lineup had at least one hitter that was a legitimate [pro-level] hitter. I have been fortunate to play pro ball for a number of years. Any time you have to take a year off, you have really put yourself behind the eight ball."

"It obviously wasn't anyone's choice to have a year off last year, but being able to still compete in what I think is still a pretty competitive league, especially with the pro and top-level college guys that were in it, it only benefited me. I treated it as a normal pro season for how I went about things. You don't take a lump in your career; you continued with the ultimate goal of trying to get back into affiliated baseball."

"I would say more guys didn't play than did," Nicely said of the York roster. "Some guys had to play in Sunday men's leagues just to get something in. It shows how much of a baseball community we have back home" in the central Shenandoah Valley with the RCBL.

Nicely said he had other pro options for 2021 but decided to return to York, where he finished the 2019 season for the Revolution. He lived with some distant relatives about 20 minutes north near Harrisburg, the state capital.

The Atlantic League in 2021 began using TrackMan, an automated system that calls balls and strikes as relayed to an actual human umpire standing back of home plate. There have been some obvious misses by the system, with one involving the nearby Lancaster Barnstormers going viral.

"You can't get wrapped up in it; it misses some [strikes] right down the middle. It is working out kinks, that is why we are testing it," Nicely said. "You have to pitch like you have pitched your entire life. Do what you normally do. They may move the mound back in a couple of weeks. But you can't get too wrapped up in" possible rule changes.

The Revolution plays its home games just off I-83 at Peoples Bank Park at 5 Brooks Robinson Way, named for the Orioles' Hall of Fame third baseman who was a founding partner and has been involved with the organization for many years.

His father, Tim, is the skipper of the Grottoes Cardinals. Cam Irvine, another Spotswood graduate, was hitting better than .400 early on for the Cardinals this season.

There is another notable pitcher who once played for the home-town Grottoes Cardinals: that would be Dell Curry, who played baseball and basketball at Fort Defiance (class of 1982) before a standout hoop career at Virginia Tech that led to a long stint in the NBA. These days, Curry is more known around the country for being the father of NBA All-Star Steph Curry of the Warriors.

Nicely, in 22 starts for York in 2022, was 3-12 with an ERA of 7.44.

Austin Nicely fires a pitch for the York Revolution of the Atlantic League. He is a graduate of Spotswood High.

64

Garland Shifflett, Hometown Star

"I'd pitch in a cow pasture if I had to," Elkton product Garland Shifflett told a newspaper in New York in 1971, his long pro baseball career winding down. "Pitching is all I know how to do and I appreciate the chance to play anywhere. I started every game my high school played beginning when I was a freshman."

Fortunately, the only Elkton native to ever play in the Major Leagues didn't have to pitch in a pasture when he made his debut on this day in 1957.

On April 22, 1957, right-hander Shifflett pitched for the Washington Senators in a 15-7 loss to the powerful New York Yankees at old Griffith Stadium in the nation's capital. It was not a successful or easy introduction—the Yankees would play in the World Series later that season and three of the first seven batters he faced were future Hall of Famers.

According to Baseball Reference, there was a crowd of 16,054 on hand as Shifflett faced his first hitter in the majors—Mickey Mantle.

Mantle walked and so did the next batter, Yogi Berra, and then Shifflett allowed an RBI single to Bill Showron. Later in the inning,

Jerry Coleman and Enos "Country" Slaughter drove in runs before Hank Bauer grounded out to end the top of the eighth. Mantle, Berra, and North Carolina native Slaughter—who grew up just south of the Virginia line—would end up in Cooperstown in the Hall of Fame.

The next outing for Shifflett would come April 28, 1957, as he made the only start of his MLB career. It was a day game in Baltimore and he allowed three runs in two innings in a game won by the Senators 7-6.

The Elkton High product, meanwhile, appeared in six games in 1957 for Washington with an ERA of 10.13 and no decisions.

It was a long way from his humble roots in Elkton, as he quit high school, joined semi-pro teams, and eventually worked as a press punch operator in a steel mill in Orange, according to thebaseballbloggess.com from a story in 2016.

Randall Snow, who graduated from Elkton High, remembers as a boy hearing about Shifflett. "I know he had a great fastball," recalls Snow, who later was the athletic director and baseball coach at Spotswood in Penn Laird.

Shifflett was born on March 28, 1935.

"I remember reading about him growing up," says John Myers, Jr., who graduated from Montevideo and coached football at Elkton High.

Shifflett was signed to a bonus of $4,000 by the Senators in 1954 and most of that money went to his parents to pay bills, according to the 2016 story. He began his minor-league career in Erie, Pennsylvania in 1955.

Of the Virginia natives to have at least one at-bat in the majors (he was 0-for-16), Shifflett is the only one born in Elkton, according to baseballreference.com. Weldon Grimsley, who grew up in Elkton, played in the minors in 1952 for the Giants but never made the majors.

Perhaps that makes Shifflett the second-most famous person to ever call Elkton home in the last 100 years. The top honor would have to go to Patsy Cline, the former country music star born in Winchester in 1932.

Born Virginia Patterson Hensley, the late singer moved around the state as a child with her poor family, according to published reports. That included time in Elkton, where she lived on her paternal grandparents' farm, according to her daughter. Cline died in a plane crash in Tennessee in March of 1963 at the age of 30.

The next year, Shifflett played in just his second Major League season and his first season since his rookie year of 1957. After several years in the minors, he pitched for the Minnesota Twins on June 3, 1964, against the Yankees and threw a scoreless eighth inning in a 3-0 loss in New York.

Shifflett picked up the only save of his MLB career the next week, getting the last three outs in the ninth in a 4-2 win in Detroit over the Tigers. Future Hall of Famer and Baltimore native Al Kaline, who died in 2020, led off with a walk for the Tigers before Shifflett retired Bill Freehan, Norm Cash, and Don Demeter for the final three outs.

It would be the only time he appeared in a game that season in which the Twins won.

The bullpen construction in the 1960s was much different than today. For the most part, relievers were failed or washed-up starters who came out of the bullpen as a last resort in a one-sided game. It was not the path to fame or riches for most pitchers and Shifflett was no different.

Shifflett would go 0-2 with an ERA of 4.58 in 10 games out of the bullpen in 1964 for Minnesota. The last game of his MLB career came on June 26, 1964 against the Chicago White Sox. He allowed two hits and no runs while retiring four batters in the top of the seventh with his team losing 7-2.

The Elkton native ended his MLB career with a record of 0-2 with an ERA of 6.31 in 16 games—with 15 coming in relief. His team lost in 14 of the games in which he pitched.

Early in 1972 he was featured in the Los Angeles Times—

profiled as a career minor-league player while the big leaguers were on strike.

"If I could make the money doing something else, I'd give this up and get out," he told the paper from spring training. "I started my career with nothing and I guess I'll end it with nothing."

He pitched in the minors for 16 years and posted a record of 144-117 in 707 games.

Shifflett lived for several years in the Denver area after his minor-league career ended there in 1972 with the top farm team of the Texas Rangers.

Shifflett, in an interview several years ago, told us he was glad to know he was the only native of Elkton to make the majors.

He died on May 13, 2020, in Colorado, according to baseball-reference.com.

Garland Shifflett

Two Teams At Rebel Field

The first pitch was more than nine hours away but that didn't keep Charles Sisler of Falls Church from stopping by Rebel Field in New Market on a glorious Saturday morning in early June of this year.

Born in New Market in 1943, Sisler recalls many trips to Rebel Park to watch his cousin, Joe Wetsel, play for the Rebels.

"He was a good player," Sisler said of his late cousin, who didn't get a chance to play at the pro level.

On a sunny day, Sisler was in town for a meeting and wanted to stop by the park that is used in the summer by the Rebels of the Valley Baseball League and the New Market Shockers of the Rockingham County Baseball League.

Although he grew up in Falls Church, Sisler would make trips to New Market with his family to see relatives.

Years later, on his visit to town in June, he happened to meet Arthur Stenberg IV – the current manager of the Rebels.

Stenberg was at the field early to get ready for the first home game of the season for the Rebels, who had won on the road the night before at Woodstock.

"They want to learn more and work hard and get better," said Stenberg, taking a break from getting the field prepared.

Stenberg was hired by the late Bruce Alger, who spent decades guiding the Rebels before he passed away in the fall of 2021.

Mike Jones is the new President and General Manager of the Rebels.

"He is doing an outstanding job filling some big shoes," Stenberg said of Jones. "Bruce was such an integral part of this organization."

Stenberg spent three months earlier this year on the baseball staff of the noted IMG Academy of Florida.

"It is a tremendous coaching staff, there is a ton of gentlemen there with a wealth of baseball knowledge," he said.

The New Market Shockers won the Rockingham County Baseball League title in 2021 by knocking off Stuarts Draft. It was the first RCBL title for the franchise in nearly 50 years. The Shockers share a field in New Market with a Valley Baseball League team, the Rebels.

The roster of the Rebels this year has players from as far away as California, Texas, and Florida.

But at least three Virginia residents were on the pitching staff – Antonio Buckley of Centreville and Southeastern Louisiana; Harrison Clifton, from the University of Richmond; and T.R. Williams, from nearby Page County High.

Williams is transferring from Virginia Tech to JMU this coming academic year; he overcame serious health challenges while in high school to return to the mound and made his first start for the Rebels in early June.

"He took us into the fourth inning; he looked good," Stenberg said.

Also on the roster early on for the Rebels was Michael Robertson, an outfielder from Fairfield and Abilene Christian; and outfielder Trevon Smith, from Barboursville and Glenville State in West Virginia.

Among the former Rebels who went on to the Major Leagues include pitcher Tom Browning, who won 123 games between 1984-95 and pitched a perfect game for the Reds; outfielder Brett Gardner, who broke in with the Yankees in 2008; and Dan Pasqua, who played for the Yankees and White Sox and hit 117 homers.

Rebel Field is home to two teams in the summer.

The other is the Shockers, who won the RCBL title last summer for the first time since 1972.

That came in the first year with Lisa Hart, a long-time New Market administrator, as the new commissioner of the RCBL. She is the first woman to hold that spot.

Her grandfather, the late RCBL Hall of Famer Bobby Strickler, helped bring a New Market team to the league in 1964. Hart played basketball at Stonewall Jackson High.

Hart remembers as a young girl sitting on the wooden bleachers at Rebel Park and watching RCBL games.

"My grandmother was sitting there crocheting," Hart said. "That is the earliest memory of actually watching a ballgame."

She took over for Randy Atkins, who held the post for two years and will stay on to work in media relations and with interns with one of the oldest amateur circuits in the country.

"Lisa truly loves the RCBL," New Market manager Nolan Potts, part of the team in some fashion since 2014, said. "She knows the bylaws of the league inside and out so she's been a great resource whenever I've had a question about anything."

"We have some great baseball in this Valley. These kids these days are so much into their cell phones they don't know the greatness of baseball played on cow pastures," Hart added. "I hope my granddaddy is looking down and knows I am doing it for him."

66

Floyd Baker, The Rt. 340 Pipeline

Route 340 starts in Greenville in Augusta County and runs northeast through Virginia, passing through Waynesboro, Grottoes, Elkton, Luray, Shenandoah and Front Royal before heading into West Virginia and eventually Maryland.

While the road goes through several small towns, the north-south route has paved the way for big (league) baseball dreams for decades.

Almost every town along the way in the region has produced at least one Major League player, from Waynesboro (Reggie Harris) to Grottoes (Daryl Irvine) to Elkton (Garland Shifflett) to Luray (Floyd Baker) to Shenandoah (Wayne Comer) to Front Royal products Dana Allison and Darrell Whitmore.

"That's crazy," says Irvine, a Spotswood High graduate who pitched for the Boston Red Sox from 1990-92. "I think we have such a great baseball area."

JMU product Allison says he pitched to Irvine and his Grottoes teammate Dell Curry—who made a name for himself in another sport, basketball—when they were American Legion baseball players in the 1980s.

Here is a look at Harris and Baker, who played long before many of the others even began youth ball:

Baker was born in Luray on October 10, 1916, and made his Major League debut on May 4, 1943, for the St. Louis Browns against the visiting Detroit Tigers. He hit into a double play against pitcher Virgil Trucks.

Baker joined the White Sox in 1945, then moved to the Washington Senators in 1952. He joined the Red Sox in 1953 and ended his career with Philadelphia in the National League in 1955. All told, the infielder came to bat 2,280 times with an average of .251.

His only homer came on May 4, 1949—six years to the day of his debut—at old Comiskey Park with the White Sox against Washington. The homer came off Sid Hudson in a game the White Sox lost 8-7. Baker died in Ohio in 2004, according to baseballreference.com.

Harris was born August 12, 1968, and was a baseball and basketball standout at Waynesboro High. One of his hoop teammates was Kenny Brooks, who would go on to play and coach basketball at James Madison University. Brooks is now the coach of the women's basketball team at Virginia Tech.

But they go back further than that, as Harris and Brooks grew up in the same area. Both graduated from Waynesboro in 1987.

"We played Whiffle ball, pickup football. We were always in the same group," Brooks said. "I played with him in Little League football. I was the safety and he was the noseguard so I never got any action. He always sacked the quarterback or tackled somebody. We grew up playing Little League, always against each other. We played on the same All-Star teams. At Babe Ruth, we won states and we went to the regionals down in Florida. I played second base and I got some action when he pitched because nobody could ever get around on him. I have known Reggie since I was about 7 years old. He was always bigger than we were."

Harris turned down a chance to play basketball for the Hokies when he was drafted in the first round out of high school by the Boston Red Sox in 1987 as a right-handed pitcher.

He made his Major League debut as a Rule V player with Oakland in 1990 and appeared in 16 games, with one start. His first game was on July 4, 1990, as he pitched two innings against Milwaukee.

Harris pitched for Oakland in 1991, the Red Sox in 1996, Philadelphia in 1997, Houston the next year and Milwaukee to end his Major League career in 1999.

67

Mark Arrington, Notable Emory and Henry Alum

After playing at William Monroe High School, Mark Arrington was a standout at Emory and Henry College.

He graduated in 2002 and then began an impressive run with the Elkton Blue Sox of the Rockingham County Baseball League.

Arrington played for more than a decade with the Blue Sox and pitched briefly for the team in 2021.

"I have never had a major injury, knock on wood," said Arrington, who first played in the RCBL in 1999. "I feel like I can go out there and at least compete."

"When I can't compete, I need to leave. That might be very soon," he said, with a laugh, last year.

He was right as he pitched in one game with the Blue Sox before shutting things down in a career that included being the pitcher of the year in the RCBL.

Arrington has also excelled off the field.

He has been a teacher at Madison County and in 2019 was named the Virginia High School Health, and Physical Education Teacher of the Year.

"He is always a leader when he is out there on the field," J.J.

Loker, his former skipper in Elkton, said of Arrington just before his career ended. "He is competitive; he is going to go out there and throw you strikes and he is going to keep you in the ballgame. Everybody who has been in the league and been around it for a while, they know who is and what he brings to the table. He is a workhorse; he likes to go out there and go nine innings when he is there."

Arrington lives in Greene County and has taught at Madison High for eight years; he teaches health, physical education and driver's education.

Elkton did not field a team this year in the RCBL.

"He tried to get people to take it over," Arrington said in June of Loker, "but I guess he wasn't able to. It's unfortunate."

J.J. Loker was a top hitter for several years for the Blue Sox; he took over managing duties from his father, David, a former star pitcher for Elkton High and for American Legion Post 27 of Harrisonburg.

Other pitchers for Elkton in 2021 included Derek Justice, who played at Mount Olive.

Will Decker, a former Roanoke College standout, hit .361 for Elkton in 2020 but then played last year for the Southern Maryland Blue Crabs in the independent Atlantic League.

Decker was playing this season for Kentucky in the independent Atlantic League.

68

The Comer Brothers

It is rare when the same family produces more than one Major Leaguer.

The Comer family did indeed produce a big leaguer in Wayne. His brother, Buddy, didn't make The Show but he was certainly a Major League person on and off the field.

Vincent J. "Buddy" Comer played baseball in the minors with the Washington Senators in the 1960s.

He won state titles a coach 30 years apart at two different schools — in different sports. His son also won a state title as a basketball coach.

But that was just part of his legacy. Comer, 79, of Shenandoah, died at his home in April of last year — leaving a slew of memories for coaches and athletes in the area.

"He was an icon," said Keith Cubbage, the athletic director at Page County High and an athlete at the school in football and track for coach Comer in the 1980s.

Comer was active for decades in the region in athletics as a coach, administrator, baseball and softball umpire, and basketball referee. He also officiated at the college level in the Old Dominion Athletic Conference.

He was the former baseball coach at Bridgewater College and was the athletic director at Spotswood High when the school opened in 1980.

Comer was a former coach at Luray High and had taught for several years at Page County. He retired as a teacher but continued to teach driver's education. He won a state title in boys' basketball as a coach at Luray in 1971 and a track title at Page County in 2001.

"He was definitely a fixture at Page County," Cubbage said. "He made a difference in a lot of people's lives."

Comer played baseball at Bridgewater College before beginning his pro-playing career, then returned to eventually coach the Eagles.

"I just remember him being a very personable, very approachable, very-caring guy," Bob Scott, who played one year of baseball in 1972 for Comer at Bridgewater, said. "He was just a gem of a guy. He was everything you wanted in a person and coach."

"He umpired baseball and was a basketball referee for maybe 50-plus years," added Scott, a former assistant baseball coach under Ray Heatwole at Turner Ashby. "Coaching just ran in his blood. He could coach anything he wanted to and he was able to motivate because he was that kind of guy."

"He was a basketball referee and also umpired baseball for years," Heatwole said. "Buddy has umpired with everybody. He was a good friend and a good person. He umpired for the right reason. I think a lot of Buddy and his whole family. His sister, Joyce, was the [athletic] secretary when I was at JMU" as the coach.

Comer officiated many boys' basketball coaches in which Jim Kramer was the Spotswood coach. Comer worked many games with his brother, Wayne, and Archie Dodson.

"He was a great official," Kramer said. "He was well-liked and always had a smile on his face. I think he really enjoyed what he did. I can't tell you how many times I had him as an official."

Buddy Comer and Dodson were very close friends and were the

best men for each other's wedding. Chris Dodson, the girls' basketball coach at state power Spotswood, is the son of the late Archie Dodson.

"Tough to put into words all the feelings when the second most influential person in your life passes," Chris Dodson wrote on Facebook.

David Rees, a 1976 TA graduate, worked several high school baseball games with Comer as umpires. "He had so many stories to tell. He was so well-respected," said Rees, adding that Comer was an umpire in Valley League Baseball as well. Rees it was just a pleasure to talk sports with Comer in the car on the way to and from games.

Comer, according to baseballreferrence.com, played minor league baseball in 1962-63 in the Washington Senators' farm system.

As an outfielder he hit .247 in 45 games in the Appalachian League with Middleboro, Kentucky, with four homers and 24 RBIs, in 1962. The next year he played in three games with the Wisconsin Rapids in the Single-A Midwest League.

Comer is in the athletic Hall of Fame at Bridgewater and in the Virginia High School League.

COMER'S BROTHER, Wayne, played Major League Baseball from 1967-72 as an outfielder for Detroit, Seattle, Milwaukee, and Washington. He had a pinch-hit in the seventh inning of Game 3 of the 1968 World Series as the Tigers won the Fall Classic over the St. Louis Cardinals in seven games.

Shenandoah native Wayne Comer was later the baseball coach at Spotswood and has been the baseball coach at Page County, which opened in 1961. Buddy Comer's son, Mark, has also been a high school coach and also won a state title as a basketball coach — at Washington & Lee in Montross in 1998.

Page County graduate Mark Comer, class of 1984, said his

father attended college in Kentucky at Berea before transferring to Bridgewater. Buddy Comer also coached at Albemarle High during the 1969-70 school year.

69

Mike Bocock, Winner, Author

Mike Bocock has won eight Valley Baseball League titles as a skipper going into this year and he has helped pave the way for some of his players to the Major Leagues.

Now the former Turner Ashby High and Bridgewater College player has written a book about his experiences.

He teamed up with local writer Bill Meade to produce "Close to the Dirt: Mike Bocock's Life and Journey Through the Dugouts and Diamonds of the Shenandoah Valley."

"*Close to the Dirt* describes Bocock's journey, showing his love of sport, love of family and love of life. Full of humorous stories, the book details Bocock's coaching strategies, interesting characters, and impactful personal losses. A portion of the proceeds from the book's sales will go to the Woodstock-Edinburg Community Baseball organization to benefit local [youth] leagues and other charities," according to the Page Valley News.

Bocock has been successful at several levels.

In 2018, the year before Bocock became the Woodstock manager, the River Bandits were 5-37 and finished 20 games back of first-place Purcellville in the North Division.

Woodstock was greatly improved in 2019 at 25-17-1 under Bocock.

Last year Woodstock advanced to the Northern Division finals before falling to Strasburg, the eventual champion.

"I do know a lot of people," Bocock said last year. "The Woodstock board has worked hard to make this go."

Bocock has also guided teams in New Market, Staunton, Luray, and Waynesboro. He has won eight Valley League titles and nurtured future big leaguers such as Daniel Murphy, Aubrey Huff, Yonder Alonso, and Brian Bocock, a fellow TA product and his nephew. Murphy played for Bocock in Luray and became a top hitter for the Mets, Nationals and Rockies.

"With his recruiting, it has just been invaluable," Woodstock general manager Robert Bowman said of Bocock. "He is very knowledgeable and that is evident with his championship rings. Mike came in and he hit the ground running and we have been better for it."

One of his top prospects last year was Edrick Felix.

Felix, as a freshman, hit .275 with six homers last year for the College of Central Florida. He is from Orlando.

"Felix is the best defensive shortstop in the league, there is no question. Offensively he has a lot to learn. I am telling you he is a can't-miss Major Leaguer," Bocock said last year.

The Woodstock roster this year includes hometown product and pitcher Kalen Hoover, from Garrett College.

Dawson Moomaw, from Mount Jackson, was also on the roster as an infielder from Ferrum.

Hunter Hoopes, from Fairfax, was also on the roster as a pitcher.

Tomas Sanchez, from Dewitt, was off to a fast start at the plate as the River Bandits won three of their first six games.

Frankie Ritter, an infielder from Shenandoah, was leading off in the early part of the year for Bocock. He is from Stephens City.

70

Jaylon Lee, Division III to JMU

Last summer, Jaylon Lee showed that a player from a Division III program could perform in the Valley Baseball League.

The outfielder who had played at EMU in 2021 had a strong season for the River Bandits in Woodstock, who ended up falling in the Northern Division playoffs to Strasburg.

Lee returned to the Royals this spring and hit .382 with 10 homers for coach Adam Posey.

But after four years with the Royals, Lee decided to test his ability. After entering the transfer portal, he told us he heard from several Division I schools but eventually decided to transfer to JMU for the 2023 season.

"I really like the coaching staff at JMU," Lee said.

Prior to the 2021 Valley League season, Posey had contacted every team to find a spot for Lee.

"No one was interested," Posey noted.

"We couldn't really find spots because teams were filling up," Lee recalled.

But then during the Old Dominion Athletic Conference tournament that spring, Posey heard from recruiting coordinator Gerald Harman of Woodstock. The rest is history.

Lee was the MVP for the North as he drove in a run with a single and robbed Mike Rosario (Miami) of the Turks of a homer in center in the third inning as the North won 5-0 over the South in Harrisonburg at James Madison's Veterans Memorial Stadium last summer in the All-Star game.

Lee said it was his first game at JMU.

"It went right over my head," Lee said of the long drive by Rosario. "I kind of stood there for a second because it was a gloomy sky; I didn't get a good read on it. Once I saw it, I thought it had a chance to go and I had to get back there."

Jaylon Lee batting with EMU

"IT WAS JUST fun to be out there," he added of the All-Star game. "I was surrounded by great players. We kind of took it seriously; we wanted to beat the South real bad." The Division III star has held his own and then some against Division I pitching.

"I wouldn't say doubts; more like nerves of how it would go for me considering I hadn't played against guys at that level," said Lee, who is from Newport News. "I seem to fit in pretty well. It has been a huge adjustment [facing pitchers] who don't throw lower than 88. It has a rough adjustment, considering off-speed and stuff like that. I am working on that."

Lee played all three outfield spots for Woodstock.

"I would like to see him get a chance to play in the minors," Bocock said of Lee.

Among the scouts at the All-Star game was Jim Farr, who is with the Kansas City Royals and is the former coach at William & Mary. Also on hand was long-time scout Bo Trumbo, a member of the Athletic Hall of Fame at Bridgewater College

The South MVP was Victor Castillo (Covington, Florida Atlantic) while Edrick Felix (Woodstock, Central Florida) won the 60-yard dash in the pre-game events with a time of 6.43.

After four years at EMU, Lee will transfer to JMU for the 2023 season after playing for the Harrisonburg Turks in the Valley Baseball League in 2022.

71

Spottswood Poles, The Black Ty Cobb

There is a very good chance you have never heard of Winchester native Spottswood Poles even though he is one of the best professional baseball players to come out of the Shenandoah Valley.

The reason you probably haven't heard of him is not just that he was born nearly 150 years ago. It's also because he was a Black player who appeared in the Negro Leagues — a circuit until 2020 relegated to second division status by some baseball historians.

Records indicate the speedy Poles, called the Black Ty Cobb, hit better than .400 against all foes with an average of .610 against Major League pitching in exhibition games. Poles — sometimes called Spot — played from 1908-23 in various leagues.

Major League Baseball tried to rectify some previous wrongs two years ago by elevating the Negro Leagues to "Major League" status 100 years after the Negro Leagues began. MLB said it will highlight seven distinct leagues from 1920 to 1948 and statistics from that era will be included in MLB records.

It was a move that won't erase a racist past. But perhaps in the future more fans, young and old, will learn more about some of those Negro League stars such as Josh Gibson and Cool Papa Bell.

Stars such as Hank Aaron, Ernie Banks and Willie Mays played in the Negro Leagues before becoming Hall of Famers in MLB.

"The Negro Leagues Baseball Museum is thrilled to see this well-deserved recognition of the Negro Leagues. In the minds of baseball fans worldwide, this serves as historical validation for those who had been shunned from the Major Leagues and had the foresight and courage to create their own league that helped change the game and our country too. This acknowledgement is a meritorious nod to the courageous owners and players who helped build this exceptional enterprise and shines a welcomed spotlight on the immense talent that called the Negro Leagues home," Bob Kendrick, president of the Negro Leagues Baseball Museum in Kansas City, said in a statement.

Spottswood Poles

"The perceived deficiencies of the Negro Leagues' structure and scheduling were born of MLB's exclusionary practices, and denying them Major League status has been a double penalty, much like that exacted of Hall of Fame candidates prior to Satchel Paige's induction in 1971. Granting MLB status to the Negro Leagues a century after their founding is profoundly gratifying," John Thorn, the official historian of Major League Baseball, said in a statement put out by MLB.

Despite a mostly feel-good announcement, there was some pushback on social media — as is normally the case. Some feel the Negro Leagues is a separate entity and can't be "bought" by MLB. Others didn't like the term "elevated" that MLB used in its release.

As for those "perceived deficiencies" of the Negro Leagues: can we truly measure statistics from one generation to the next, no matter the league?

Poles, the Winchester native, once hit .406 in a season. That was the same average that Ted Williams compiled for the Boston Red Sox in 1941.

Williams reached that mark while not facing any Black pitchers. Poles hit .406 while not batting against any White pitchers. Either way, .406 is pretty darn good no matter the league or decade.

According to The Negro Leagues Book, published in 1994, other natives of Virginia to play in the league included:

• Hall of Famer Ray Dandridge, a third baseman who was born in Richmond in 1913 and played pro ball from 1933-53. He went into the Baseball Hall of Fame in 1987 and died seven years later in Florida.

• Johnny Davis, who was born in Ashland in 1917 and died in Florida in 1982. The outfielder-pitcher played from 1940-48, including a long run with the solid Newark teams.

• Hall of Famer Leon Day, a pitcher who was born in Alexandria in 1916 and spent most of his youth in Baltimore. Day went into the Baseball Hall of Fame in Cooperstown in 1995 — the same year he died in Baltimore. He played from 1934-49.

• Wilmer Fields, who was born in Manassas in 1922 and was a two-way player from 1940-51 in various leagues.

• Stanley Green, a catcher born on the Eastern Shore in 1926. He played in Philadelphia in the Negro Leagues starting in 1943.

• Louis Louden, a catcher born in West Point, King William County in 1919. He broke in with a team in New York in 1942 and played through 1950. He died in New Jersey in 1989.

• Charles Peete, an outfielder who was born in 1929 in Franklin in southwest Virginia and played from 1950-56.

Negro League players from West Virginia included Lawrence Raines, born in St. Albans in 1930. Another Negro League player born in West Virginia was Bluefield native Toni Stone, one of three women to play in the league in the 1950s.

The other women to play in the league were Connie Morgan and Mamie "Peanut" Johnson, who was born in South Carolina and was a long-time resident of Washington, D.C. before she passed away in 2017.

An AP story was written by Joseph White, a former Staunton resident who died in 2019, and helped lead to Johnson being interviewed on national TV outlets. "I played with the fellas most of the time because the girls did what the boys did, because there was nothing else to do," Johnson said of her youth in South Carolina.

Country singer and pioneer Charley Pride, who died in 2020, played in the Negro Leagues and in the farm system of the Reds in 1960. Some fans weren't aware he had played baseball at a high level until after he passed away. Perhaps in the future, thanks to the MLB announcement two years ago, those facts won't be overlooked as much from now on out.

As for Poles — he excelled off the diamond as well. Born in 1887 or 1889, depending on the source, he earned five battle stars and the Purple Heart, according to baseballreference.com, as a sergeant in World War I then resumed his baseball career. He was buried at Arlington National Cemetery with full military honors in 1962 after his death in Harrisburg, Pa.

There are at least four natives of Virginia from the Negro Leagues now in the Baseball Hall of Fame: Leon Day, who was born in Alexandria and grew up in Baltimore; Dandridge; Pete Hill, who was born in Culpeper; and Jud Wilson, who was born in Remington in Fauquier County.

Rick Croushore, Pitching-In At Shenandoah

This past season, Division III Shenandoah posted a team ERA of 3.78 while opponents had a mark of 8.28.

The Hornets pitchers held foes to an average of .269 while Shenandoah hit .333 as a team.

Those numbers reflect well on Rick Croushore, who just ended his second season as the pitching coach for head coach Kevin Anderson in Winchester.

That pitching helped Shenandoah advance to the Division III national tournament. The Hornets hosted a regional which was won by Catholic, which advanced to the Division III College World Series in Iowa.

As for Croushore, the former Major League pitcher stopped in Harrisonburg nearly three years ago to check about the possibility of being a volunteer coach with the JMU program – his alma mater.

A side trip to Winchester to see his former JMU coach, Anderson, turned into an even better opportunity — a part-time paid position as the pitching coach and recruiting coordinator for Shenandoah.

"He was looking to get back into the (college) game," said Anderson, the long-time coach at Shenandoah. "The kids love him. He is very knowledgeable about the sport. He hit the ground running and has not looked back."

"He was fun to play for but at the same time he kept us accountable," said Harrisonburg graduate Cade Templeton, a senior pitcher this past season for the Hornets.

Croushore had been coaching youth baseball in Arkansas for about 20 years. With his two children (Jake and Kaylee) now in college, the Mount Vernon High graduate sought the opportunity to coach at the college level and looked to return to Virginia.

"I felt like it went well; my first recruiting class I feel is going to be pretty strong," Croushore said. "I got along great with the kids."

Anderson was the pitching coach at JMU when Croushore was with the Dukes for two years in the early 1990s. The head coach was former Turner Ashby mentor Ray Heatwole, who saw Croushore pitch in an amateur league in the nation's capital after two seasons at Hutchinson Community College in Kansas.

Croushore said he and his father visited JMU the next day and Heatwole offered him a scholarship. A right-hander, Croushore accepted even though George Mason University had expressed interest before the Dukes.

Even though he was not drafted out of JMU, Croushore signed a contract with St. Louis in 1993 and worked his way up the minor-league ladder. He made his MLB debut with the Cardinals on May 18, 1998, with two innings out of the bullpen against the Marlins.

His most memorable appearance came later that year in the game that Mark McGwire of the Cardinals hit his 62nd homer of the season to break the mark of 61 set by Roger Maris in 1961. (McGwire was later found to use steroids during part of his career).

On Sept. 8, 1998, Croushore gave up two hits and one walk while retiring two batters as he came on in the seventh for St. Louis starter Kent Mercker. One of the batters he retired was Sammy

Sosa, the Cubs' slugger who was also chasing McGwire for the homer record held by Maris.

In the fourth inning of that game, McGwire hit a solo homer off Steve Trachsel for his 62nd round-tripper of the season.

"There are only two people in the world who have that on video camera," Croushore said. "And that is me and Dave Duncan, the pitching coach. I have a different perspective. He got it from the dugout and I got it from the bullpen. I ran in and got the whole ceremony with Mark and Sammy."

Croushore was the only rookie to pitch in the game — a nod from then-Cardinals manager Tony La Russa for past success.

"That was pretty cool," Croushore said.

That came in his 34th appearance as a rookie for the Cardinals. He recorded the first save of his career on June 18, 1998, as he gave up one run in two innings in a 7-6 win at Houston over the Astros.

The JMU product was 0-3 with an ERA of 4.97 in 41 games with eight saves that season.

Croushore was 3-7, 4.14 in 59 games with three saves in 1999 for St. Louis.

He split the 2000 season between Colorado and Boston, as he went 2-0, 8.74 in six games for the Rockies and 0-1, 5.79 in five outings for the Red Sox.

His last MLB outing came October 1, 2000, as he gave up the winning run in the last of the 10th as Tampa Bay won 3-2 over the Red Sox.

The right-hander was 5-11 with an ERA of 4.88 with 11 saves in 111 games in the majors and also appeared in the minors with the organizations of the Baltimore Orioles, Cincinnati Reds, Florida Marlins, and Tampa Bay Rays. He pitched in 2003 with the Orioles in the Gulf Coast League and ended his pro career in the minors with Triple-A Louisville.

Croushore made it to the majors even though he didn't play for a college team the year after he graduated from Mount Vernon

High in Fairfax County. That was because he was injured just before his senior year of high school.

He lived with his mother that year in Texas and took classes at the University of Houston, with an eye on becoming an accountant. Then he was spotted by coaches at Hutchinson, a top program in Kansas.

"It is funny how things work out," said Croushore, who was born in New Jersey.

After coaching in Arkansas, where he also played in the minors and met his former wife Tami, Croushore wanted to get into the college game. He met with JMU coach Marlin Ikenberry about the possibility of being a volunteer.

"The next day I had lunch with Kevin (Anderson). He said, 'Are you serious about this? Well, my recruiting and pitching coach positions are open. You can have both of them.' Things have worked out," Croushore said.

The spot opened at Shenandoah after former assistant coach Michael Scimanico became a volunteer assistant coach at Division I Seton Hall in his native New Jersey.

Templeton, who has played for New Market this summer in the Rockingham County Baseball League, said Croushore helped him work on his cutter and other facets of his game. "We definitely did a lot more running," said Templeton.

The Hornets had an ERA of 4.75 in 2021 in the first year under the former JMU hurler.

"I could not be happier," Anderson said of Croushore.

Croushore, in the summer of 2022, stepped down as the pitching coach at Shenandoah.

73

Dana Allison, Oakland A's For One Year

Dana Allison was born in Front Royal in 1966 and played at Warren County High before joining the baseball program at JMU in 1985. He played in the Valley Baseball League for Front Royal from 1986-88 and some of his teammates included future Major League catchers Steve Decker and John Flaherty.

A lefty pitcher, Allison was drafted in the 21st round out of JMU in 1989 by Oakland. He made the Opening Day roster of the A's in 1991 under manager Tony La Russa, a Hall of Famer who now guides the White Sox.

"I was at the right place at the right time," Allison said.

Allison said he made the team after an injury to veteran lefty pitcher Rick Honeycutt, a former pitching coach for the Dodgers.

Allison's first Major League game was April 12, 1991, as he retired Omar Vizquel on a flyball and then walked Harold Reynolds of Seattle in a 6-1 Oakland win.

Allison pitched in 11 games with Oakland that year—all out of the bullpen—in his only Major League season.

He was roommates with Reggie Harris of Waynesboro at Tacoma in 1990. Allison eventually moved back to Warren County and became a security officer at Skyline High. He and his wife, Stacey, have a son, Dylan, who was a junior at JMU in the fall of 2021.

Darrell Whitmore also went to Warren County High and then was drafted out of West Virginia University by the Indians in the second round in 1990. He also played football in college.

The outfielder started in his first Major League game, on June 25, 1993, against the Montreal Expos. Whitmore played in 76 games with the Marlins that year, nine in 1994 and 27 in 1995. He hit .203 in 330 at-bats with five homers in the majors.

Dana Allison with his wife Stacey and son, Dylan, a JMU student.

He played in the minors with Pittsburgh, Toronto, Cincinnati, and St. Louis before his last pro year with independent Long Island in the Atlantic League in 2002.

Front Royal, like Waynesboro south on Rt. 340, also sent many players to the majors with its Valley League affiliate. Just one of them is pitcher Randy Dobnak, who has been with the Twins for the past few years.

As for the 2022 Valley League team, the roster of the Cardinals includes pitcher Jackson Arnold, from nearby Linden and a product of Emory and Henry College; Justin Rebok, a pitcher from Ashburn and Towson University; pitcher Michael Schultz, from Centreville and the College of Charleston in South Carolina; Longwood product Kevin Warunek, a pitcher from Gainesville; and infielder Drew Camp, from Longwood and South Chesterfield.

Infielder Riley Frost had three hits in a win on June 10 as Front Royal improved to 3-3 on the young season.

Part VI

NORTHERN VIRGINIA AND BACK TO
RICHMOND

74

Mike Wallace, Among Madison High Quartet

Mike Wallace, a long-time resident of Remington, was born in Gastonia, North Carolina in 1951.

His family eventually moved to Virginia and he was a standout pitcher at James Madison High in Vienna before he was drafted in the fourth round by the Phillies in 1969.

Wallace is one of four Madison High alums to appear in the Majors, including pitcher Jay Franklin, outfielder Bob Brower, and catcher Jim McNamara. "We moved from Gastonia to Vienna in 1959, when I was 9," Wallace said earlier this year. "I still have relatives on both sides of the family from Gastonia."

Franklin was the second overall pick in the 1971 draft, going to the Padres, and he pitched in his only three Major League games that year for San Diego.

Brower went to Duke and played for the Rangers and Yankees from 1986-89. McNamara went to North Carolina State and played for the Giants from 1992-93.

A lefty, Wallace broke in with the Phillies in 1973 and also pitched for the Yankees and Cardinals before ending his career with the Texas Rangers – formerly the Senators – in 1977.

In his career, Wallace was 11-3 with an ERA of 3.91 in 117 games with four starts and three saves.

After his playing days, Wallace was an assistant coach at George Mason University, in the Clark Griffith League and has appeared in the past on baseball shows with the Mid-Atlantic Sports Network (MASN) as he discussed the Nationals and the majors.

At least two former Senators share a February 3 birthday with Wallace: one-time outfielder Wayne Comer and former pitcher Joe Coleman. Comer was born in Shenandoah and went to Page County High.

Page County was back in the limelight last year when alum Katie Gordon, a slugger for JMU softball, helped the Dukes make the Softball College World Series for the first time.

The star pitcher for that Dukes squad was Odicci Alexander, from tiny Boydton in Mecklenberg County.

Coleman was born in 1947 in Boston and was a first-round pick out of nearby Natick High by the Senators in 1965. He made his debut in the majors later that year at age 18 and was with the Senators through 1970. In his first year with the Tigers the next season, he won 20 games then won a career-high 23 games three years later. Coleman ended his career with the Pirates in 1979 and he won 142 games in the majors.

Wallace remembers one spring training when Coleman was almost hurt seriously. "Ted Simmons hit a line drive off his head; Coleman was with the Tigers at the time," Wallace said.

Earlier this year, Wallace attended a baseball game at JMU in Harrisonburg and chatted with fans of visiting William and Mary, who learned of his Major League past.

The Madison High legacy continued in the summer of 2022 as Bryce Eldridge, a class of 2023 star for the Warhawks, was named the MVP as he helped the USA national team win the U-18 world title in the WBSC. He has committed to the baseball program at Alabama but some consider him a possible first-round pick in the 2023 MLB draft as a two-way player.

75

Steve Brodie, What A Character

It has been more than 100 years since Steve Brodie played for the Baltimore Orioles – the Orioles of the 1890s, that is – but there is little doubt that the Warrenton native is one of the greatest Virginia players of all time.

Brodie was born in Warrenton on Sept. 11, 1868, according to baseballreference.com.

"His father, Alexander Marr Brodie, an immigrant from Scotland, named his son after the most famous author of his native soil, Sir Walter Scott. His mother, Jennette LaMarque was a Virginia native of French heritage. The elder Brodie was a tailor by vocation and a Shakespearean actor by avocation. During his adult years, the younger Brodie enjoyed reciting lengthy passages from the Bard to the surprise of teammates and fans," according to the Society of American Baseball Research (SABR). "As a teenager, Walter moved to the bustling railroad center of Roanoke, Virginia, in 1885 to play ball on semi-professional teams in the local industrial leagues. Teams found jobs for him, but they were secondary. He began as a catcher and sometimes outfielder. He acquired the nickname "Steve" after a famous daredevil named Steve Brodie gained fame by jumping off the Brooklyn Bridge and surviving in the summer of 1886. The sobriquet seemed to fit and never left him."

Brodie ended his career with the New York Giants in 1902 – the year before the first World Series took place.

He had 1,728 hits in his career – among the most of any player born in Virginia.

Brodie died in Baltimore in 1935.

Steve Brodie

76

Nick Wells, Valley League Memories

Nick Wells got an early start with baseball in Northern Virginia.

"My neighbor got me into it," Wells said. "He was a little bit older than I was and we were pretty good friends growing up."

Wells eventually played for the Gainesville Cannons, Haymarket Bulls, and Richmond Braves and was a standout at Battlefield High.

As a boy, he went to Valley Baseball League games at Haymarket, which used to play home games at Battlefield.

"As a kid, we used to go with the neighbors and chase foul balls and stuff like that," said Wells earlier this season, while wearing a Virginia Tech T-shirt.

He was drafted in the third round out of Battlefield High in Virginia in 2014 by the Blue Jays.

In July of 2015, Seattle Mariners traded RHP Mark Lowe to Toronto Blue Jays for LHP Rob Rasmussen, LHP Jake Brentz, and Wells.

Wells appeared with Double-A Harrisburg and Triple-A Rochester last season in the Washington system but was then released in late March. A few weeks later he signed with the

Southern Maryland Blue Crabs of the independent Atlantic League.

"Going in you don't really have any idea what to expect," said Wells, after a home game in Maryland this spring. "You just got released, so you are a little bitter. Honestly, it has been a blast; great group of guys that have been very welcoming."

"I am having fun playing the game again," added the lefty. "That is one of the main things. It is looser; it is hard to describe honestly. It is just a fun atmosphere, you know what I mean? I can't really describe it. The group of guys, there is no ego to it. Everybody is here for the same reason."

He posted an ERA of 2.16 in his first 15 outings for the Blue Crabs this season out of the bullpen.

Nick Wells

"Just keep going. Throw strikes, attack hitters," he said of his goals. "This is where my feet are right now. Sometimes in the affiliated ball you start pressing and try to get there quicker and quicker (up the ladder). This is where my feet are now and where I will be until something (else) happens."

Wells elected to be a free agent after the 2021 season.

The Virginia native had an ERA of 2.12 in 10 games with Harrisburg last year and a mark of 6.47 in 22 outings for Rochester out of the bullpen.

"I have a lot of good friends there," he said of his time with the Nationals. "I still have a good relationship with them. There is some talent there for sure."

77

Clay Kirby, Arlington Ace

According to baseball-reference.com, more than 100 players born in Washington, D.C. made it to the Major Leagues.

And several of them had ties to Virginia – including pitcher Clay Kirby of Arlington.

Here is a look at one person's all-time team of D.C. natives.

One caveat: a player had to spend at least three years in the majors and had to play at least one season in 1947 or after – 1947 was the year Jackie Robinson broke the color barrier.

Vic Correll, Catcher

Correll was born in D.C. in 1946, was drafted out of Georgia Southern by Cleveland in 1967, and made his Major League debut five years later with Boston.

He spent most of his career with Atlanta and was with the Braves in 1974, the year Hank Aaron broke the career homer mark of Babe Ruth.

Correll ended his career with the Reds in 1980. He hit .229 with 29 homers in the majors.

Ryan Hanigan, Catcher

Hanigan was born in D.C. in 1980 and went to a high school near Boston.

He played at Rollins University in Florida and then broke in with the Reds in 2007.

Hanigan ended his career with the Rockies in 2017; he had 30 homers in his career and hit .251.

Justin Bour, First Base

Born in 1988, the left-handed slugger went to Westfield High in Northern Virginia and was drafted out of George Mason University by the Cubs in 2009. He was signed by Billy Swoope, a long-time scout based in Virginia and the former coach at Virginia Wesleyan.

Swoope signed several players who made the majors, including Herndon High and University of Virginia product Brandon Guyer; Brendan Harris out of William and Mary; and VCU product Jason Dubois.

Bour broke in with the Marlins in 2014 and hit at least 19 homers in a season four times.

Bour had great success late in his career against the Nationals and at Nationals Park, with several homers off Washington pitchers.

He last played in the majors in 2019 with the Angels. He hit .253 in his career with 92 homers – among the most of any D.C. native.

Bump Wills, Second Base

The son of Maury, the younger Wills was born in D.C. in 1952. He went to high school in Washington state, played in college at Arizona State and then broke into the majors with Texas.

He ended his career with the White Sox in 1982.

Wills had 196 steals in his career with 36 homers. He had a career-high 52 steals in 1978 with the Rangers.

Maury Wills, Shortstop

Perhaps the best player from D.C., he was born in 1932 and went to Cardozo High and broke in with the Dodgers in 1959.

Wills stole 104 bases with the Dodgers in 1962 and that record stood until Lou Brock of the Cardinals came along in 1974.

The elder Wills had 586 steals in his career, which ended with the Dodgers in 1972.

He managed Seattle in 1980 then was let go early the next season.

Don Money, Third Base

Money was born in D.C. in 1947 and went to La Plata High in southern Maryland.

The right-handed hitter broke in with the Phillies in 1968 but spent most of his career with the Brewers.

He was a three-time All-Star in Milwaukee and was part of powerful offensive teams with the Brew Crew.

Money helped the Brewers hold off the Orioles to win the American League East in 1982 as Milwaukee made it to the World Series that year against the Cardinals.

He ended his career in 1983 with the Brewers; he hit .261 and had 176 homers, the most of any player born in D.C.

Milt Thompson, Outfield

Thompson was born in 1959 and starred at Magruder High in Rockville, Maryland, and at Howard University.

Drafted in the second round by the Braves in 1979, Thompson made his Major League debut in 1984 with Atlanta.

He had a career-best 47 steals with the Phillies in 1987.

Thompson ended his playing career with the Rockies in 1996. He had 214 steals in his career and was a coach for several years with the Phillies after his playing days.

Curtis Pride, Outfield

Born in 1968, Pride was a baseball and basketball standout at Einstein High in Montgomery County, Maryland and played both sports at Division I William & Mary in Virginia.

He was drafted in the 10th round by the Mets in 1986 and made his major league debut with Montreal in 1993.

Pride played in a career-high 95 games with Detroit in 1996 and was back with the Expos in 2001.

He ended his career with the Angels in 2006. Pride hit .250 with

20 homers in his career; for more than a decade, he has been the baseball coach at Division III Gallaudet in northeast Washington and has been part of diversity programs with Major League Baseball.

Sonny Jackson, Outfield

Jackson was born in D.C. in 1944 and went to Blair High in Silver Spring.

He broke in with Houston in 1963, then played for the Braves from 1968 through the end of his career in 1974.

Jackson was teammates in Atlanta with Aaron and fellow D.C. native Correll.

The left-handed hitter had 126 steals in his career and batted .251.

Emmanuel Burriss, Utility

The infielder was born in D.C. in 1985 and went to Woodrow Wilson High in northwest D.C.

He played at Division I Kent in Ohio and then was drafted in the first round by the Giants in 2006.

When he made his debut two years later with San Francisco, he became the first product of a D.C. public high school to make the majors since Willie Royster (Spingarn) of the Orioles in 1981. Royster was born in Clarksville, was drafted by the Orioles out of high school, and died in New Jersey in 2015.

Burriss was with the Giants through 2012, then played in five games with the Nationals in 2015. He also played in the minors while with Washington.

His career ended with the Phillies in 2016. Burriss hit .237 with 41 steals in 325 games.

L.J. Hoes, Utility

Hoes was born in D.C. in 1990 and starred at St. John's College High of the powerful Washington Catholic Athletic Conference.

He was drafted in the third round by the Orioles in 2008 and turned down a scholarship offer from North Carolina to sign with the Orioles.

Hoes, who grew up near Bowie, Maryland, made his Major League debut with the Orioles in 2012 in two games and played one game for the Birds the next year. He played infield and outfield as a pro player.

He played in a career-high 55 games in 2014 for Houston and ended his Major League career with the Astros the next year.

Hoes recently began working at a sports facility in Northern Virginia as the Director of Baseball at the St. James program.

He played for Double-A Bowie for parts of three years in a row, from 2010-12.

He was with Triple-A Norfolk for part of 2012, 2013, and 2016 and ended his career with Southern Maryland in the independent Atlantic League in 2017.

He turned 32 on March 5.

Clay Kirby, Starting Pitcher

Kirby was born in D.C. in 1948 and was a star at what was then Washington-Lee High in Arlington, a school now named Washington-Liberty.

He was a third-round pick in 1966 out of high school by the Cardinals then broke in with the Padres three years later; he lost a league-high 19 games that season.

Kirby also pitched for the Reds and ended his career with Montreal in 1976. He had a record of 75-104 with a decent ERA of 3.84.

Kirby died in Arlington in 1991 at the age of 43; according to baseball-reference.com, he is buried in Falls Church.

Johnny Klippstein, Starting Pitcher

Born in 1927, Klippstein also went to Blair High in Maryland. He made his debut in the majors in 1950 with the Cubs.

He won a personal-best 12 games for the Reds in 1956 and had a career-best 14 saves for Cleveland in 1960.

The next season he played for the hometown Washington Senators, going 2-2 with an ERA of 6.78 in 42 games, with one start.

He ended his career in 1967 with the Tigers; he went 101-118 with 65 saves in his career. He won a World Series ring with the Dodgers in 1959 and also pitched in the World Series with the Twins in 1965.

Klippstein died in Illinois in 2003.

Frank Funk, reliever

Funk was born in D.C. in 1935 and went to American University and Shepherd University in West Virginia, according to baseball-reference.com.

He pitched for Cleveland from 1960-62 then ended his career in 1963 with the Milwaukee Braves.

Funk won 20 games with 18 saves and posted an ERA of 3.01 in the majors.

Clay Kirby

78

Leon Day, Hall of Famer

Leon Day was born October 30, 1916, in Alexandria – but he didn't stay there long.

Geraldine Day, his widow, told us in a telephone interview in February of this year that Leon Day's father found a job in Baltimore soon after he was born.

She read his acceptance speech when he was inducted into the Baseball Hall of Fame in Cooperstown in the summer of 1995. Day had been elected earlier that year and died less than a week later at a hospice in Baltimore.

"That day was like happy and sad," she said from her home in Catonsville, Maryland, just south of Baltimore of that day in Cooperstown. "I was sad because he wasn't there to say his own speech. But his dream came true."

The Negro League star pitcher met his future wife in 1962 while working as a bartender in Newark, N.J. "It took me two years to know he even played baseball," she said.

The only way she found out was when he showed her two tickets for a trip to Mexico, where Day was asked to play in an Old-

Timers' game there. That was the first day Geraldine Day saw him pitch.

The couple moved from New Jersey to Baltimore in 1980, the year they got married.

Day was honored by the city of Baltimore and the state of Maryland before he was elected to the Hall of Fame.

Geraldine Day said she was able to meet several Negro League stars, such as Satchel Paige and Cool Papa Bell.

One year, the couple drove to Florida and spent time with the family of Richmond native Ray Dandridge, another Negro League star who is in the Hall of Fame.

Geraldine Day said she never met Jackie Robinson, but did meet his wife and other family members.

Day was a star in the Negro Leagues and began his career in 1934 and played in various leagues for about 10 years.

The right-handed pitcher played in Mexico City from 1947-48 and was part of the St. Louis Browns' system in the early 1950s, though he never got a chance to play in the Major Leagues.

His last season, according to baseballreference.com, was in 1954 in the Manitoba-Dakota League.

Day was named to the Baseball Hall of Fame in March of 1995; he was the 12th Negro League representative to make the Hall and the first since 1987—when Dandridge got the nod.

"I thought this day would never come. I'm feeling pretty good," he said when he received word from the Hall at his hospital bed on March 8, 1995, according to SABR. "I'm so happy, I don't know what to do. I never thought it would come."

And it began in Alexandria.

"Looking further back in Leon's life, to his earliest years, it was his family's move from Alexandria to Baltimore when he was 6 months old that would pair him forever with what would become one of his two hometowns—Baltimore (with Newark as the other). His father, Ellis Day, got a job at the Westport glass factory so that he and his wife, Hattie, could make enough to help raise their six children. They lived in nearby Mount Winans, then a poverty-stricken, all-black community in Southwest Baltimore in a house with no electricity or running water. For Leon, baseball became an early fixture. He would do anything to see the Baltimore Black Sox play at Maryland Baseball Park in Westport," according to the Society of American Baseball Research.

Day's widow appeared in August of 2022 at the home of the Double-A Bowie Baysox on a night the Orioles' farm team honored the Negro League. Others on hand included the great-grandson of former Negro League star Josh Gibson.

Sean Gibson played Division I basketball at Robert Morris near Pittsburgh, where the elder Gibson was a star in the Negro Leagues.

Leon Day

79

Mike Venafro, From Reliever To Scout

Mike Venafro grew up in Northern Virginia and played baseball at Paul VI High in Fairfax.

He was not a top prospect and had already decided to attend JMU for academics when he was invited to try out for the Dukes.

That led to a long career in professional baseball – he has been a scout for several years for the San Diego Padres.

"I was never going to college (just) to play baseball," said Venafro, who first studied graphic design in Harrisonburg. "I was already going there academically."

Used sparingly during his first three seasons, Venafro was part of a strong team in his senior year in 1995.

A big key was when Venafro dropped down his arm slot to almost an extreme level while at JMU.

"That was a big move," said Ray Heatwole, the former Dukes' coach, and pitching coach. "It really gave him a weapon that he could use to get people out that he did not have. I followed his Major League career; I knew he could get people out and get groundballs."

Kevin Anderson, also a former head coach and pitching coach for JMU, helped Venafro lower his arm slot.

"When he first started with it, he couldn't get anybody out," said Anderson, now the coach at Shenandoah University in Winchester. "Each year, because of his work ethic and willpower, he got better and better. By his senior year, he was one of the best relievers in the CAA and the state. His velocity got up to 86 (miles-per-hour) from the mid-70s. You talk about a rags-to-riches story."

The lefty, who also played for New Market in the Valley Baseball League, was drafted by the Texas Rangers that year in the 29th round. He was signed by scout Mike Toomey, the former coach at George Washington University and a member of the front office with the 2015 World Series champion Kansas City Royals.

"It was a surprise," Venafro, a self-proclaimed late bloomer as a lefty pitcher, said of being drafted.

Venafro worked his way up the minor-league ladder and made his MLB debut for Texas on April 24, 1999. In one inning out of the bullpen, he retired all three Minnesota batters he faced: Todd Walker, Torii Hunter, and Matt Lawton. "I remember being excited, very excited," he recalled.

He had been with Triple-A Oklahoma in the Texas system when he learned of his promotion. Venafro flew to Minnesota to join the Rangers.

Venafro made 65 appearances as a rookie that year and was 3-2 with an ERA of 3.29. He played for the Rangers through the 2001 season, when he pitched in 70 games out of the bullpen with four saves.

The Maryland native played for the Oakland A's in 2002, Tampa Bay in 2003, the Los Angeles Dodgers in 2004, and the Colorado Rockies in 2005.

He was teammates with former JMU pitcher Travis Harper, a product of Circleville High in West Virginia, with Tampa Bay.

"Mike was a senior when I was a freshman," Harper said of their JMU days. "I got to know him a lot better in the bullpen (in the majors). He is a dynamic person. I really enjoyed my time with him."

Venafro ended his MLB career with a record of 15-10 and had an ERA of 4.09 in 307 outings as a reliever, with five saves.

"I wanted to pitch every day. It was such a blitz" of memories, he said. "I think I am more of a day-to-day guy instead of a guy that looks back."

He was pitching at Triple-A during the 2007 season when family health concerns forced him to stop playing. After about two years away from the game, he joined the Padres as a scout 12 years ago with some help from veteran scout Toomey.

Venafro went to the winter meetings in Florida after his playing career and was able to get into pro scouting. He was hired by AJ Hinch, who used to work in the front office of the Padres and then was let go as Houston manager due to sign stealing before the 2020 season.

The JMU graduate had studied economics and social sciences while in college—Heatwole feels Venafro was bright enough to earn a living outside of baseball.

"He is just a very unique person," said Heatwole. "Not only was he intelligent about a lot of things but he was intelligent about pitching."

80

Shawn Camp, Back To Mason

Shawn Camp has indeed come home again.

After playing at Robinson High in Fairfax, he had a long career as a reliever in the Major Leagues.

Then in 2020, he became an assistant coach at George Mason University, where Camp played for Coach Bill Brown before heading to pro ball.

Camp finished his third year with the Patriots this year and his first as the Associate Head Coach under Brown. The Patriots were 23-33 overall and 13-11 in the Atlantic 10 Conference. Other state schools in the Atlantic 10 are VCU and Richmond.

"I am extremely excited to reunite with Coach Brown and the George Mason University Baseball staff," Camp said when he joined the coaching staff. "Coach Brown was a huge influence on my career as a young athlete and taught me from an early age the importance of hard work and dedication to the game of baseball. I was truly blessed to play 18 years of professional baseball and spend 11 seasons in the Major Leagues. With my experience in the game and to be able to teach collegiate players the lessons I learned is something I am looking forward to."

"I am incredibly excited to have Shawn coming back home, it is a great day for Mason Baseball," Brown said when Camp was hired. "He has a passion for teaching the art of pitching and his impact will be obvious from day one with our pitching staff. Shawn has had an impressive Major League career and will now bring a resume and expertise that is very unique to a college program. Having Shawn join our staff will also have an immediate impact on recruiting as he has developed numerous relationships with Washington, D.C. area high school and travel ball coaches. His credentials bring immediate credibility in the baseball world and his addition to our staff instantly changes the trajectory of Mason Baseball."

Washington manager Dave Martinez also praised the hiring of Camp. "I've known Shawn for many years. As I look back at our time together, I think of what a fierce competitor he was," he said in a statement. "He was always willing to learn to strive to get better. Shawn is a student of the game and developed into a team leader who was a positive influence in the clubhouse. He will be a tremendous asset to the student-athletes, the baseball program, and George Mason University."

Javier Lopez played at Fairfax High, at the University of Virginia and had a long career in the majors. A lefty reliever, Lopez won four World Series rings as a player.

"I am very happy for Shawn. Everything has come full circle for him with his return to George Mason. He is not far removed from playing so he will do an outstanding job connecting with his players. He knows the area very well and has a strong baseball acumen. Shawn has the great ability to help with the mental state of the game and with the overall preparation. He has tremendous energy and will do an outstanding job with the George Mason baseball program," Lopez said in a statement on Camp.

Camp was taken in the 16th round of the 1997 draft by the San Diego Padres and played from 1997-2014 for nine different organizations.

In his 11 seasons in the majors, Camp appeared in 541 major league games for the Royals, Rays, Blue Jays, Cubs, and Phillies. He finished his MLB career with a 29-33 record and 12 saves.

During the 2012 season, Camp led the MLB with a career-high 80 appearances for the Cubs. Camp was not surprised to see manager Dave Martinez lead the Nationals to a World Series title in 2019.

Martinez ended his major league playing career in 2001 and was getting started with coaching in 2006-07 when Shawn Camp was pitching for Tampa Bay.

"Davey would help pitchers for how to stop the running game," Camp said. "He was around the ballpark; it was what Joe [Maddon] wanted. He let him be himself. That is one thing Joe does really well: there are certain times when guys have to fall in certain lanes as coaches."

Camp was named the interim head coach at George Mason on July 8, 2022, when Brown stepped down after 41 years at the helm. Brown won 1083 games and six of his Mason players made the majors - Camp, Justin Bour, Mike Colangelo, Mike Draper, Chris O'Grady and Chris Widger.

Shawn Camp

81

Samantha Gjormand, Early Start With Baseball

It didn't take long for Samantha (Sam) Gjormand to find herself at a baseball game.

And 23 years later that is still the case for the James Madison University graduate.

Gjormand was born at a hospital in Arlington on April 29, 1999. The next day she was taken by her mother, Beth, to a baseball game in Vienna at Madison High, where her father Mark has been the head coach for more than two decades. A foul ball came her way when she was two days old and someone nearby ran over to make sure the baseball didn't hit her.

"You can quite literally say I was born into the game," said Gjormand, who just finished her first season as the Director of Operations for the baseball team at Division I College of Charleston. "We joke about that all of the time."

The Cougars were 37-20 and 19-5 in the Colonial Athletic Association this past season. College of Charleston has regularly sent several players to the pro ranks over the years.

Last summer, Gjormand was the de facto general manager of Wareham in the prestigious Cape Cod League.

She has been around baseball her whole life — even though she gave softball a whirl as a player.

"She just didn't like it," says her father, who went to Oakton High.

Gjormand's mother has been an athletic trainer at high schools after attending Madison High and West Virginia University, so sports runs deep in the family.

"I played baseball until I was 13 years old and I played softball a little bit," Sam Gjormand said. "My heart wasn't in it; I liked baseball a lot more. It drew me back. I took a big role with my dad at Madison with summer camps. I was running his summer program for him. We have a program called MVP International Athletics and we send teams overseas to play games. I took on a pretty big logistic role when that company got started in 2013. It just kind of grew. I had to do a lot of work to prove myself."

That company has led to baseball trips for her to Germany, Italy, the Czech Republic, Spain, The Netherlands, Puerto Rico, and the Dominican Republic.

Her father has known Marlin Ikenberry, the JMU coach, for many years. And Ikenberry made it clear when she was in high school he wanted her to come to Harrisonburg to work with the Dukes.

Gjormand spent four years assisting the baseball team at JMU, as she rose to the director of student managers for the Dukes this past season. Her duties also included set up and break down on games days and assisting with video and team organization.

She graduated last year with a BS in sport and recreation management.

"I was really lucky with the role they ended up letting me take," said Gjormand, who also attended a lot of Washington Nationals games at an early age since her father had prime tickets. "We were not sure what I was going to be able to do within the program. I think I worked pretty hard to earn that respect to have the on-field role that I did by my senior year. I just had a blast. I am so thankful for the opportunities they gave me. I am lucky. My dad has a lot of connections in the game."

And she has made the best of those connections and impressed those around her.

"She is very energetic about her job," said JMU slugger Chase DeLauter, who played for Orleans in the Cape Cod Baseball League last year. "You never see her in a bad mood."

"Sam is the best," says Jimmy Jackson, the Associate Head Coach/Pitching for JMU. "She does anything and everything. She went above the call. From being a coach's daughter, she has a good idea of what is needed to do. She is really persistent. From a manager's standpoint, she never looks at anything that is beneath her. She leads by example" with other student managers.

Gjormand was supposed to work for Wareham in 2020 but the pandemic wiped out the summer season in one of the top amateur circuits in the country. One of her duties last summer was as a coordinator for Major League scouts, who flock to the Cape every season.

"I got a phone call from Andrew [in 2020] and he offered me the job up here," she said of 2021 Wareham general manager Andrew Lang.

Said Lang, who played at Division III Southern Maine and is an attorney: "She has done a great job. She proved herself the first week."

More than 1,400 players from the Cape have gone on to play in the majors.

Former JMU star Scott Mackie played for Wareham in 1986-87 and Fort Defiance and JMU product Chris Huffman pitched for the Gatemen in 2012-13. Former Virginia Tech and Major League pitcher Brad Clontz was with Wareham in 1991 and University of Virginia product Pat Daneker, who also pitched in The Show, played for the Gatemen in 1995-96.

Ty McFarland, a Turner Ashby and JMU product, was with Wareham in 2012, as was former JMU pitcher Brian McNichol in the 1990s. Harrisonburg native Tyler Zombro, a Staunton High graduate, pitched for Wareham in 2015.

Gjormand has been motivated by the career of Kim Ng, who became the first general manager of a Major League team when she was hired by the Marlins last year. Other women have been hired by Major League teams to be coaches, and the Boston Red Sox hired the first Black female, Bianca Smith, to work as a coach in the minors.

"A lot of women have broken through that glass ceiling and made a name for themselves the last few years," Gjormand said.

The JMU graduate plans to put in the time that is needed.

"Any task that is thrown at me, I am going to be the hardest-working person doing it. I will do what I can to be successful and put the best product out on the field," Gjormand said.

In late June of 2022, the College of Charleston announced Gjormand would be one of the staff members out the recruiting trail for the summer – making her one of the few women to have that role at the Division I level.

Samantha Gjormand

82

Kyle Novak, Early Love Of Madison High

Kyle Novak began taking lessons when he was about 10 from Mark "Pudge" Gjormand, who would later become his coach at James Madison High in Vienna.

The Novak family eventually moved from Great Falls to Oakton and the left-handed hitter became a four-year player for the Warhawks, who have produced dozens of college and pro players for several decades.

Gjormand was recently inducted into the National High School Baseball Coaches Association Hall of Fame and the school has won three state titles in the last 20 years under his leadership.

Overall, Madison has won five state titles – the most of any school in the Northern Region.

Novak certainly knew about the legacy at Madison High, which has produced four Major League players: Mike Wallace, Jay Franklin, Jim McNamara, and Bob Brower.

Wallace was drafted in the fourth round by the Phillies in 1969 and pitched in the majors from 1973-77. The second overall pick in 1971, Franklin pitched in three games that season for San Diego.

Brower went on to play at Duke and was an outfielder with

Texas from 1986-89. A catcher, McNamara saw action with San Francisco from 1992-93 after playing in the Valley Baseball League while in college.

"I grew up watching Madison High baseball games since I was 12 years old," Novak said. "I went to Madison High and that was the best decision I ever made."

One of the Madison High products that Novak remembers watching as a young boy was Andy McGuire, who was drafted out of high school by the Rockies in 2013 but opted to play at the University of Texas.

McGuire signed with the Blue Jays five years later after going in the 28th round of the draft. He reached the Single-A level with Toronto and played independent ball in 2021 with Kane County in Illinois.

"When he was a sophomore, I was probably 13. When you are that young, every guy in high school looks like they are men," Novak said.

Zach Perkins grew up in Vienna and also played at Madison High. As a young boy, he recalls getting the autograph of Kyle Werman, who played at the University of Virginia, in the Appalachian League in the Mets' system in 2005 and later became the coach at La Salle in Philadelphia.

Kyle Novak led the CAA in RBI in 2022 while playing for JMU.

"Growing up in Vienna, every kid wanted to play at Madison," said Perkins, who hit .339 this past season for Washington & Lee University in Lexington.

Novak, meanwhile, has become one of the most consistent hitters in recent years for JMU in Harrisonburg.

In April of this season, Novak reached base for the 35th game in a row to set a JMU record.

Novak hit .303 as a freshman in 2019, .317 as a sophomore, and

.315 last year as a junior at the Harrisonburg school. This season he batted .292 and had a team-high 49 RBI while starting all 53 games for the Dukes.

"He is a professional hitter," said Marlin Ikenberry, the JMU head coach. "He has been a workhorse all year and has been consistent for us all year."

Novak is one of several Madison High graduates who has played for Ikenberry during his coaching stints at VMI and JMU.

Another Madison High grad with JMU this year was Ryan Murphy, a sophomore pitcher.

Kyle Hayes, another Madison High alum, played in college at JMU and is now a catcher in the Kansas City minor league system. He was with Columbia when his team had a series in Salem against the Boston affiliate in early June.

Infielder James Triantos was drafted in the second round by the Cubs last year out of Madison High and began this season at Single-A Myrtle Beach.

He is aiming to be the fifth Major League player to come out of the prep powerhouse in Vienna. He was hitting .309 in June after batting .327 in his pro debut in 2021 at the rookie-level in Arizona.

"I think he coaches his guys hard and prepares them," Ikenberry said of Gjormand. "Baseball is a hard game anyway but he prepares them to execute and compete. That is what you want out of a high school player coming to college."

Novak has one more year of eligibility left for college; he is playing this summer in a wooden-bat league for a team in Vermont. Novak went to the Dominican Republic in 2018 and on other trips with MVP International, which was founded by Gjormand. (Note: Novak's mother, Tara, works for MVP International, as does this reporter, Driver, on a part-time basis.)

The Vienna Inn, on Maple Avenue near Madison High, is a popular spot for fans of the Warhawks before and after games. The eatery opened in the 1960s in Vienna and owner Marty Volk is a big fan of Madison.

83

Brandon Guyer, Hometown Hornet

It was less than 20 years ago that Brandon Guyer graduated from Herndon High and headed south to Charlottesville to begin his college baseball career. The move paid off well.

Guyer was drafted in the fifth round out of the University of Virginia in 2007 by the Chicago Cubs.

He worked his way up through the minors then before the 2011 season was traded by the Cubs to Tampa Bay.

The outfielder made his Major League debut for Tampa Bay on May 6 of that season. Playing before family and friends in Baltimore, Guyer hit a homer off Zack Britton in his first game as Tampa Bay beat the Orioles.

Guyer was traded by Tampa Bay to Cleveland during the 2016 season and that turned out well for the Herndon High product.

He played in all seven games of the World Series in 2016 for the Indians against the Cubs, who won in seven games. Guyer hit .300 in the Fall Classic against his former organization.

He ended his Major League career in 2018 with Cleveland. Guyer was released by the Giants before the 2020 season.

He is married to the former Lindsay Murphy, who was working

as a sports broadcaster for Channel 7 in Washington when they met. Murphy interviewed Guyer when he was at the University of Virginia.

These days, Guyer by his own social media account is a "Former MLB player turned Mental Skills Coach now helping athletes excel ON and OFF the field with a Major League Mindset. Welcome To Excellence." He can be reached at brandonguyer.com.

His alma mater continues to produce quality baseball.

Herndon High upset Colgan in the state semifinals and then lost 2-1 to Freedom of South Riding on June 11 in the Class 6 title contest the next day.

It was Freedom/South Riding that advanced to the Little League World Series in Pennsylvania in 2019. Tuckahoe of Richmond lost to Japan in 1968 in the title game of the Little League World Series.

That Virginia team included Pennington Gap native Jim Pankovits, who went on to play at Douglas Freeman, the University of South Carolina, and for the Astros and Red Sox in the majors.

Freedom was second in the final Top of The Washington Post baseball poll in 2022 and that includes schools from Maryland and D.C. Herndon was No. 8 and Colgan was No. 9.

Another top program for years in Northern Virginia is West Springfield High. Former coach Ron Tugwell won more than 400 games with the Spartans and one of his players, Joe Saunders, pitched at Virginia Tech and in the Major Leagues.

The University of Virginia announced on Sept. 23, 2022, that Guyer "is is joining our staff as our newest resource to help our players maximize their full potential through his Major League Mindset training program."

84

Transplants

Ryan Zimmerman and David Wright both grew up in the Tidewater region of the state and both became All-Star third basemen in the majors. Both also have spent a lot of time in Northern Virginia during and after their careers. Zimmerman and his wife, Heather, put their Great Falls home on the market in April, according to published reports.

Wright, meanwhile, spent significant time in Northern Virginia during his career with the New York Mets as his team would fly into area airports before and after a series with the Nationals at either RFK Stadium or Nationals Park. He began his career in the majors with the Mets in 2004.

Before Wright embarked on a 14-year major league career and became known as Captain America, he was blessed to play in a Hampton Roads area that was as good a place as any in the U.S. to learn the game of baseball.

"This community has raised me and introduced me to a support system that lasted my entire career and continues to show me love and support," Wright said in 2022 in his induction speech at the Virginia Sports Hall of Fame in Virginia Beach.

The 6-foot, 205-pound Wright wasn't the biggest or tallest player growing up, but his work ethic helped him star at Chesapeake's Hickory High. The New York Mets took him in the supplemental first round of the 2001 draft (38th overall), and he went on to play his entire career in their organization. He's the franchise's all-time leader in numerous categories, including wins above replacement (49.2), at-bats (5,998), runs (949), hits (1,777), doubles (390), and RBI (970). Wright's 242 home runs trail only Darryl Strawberry's 252 in Mets history.

In his career, Wright hit .296, had a .376 on-base percentage, and slugged .491. He was a seven-time All-Star, four-time top-10 NL MVP vote-getter, two-time Gold Glove winner, two-time Silver Slugger winner and two-time Home Run Derby champion. Wright earned his patriotic nickname when he led the 2013 World Baseball Classic with 10 RBI for the U.S. team.

Wright said in his state Hall of Fame induction speech that he started to have big-league dreams after seeing Michael Cuddyer, of Chesapeake's Great Bridge High, go in the first round of the 1997 draft. By the time Wright made the Mets in 2004, he was part of a cadre of Hampton Roads players in the major leagues.

"We'd beat our chest pretty hard when we'd meet in center field and shake hands with the other guys from the area because it meant a lot that this relatively small area of the country created such great baseball players and athletes in general," Wright said. "I think we wore that with a badge of honor that we took to heart, and we were very proud about that."

Wright and his wife, Molly Beers, continue to make an impact in the area. The eighth-floor playroom at the Children's Hospital of the King's Daughters in Norfolk is named in their honor. He is among the leaders among Virginia natives in career homers.

Willie Horton hit 325 in his career while Justin Upton, a Norfolk native, also had 325 as of July 7. Upton hit a homer in early July with Seattle to tie Horton.

85

Brian McNichol, Wrigley Field, Tragedy

After getting called up to the Major Leagues, Gar-Field High grad Brian McNichol took a flight from Edmonton to Chicago and was dropped off by a taxi driver in front of storied Wrigley Field.

The lefty pitcher had to convince stadium staff he was starting pitcher for the Cubs in the nightcap of a doubleheader after spending several years in the minors. "I need to get there because I am starting the second game," he told anyone within earshot.

The Fairfax native finally made it to the home clubhouse. It was on Sept. 7, 1999—about four years after he was drafted out of JMU by the Cubs.

In his first MLB outing, McNichol gave up six runs on eight hits (including three homers) in four innings and suffered the loss, 10-3 to Cincinnati. McNichol's LinkedIn bio in the past has noted the scorecard from that game, which featured Sammy Sosa as the starting right fielder for the Cubs.

Shaun O'Neal was among former JMU teammates who were at that game. "I would follow all of his (pro) starts," said O'Neal, who used to work in the front office of the Frederick (Md.) Keys in the minors and had access to such details back then.

McNichol fared much better in his second MLB start and fourth appearance overall in what turned out to be his last game in The Show on Sept. 30 of that year. Starting in Philadelphia, he gave up just two runs in five innings but was charged with the 2-1 loss to the Phillies at old Veterans Stadium. Unfortunately, it turned out to be his last game in the majors.

McNichol went to spring training the following year, in 2000, hoping to make the Cubs' Opening Day roster. But the team had fired manager Jim Riggleman and brought in skipper Don Baylor, whose staff didn't give McNichol many looks during spring training in Arizona. McNichol was back at Triple-A Iowa in 2000 and spent the next six seasons in the minors with several organizations trying to get back to the bright lights of The Show.

After pitching for the Orioles' Triple-A team in Ottawa in 2005, the former Dukes' standout called it a career. He was 0-2 with an ERA of 6.75 in the majors with the Cubs. In 10 seasons in the minors, he won 59 games in 290 appearances, with 124 starts, and posted an ERA of 4.38.

By the end of his career, McNichol, now 48, had settled in Arizona after spending a lot of time there in spring training with the Cubs.

McNichol got married in 2001 and he and his former wife had a son and daughter. Tragedy, however, struck less than two years ago. His son, Ryley, was killed in a car accident at the age of 13 on the way to hockey practice on January 16, 2019, in Phoenix. McNichol was driving as the only other person in the vehicle and suffered injuries, including to his hip and a concussion. His son, who also played baseball, would have been 15 next month.

"He was a stud," said McNichol.

"He had a tragedy, I reached out to him," said Shenandoah University Coach Kevin Anderson, his former pitching coach and head coach at JMU.

After taking time off following the death of his son, McNichol—who had divorced in 2016—has returned to coaching baseball to youth in his area. McNichol has given private coaching lessons for several years and works mostly with high-school players.

"I really enjoy it. I have done lessons; I stick with a core group of about five kids who are good," he said from Arizona. "I talk to them differently if you will, about facing different hitters and see what their baseball IQ is. I enjoy that."

McNichol also took some time professionally and took a job as a salesman for a real estate company—Destin—in Arizona. He has worked in sales in the past.

McNichol grew up in Woodbridge. His sister, who also attended Gar-Field High, has worked for the FBI.

After looking at schools such as Clemson, Virginia Tech, VCU and Radford, McNichol headed to Harrisonburg to play for the Dukes. As a freshman, the JMU coach was Ray Heatwole. He then played for Anderson as a sophomore and junior.

"He was the hardest worker on his craft than anyone I had," said Anderson. "He did countless hours on aerobics, long toss and video. He eventually developed a change up (at JMU) and his fast-ball kept getting better and better and better. Then he developed a slider that had real good bite to it. It is a tribute to good old-fashioned work."

As a junior in 1995, he was part of a JMU team that featured two other future MLB pitchers: Mike Venafro, a senior from Chantilly; and freshman Travis Harper, who was born in Harrisonburg.

Another member of the 1995 team was sophomore pitcher O'Neal, who has remained good friends with McNichol. "There were several times my junior year I would pop out of the dugout to throw and scouts would perk up since they thought I was Brian. We were the same height and about the same weight," O'Neal said.

While at JMU, McNichol pitched in the Valley Baseball League for the Winchester Royals. He was the highest pick in JMU history when he was taken in the second round in 1995 as the 34th overall pick.

"Left-hander from JMU, made it to the big leagues," recalled Billy Swoope, the Cubs' scout that signed him.

McNichol began his pro career in 1995 in Williamsport, Pa., in the New York-Penn League and three years later he was at Double-A, where he won a career-high 12 games with West Tenn. He was with Triple-A Iowa late in that 1999 season when manager Terry Kennedy told him he was being promoted to the majors for the first time.

But on that day in September, Kennedy also informed McNichol he was starting for Iowa and would throw about 35 pitches since he would start the second game of a nightcap for the Cubs a few days later.

"I hit a guy, gave up a triple and two walks," McNichol said of that rough Triple-A outing.

The lefty retired just one batter before he was lifted by Kennedy, a former Orioles catcher. A few days later he was in Chicago, pitching for the Cubs in his first MLB appearance.

"Steve Stone (on Cubs TV) said 'In his last start he lasted a third of an inning.' That was funny," McNichol said.

But at least he had made it to the majors—if only for four games.

Brian McNichol (center), with his fiance Stephanie Flaherty and daughter, Mia, 13,

86

Jin Wong, A World Series Ring

Jin Wong, a graduate of the University of Mary Washington, has been part of the front office of the Kansas City Royals for several years as Vice President, Assistant General Manager: Baseball Administration.

He works under President of Baseball Operations Dayton Moore, a former infielder at George Mason University.

It will be hard to top what happened for Wong and the Royals in 2015 as the Royals won the World Series over the New York Mets. It was the first time for Kansas City in 30 years. "It was overwhelming," Wong said.

As for the victory parade, which he participated in with his wife, Libby, and sons Kai and Tate, "It was an amazing sight to see. Fans came out in droves. A championship brings every walk of life together. Everyone was wearing Royals blue," Wong added. "I could not be more proud to be a part of it."

A former All-American as a center fielder at the University of Mary Washington, Wong – who grew up in Northern Virginia – had gone to Atlanta as a college senior for a job interview with Hall of Famer Hank Aaron, the late slugger of the Braves.

Wong became a baseball operations trainee with Atlanta, then landed a position with the minor league Richmond Braves, as a group sales manager. At one of the games, he crossed paths with Moore.

Moore, who was working in the front office of the Atlanta Braves, was in Richmond to see the minor league affiliate. He let Wong know that a job was open with the Royals as Scouting Operations Coordinator. He got the job, and has steadily moved up during the past two decades in the Royals' organization.

"Jin is a tremendously driven and detailed individual who has talents that extend to all areas of a major league front office," said Scott Sharp, who works in the front office of the Royals.

The Royals will have more Virginia ties in 2023. While Moore was let go by the team in September, the Royals hired former Tampa Bay bench coach and ex-ODU standout Matt Quatraro as their manager in early November.

Jin Wong

87

Al Bumbry, Aided Last
Orioles Champs

The Baltimore Orioles had a strong Virginia connection in the 1970s and 1980s.

That included pitcher Ken Dixon, who grew up near Lynchburg, and outfielder Larry Sheets, who was born in Staunton. Dick Bowie, the late Baltimore scout, spent a lot of time in Virginia back in those days.

And one of the players he scouted was Al Bumbry, who was born in Fredericksburg and went to Ralph Bunche High in King George.

Bumbry headed to Virginia State to play basketball and didn't play baseball until his senior year.

"Teaching didn't dawn on me until after my second year in school and I began thinking about what I'd be doing after I got out," he told the Society of American Baseball Research. "The more I thought about it, the less I wanted to teach."

Bowie saw Bumbry play and the outfielder was taken in the 11th round in 1968. Bumbry spent time in Vietnam in the U.S. military and was awarded for his actions there.

He broke in with the Orioles in 1972 then led the league in triples with 11 the next year.

Bumbry was the starting center fielder for Baltimore in 1979 as the Orioles beat the Angels for the American League pennant, then lost in seven games to the Pirates in the World Series.

He led the league in hits with 205 in 1980 as the Orioles won 100 games. But the Yankees won 103 and captured the American League East title.

The Orioles got back to the World Series in 1983 and this time, with Bumbry spending time in center along with John Shelby, Baltimore beat the Phillies for the title in five games.

Bumbry was with the Orioles the next year and then ended his career with the Padres in 1985.

He had 254 steals, among the most of any Virginia native. His son, Steve, played baseball at Virginia Tech.

Al Bumbry

88

Brady House, Nats' Phenom

In spring training this year, Brady House told us he was able to meet Major Leaguer Carter Kieboom in West Palm Beach, Florida.

The Nationals certainly hope the career of House doesn't have the twists and turns that have hit Kieboom, a first-round pick out of a Georgia high school by Washington in 2016.

Kieboom has been hit by injuries the past few years and will miss all of this season after playing in 62 games for the Nationals last year.

The sky appears to be the limit for House, also a first-round pick out of a Georgia high school by Washington. Drafted last year by the Nationals, House was bringing fans to their feet in Fredericksburg this year at Single-A games at the new stadium just off I-95.

"The only way to describe it was learning," House said of Spring Training. House played mostly shortstop early on for Fredericksburg.

After a torrid start at the plate, he was batting .278 with three homers and 31 RBI with an OPS of .731 in his first 176 at-bats.

The pitching coach this year for Fredericksburg is Joel Hanrahan, a former reliever for the Nationals.

Among his three top starters early on at the Single-A level were Rodney Theophile, Dustin Saenz, and Andry Lara.

Lara made two starts last season for Fredericksburg while Saenz was taken in the fourth round out of Texas A&M last year.

"There is a lot of big, physical arms" in the system, Hanrahan said after a light workout for pitchers. Hanrahan was formerly a minor league pitching coach in the Pittsburgh system.

Theophile had an ERA of 1.29 in nine starts for Fredericksburg before he was promoted to Wilmington in June.

Brady House

The manager for the Virginia team is Jake Lowery, who finished his playing career at Double-A Harrisburg in 2019 in the Washington system.

Lowery also had House when both were with the Florida Complex League team last year.

A standout catcher at JMU, Lowery went to Cosby High near Richmond. "A first-rounder for a reason," Lowery said of House.

Former JMU infielder Jeff Garber, an instructor with the Nationals, also worked with House last year in Florida. House went on the 7-day Injured List on June 23, 2022, and didn't play in a game the rest of the season for Fredericksburg.

The Single-A farm team of the Nationals was knocked out of the playoffs by Lynchburg, who lost in the championship series to the Charleston (SC) RiverDogs.

Cortland Lawson was an infielder from Virginia who hit .167 in his first season in the minors with Fredericksburg. He went to high school at Paul VI in Fairfax and Dominion in Loudoun County and was drafted by Washington out of the University of Tennessee in the 14th round in the summer of 2022.

89

Gregg Ritchie, From Pirates
To GW

Not many people would leave a job in the Major Leagues for a college post.

But that is what Gregg Ritchie did and the move has worked out.

A former hitting coach for the Pittsburgh Pirates, Ritchie just finished his 10th season as the head coach at George Washington University of the Atlantic 10 Conference.

The Colonials were 22-30 and 10-14 in conference play in 2022 and he has helped several players sign pro contracts during his decade in Foggy Bottom, the GW neighborhood near the White House.

North Stafford High School graduate Ritchie had a long pro career as a minor league player and coach but didn't lose touch with GW.

"I have kept myself part of GW. I was always a part of it. You never get far away. I never left," said Ritchie, who would return to the school in the off-season to help out with former coaches John Castleberry, Jay Murphy, Tom Walter and Steve Mrowka.

Ritchie spent the previous two Major League seasons as the

hitting coach for the Pittsburgh Pirates, and before that he was a minor league instructor with the Pirates and Chicago White Sox.

"GW is heading in a good direction and I am glad to be a part of it. GW is making a huge commitment to athletics, and not just baseball," Ritchie said when he got hired. "My family is involved a lot more in my life now" than when he was a pro instructor.

The Colonials have sent several former players and coaches to the professional ranks. That list includes former players Mike O'Connor, who pitched in the big leagues for Washington; John Flaherty, an ex-big league catcher; and Sam Perlozzo, the former manager of the Baltimore Orioles.

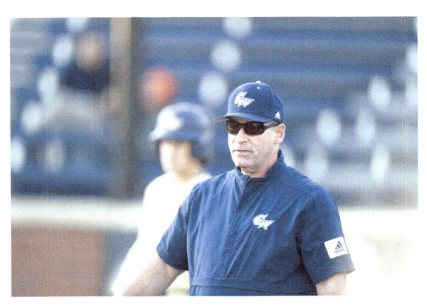

Gregg Ritchie has been the head coach at GWU for more than a decade. He is a graduate of North Stafford High School

Former GW head coach Mike Toomey was a long-time pro scout and John Castleberry, another former head coach for the Colonials, is a veteran pro scout. Scott Sharp, a former GW catcher, has worked for years in the front office of the Royals.

"I have spoken to a lot of alumni," Sharp, a former minor

league catcher who grew up in Maryland, said. "We were really excited when Gregg got the position."

Ritchie took over for Mrowka, who was let go after the 2012 season.

"The GW community is excited to welcome Gregg back to Foggy Bottom," noted former George Washington President Steven Knapp when Ritchie was hired. "His experience as a professional coach and player will be a tremendous asset to our program."

"Gregg's ability to teach the game was evident even when he was playing at GW," said in a statement former teammate, Major Leaguer and GW Athletic Hall of Famer John Flaherty, who served on a search committee to identify GW's new baseball coach. "I've had the opportunity not only to play with him at GW, but to observe his career while we were both playing professionally."

The move to GW certainly worked out well for Ritchie and his family.

He has won more than 250 games in his 10 years with the D.C. school.

90

Ken Califano, Veteran MLB Scout

After more than 10 years as a scout for the Houston Astros, Ken Califano changed teams as a veteran pro baseball scout.

The former Stafford resident joined Tampa Bay as a scout in 2015 and once again this season has done pro coverage for the Rays.

Tampa Bay has excelled in scouting and player development while competing in the American League East with the New York Yankees and Boston Red Sox – teams with a lot more money to spend than Tampa Bay.

"I have most of the teams in the mid-Atlantic," Califano said soon after he joined Tampa Bay. "I have the Washington Nationals, from the major league team on down to their teams" in the low minors.

Califano graduated from Milford Mill High near Baltimore in 1971 and played amateur baseball for Walter Youse, a long-time scouting legend, in 1972. He played in the minors with the Orioles in 1973 and 1974.

His son, DJ, played baseball and football and ran track at North Stafford High School and graduated from George Mason University. Califano's daughter, Kerri, played softball and tennis in high school.

Califano moved to Aberdeen, Maryland, several years ago in order to be closer to extended family. The director of pro scouting for the Rays is Kevin Ibach, who used to work for the Orioles.

Califano said he drives about 25,000 miles each year for coverage of games in the mid-Atlantic region.

"We have to report on everybody (in the minors), whether they are the best player or worst player," he said. "When you make trades, you go through reports and there will be multiple scouts seeing each player."

Among the many players Califano has scouted was John Maine, a graduate of North Stafford High who played in college at Charlotte before he was drafted by the Orioles. Maine pitched in the Major Leagues for Baltimore and the New York Mets from 2004-10 and he posted a record of 41-36.

The Rays lost to the Dodgers in the World Series in 2020.

Tampa Bay has had several players with Virginia ties on the 40-man roster the past few seasons.

That includes slugger Brandon Lowe, a Virginia native; lefty pitcher Ryan Yarbrough; and Mike Brosseau, who played for Waynesboro in the Valley Baseball League in 2016 and was traded to the Brewers prior to this year.

Lowe went on the Injured List earlier this year while ODU product Yarbrough was sent back to Triple-A Durham after a rough start. The pitcher played for Luray in 2012 in the Valley Baseball League.

91

Division III Power

Ray Hedrick has been involved in baseball at three key regions of Virginia.

He was born in Springfield in Northern Virginia and was the coach of the New Market Rebels in Valley Baseball in 2003 when one of his players was Brett Gardner, who would have a long career as an outfielder for the New York Yankees.

But it is the small city north of Richmond where Hedrick has made his mark at Division III Randolph-Macon.

"What Ray has done there is pretty crazy," said Travis Beazley, one of his former players who went on to pitch in the minors.

Hedrick just finished his 18th season as the head coach at Randolph-Macon, part of a strong Division III Old Dominion Athletic Conference.

The Yellow Jackets were 26-12 overall and 14-6 in the ODAC this past season while Hunter Cole, from Granby High, led the team with nine homers and a batting average of .424.

"Macon has been the barometer, the measuring stick" in the ODAC, noted Beazley.

Randolph-Macon has certainly set the standard in the ODAC,

which sent Shenandoah and Lynchburg to the national tournament this year.

Under Hedrick, the Yellow Jackets have won more than 400 games, have made five NCAA appearances, and advanced to the College World Series in 2018.

The Virginia resident has been the Coach of the Year in Virginia five times and three times in the ODAC. After playing at Randolph-Macon, Hedrick worked for the Double-A Bowie Baysox of the Baltimore system

Among the former Yellow Jackets to play at the pro level include Beazley, who pitched in the Red Sox farm system; and pitcher Nick Roth, who was drafted by the Orioles out of Ashland in 2019.

Beazley has been part of the coaching staff at Lynchburg for several years, and Roth had pitched in nine games out of the bullpen for Single-A Aberdeen in Maryland through mid-June of 2022.

After an injury at Methodist, Beazley didn't play for two years before doing a year at a community college. He eventually returned to Ashland – where Beazley went to high school at Patrick Henry.

"I was at Macon for three years and I played for Ray for two years," Beazley said. "He was awesome; he was exactly what we needed. He was really tough. The program needed a little bit of culture change. Ray scared us, he was intense. The culture changed immediately year one; we were certainly better. My senior year we made the NCAA tournament for the first time in a long time."

While in the minors, Beazley worked out with Chris Ray, a product of William and Mary and a former closer with the Orioles.

"Ray was really cool about that," said Beazley, who was drafted by Boston in 2006.

The head coach at Lynchburg is Lucas Jones, a former assistant for the Yellow Jackets. "That is how we connected," said Beazley, who reached the Double-A level with the Red Sox in 2009 as a pitcher after playing infield early in his college career.

The top pitcher in 2022 for Randolph-Macon was Hayden

Snelsire, who paced the team in wins with six and innings pitched with 60.2.

Several former Macon assistants have gone on to the Division I level and some are pro scouts.

The Yellow Jackets are certainly strong in other sports as well. The men's basketball team, for instance, won the Division III national title for the first time in 2022.

Travis Beazley (left) went to high school and college in Ashland and is an assistant coach at Lynchburg

92

Josh Tutwiler, Survivor Story
For Ex-VCU Coach

(Editor's note: We end up where we started – in the state capital – for perhaps one of the most inspiring baseball stories we have heard.)

Josh Tutwiler, a former suburban and city Richmond resident, took a drive in September of 2012 after a life-changing event.

That drive back to Virginia, with his former girlfriend, came after he almost lost his life in a fall while hiking in Missouri.

"I was in Missouri visiting my girlfriend at the time. She was getting her doctorate in physical therapy from the University of Missouri," said Tutwiler, a baseball standout at ODU and ex-VCU assistant coach.

On a Sunday, they were near the end of a hike of about eight miles when they stopped to admire the view.

"I climbed up the side of the bluff as part of the trail," he said. "I kind of pitched forward. ... I went out over the edge and fell about 40 feet. I went through a tree and landed on an outcrop about six or seven feet around. I looked out over the edge and there was another drop."

His former girlfriend went to her car to call 911, and emergency personnel arrived. "I broke my neck in four places," he said.

During the ordeal, Tutwiler—whose Christian faith is very important to him—said he heard a distinct voice three times that guided his thoughts and actions. He also thought of his high school friend, Eli Lehman, who died in a fall in Nelson County in 2010.

Tutwiler was eventually taken to the hospital at the University of Missouri campus and had two surgeries in the days after his fall.

Five days after the fall, he was discharged from the hospital in Missouri and began the drive back to the Shenandoah Valley with his parents, Don and Vickie.

When Tutwiler met his regular physician, Dr. Ronald Schubert, in Dayton less than two weeks after the fall he was told he was lucky to be alive.

"I grew up in the church, but the fall (and recovery) certainly strengthened my faith," Tutwiler said.

A few months later, Tutwiler was in the first-base coaching box for William & Mary when the Tribe began the 2013 season at powerhouse Clemson.

Tutwiler grew up in Bridgewater, and after leaving Turner Ashby High in 2007, he played at St. John's in New York, a junior college in Tennessee, and then was an all-Colonial Athletic Association catcher at ODU.

He was the offensive MVP of Staunton in the Valley Baseball League in 2011 and was later part of the coaching staff for Waynesboro when the Generals won the league title in 2014. Tutwiler also played for the Harrisonburg Turks while he was in college, in 2008.

Tutwiler has been around baseball since a young age, as his father also played baseball at TA, in the early 1970s.

"That is something that comes from my dad and grandfather; I am sure that is genetic in my blood," Tutwiler said of baseball. "There is no shortage of baseball; I played in the County League before I could drive."

He played in the Rockingham County Baseball League for Broadway and Clover Hill.

Tutwiler graduated from ODU in 2012 with a degree in Political Science and a minor in Philosophy of Religious Studies.

Less than two years ago, Tutwiler learned about a job with RMC Events through Dan Schmitt, who founded the company in 1999 and now has about 2,000 employees.

They also connected via the Center for Sport Leadership (CSL) at VCU, where the TA graduate got his master's degree in 2017. Schmitt was the former president of Glen Allen Youth Athletics near Richmond, where his two children and wife have been involved in the past. Schmitt's son, Carter, plans to play baseball at Randolph-Macon in the spring of 2023.

"We would always run a baseball camp through VCU in the summer at Glen Allen, and he was my point of contact there," said Tutwiler, now an accounts manager for RMC.

Schmitt said RMC Events has worked with JMU for nearly a decade but never had an employee with an office on campus. RMC has offices in Charlottesville and Mechanicsville.

"I think (RMC) is a good fit for him. I think he is looking to expand his career," Schmitt said. "Coaching baseball is probably a blast, and he was very good at it. This is a way to stay uniquely attached in the industry, to sports. I think this will fulfill some of those needs to be around sports."

For now, the new team for Tutwiler is RMC Events.

"It was almost too good to be true," he said of the new job that brought him back to his roots.

Tutwiler had been part of the coaching staff at VCU since 2016 before taking the job with RMC.

Before that, he was a coach with William & Mary for three years after playing in college at the Division I level at St. John's and ODU.

RMC Events is also very involved with events at the University of Virginia, wineries in the region, and other schools and locales around the state. His office is at the Atlantic Union Bank Center on the JMU campus.

"It wasn't something I was actually pursuing too much," Tutwiler said. "The job came open, and it was a great company that I never heard anyone say anything negative about. We are unarmed security; we help events run smoothly for the clients."

"He is engaging. He gains energy from other people. That is critical in this field," Schmitt said. "He has always been a detail guy."

And very fortunate, for which Tutwiler is grateful.

Josh Tutwiler was a standout player at ODU and coached at VCU.

Afterword

By David Driver

Ray Heatwole walked slowly into Veterans Memorial Park at James Madison University in Harrisonburg early in the 2022 baseball season, heading to yet another college baseball game in his native Shenandoah Valley.

"I don't know about places like Chicago and Los Angeles," he told me. "But we have it pretty good here."

Standing just a few miles east of where he grew up, Heatwole wasn't talking about a comparison in the housing market, crime, or even the cost of a gallon of milk.

Heatwole was discussing what he knows best—baseball, specifically amateur baseball in the Valley. And his knowledge has been passed on to several generations, with Heatwole's grandson—Justin Showalter—a regular starting pitcher in 2022 for JMU.

Without ever having to leave his native county, Heatwole was the head baseball coach at three schools within just a few miles of each other: Turner Ashby High School, Division III Bridgewater College, and Division I JMU.

And he pointed out that in addition to three colleges in the

Harrisonburg area, the aforementioned two and Eastern Mennonite University, the Valley Baseball League and Rockingham County Baseball League (RCBL) have been around for nearly a century in the same area.

Heatwole (pictured on the cover), whose father was a farmer in Rockingham County, is a product of a region that is crazy about baseball. He played at Turner Ashby, then performed in three sports at Bridgewater, including as captain of the baseball team.

As a coach, he led Bridgewater to the Virginia College Athletic Association title in 1973. He later took the helm at Turner Ashby, posting a record of 303-66-2 in 17 seasons and winning three of the school's seven state championships. Turner Ashby's baseball field is named for him, and he was inducted into the school's Hall of Fame in 2006. He was the assistant coach at JMU from 1986 to 1989 before taking over for Brad Babcock and guiding the Dukes from 1990 to 1993.

In addition:

*Heatwole, hesitant to talk about his honors, received the Virginia High School Coaches Association Distinguished Service Award in 1985.

*in 2002, he was named the High School Coach of the Year by the Middle Atlantic Baseball Scouts Association and was honored at an event in Baltimore that this reporter attended.

*Heatwole was inducted into the Bridgewater College Hall of Fame in 2008 and is also in the Virginia High School League Hall of Fame.

Tyler Bocock played at TA but not for Heatwole. But his father, Mike, played for the veteran mentor and so did two uncles: Tom Bocock, who played in the minors for the Cardinals, and brother Tim.

So the former Stetson player has heard plenty of stories about Heatwole.

"Basically an extended family member," says Tyler Bocock, sitting in the bleachers at Clover Hill before his game in the Rockingham County Baseball League. "He is THE baseball guy – he is the godfather of baseball around here."

Bocock is a former assistant coach at Sarasota High in Florida to long-time coach Clyde Metcalf, who retired in the spring of 2022 after two national titles and a slew of players sent to the Major Leagues.

In some way, Bocock compares the Sarasota program to TA – and vice versa. "Of course, they play all year in Florida," Tyler Bocock noted.

Along with those honors, perhaps the Heatwole legacy comes down to this: He has had a hand in the development of nearly every future Major Leaguer to come out of the central Shenandoah Valley since the 1970s.

Of the 12 JMU players to make the Majors, seven of them were there during the same time as Heatwole. While at Turner Ashby, he coached Alan Knicely — the first graduate of the school to make The Show.

Heatwole even had a role in the development of Larry Sheets, who played eight years in the Major Leagues, including 1987, when he was named the Baltimore Orioles' Most Valuable Player. In high school, Sheets played at Turner Ashby rival Robert E. Lee (now Staunton), but he spent a summer with American Legion Post 27 in Harrisonburg when Heatwole was the coach there.

In the Valley League, Heatwole made the drive out Route 33 east to coach Madison County, and one of his players was Chris Finwood, the long-time head coach at Old Dominion University. All told, Heatwole coached at least 30 players who signed to play at the pro level.

At Turner Ashby, I got an inside view of Heatwole at work, though I played a very small role as a marginal high school player.

I was a reserve outfielder for the junior varsity team in 1977 and 1978 when Heatwole was the varsity coach. As a junior, I was a reserve outfielder for a rare TA team that didn't win the Valley District title.

The following year, I was fortunate to split time as a starter between third base and left field as we won the 1980 Valley District crown. We twice beat a Western Albemarle team that was probably better at us at nearly every position. I'm pretty sure the Crozet team was out-coached.

What I saw in those years is that a lot of the credit for Turner Ashby's success could be attributed to the emphasis by Heatwole and his long-time assistant, Bobby Scott, on teaching the fundamentals of the game. It also helped that Clint Curry, then a sophomore, hit two homers in a victory at Western Albemarle in 1980. Two years later, he would be drafted in the third round by the Texas Rangers.

Heatwole and Scott were actually at their best before the season began, on cold days in February when we had to practice at the old school gym in Dayton. Sometimes those practices were before school at 6 a.m. since the girls and boys basketball teams needed the small arena for practice or a game after school. (Note: Turner Ashby is now in Bridgewater.)

With a batting cage at one corner and a pitching machine set up in the middle of the hardwood floor, we practiced hitting and bunting over and over again. In another corner was an elevated mound, where pitchers got in their work before heading outside when the weather warmed up a few weeks later.

It wasn't a practice — it was a three-hour clinic every day.

Heatwole was demanding to play for, certainly. I remember hearing the story—while on the JV team—when he made the varsity stay after a game and take batting practice after a low-hitting win over rival Broadway, at the time not known for baseball prowess. But Heatwole also made you show up in his office the morning after grades came out to let him know where you stood academically.

Another story stands out from that 1980 season.

As one of three senior captains, I struck out all three times I appeared at the plate in a win over rival Harrisonburg on a Friday night as the starting left fielder. I spent all weekend in my room in frustration — certainly worrying my parents.

Back at school on Monday, I went to Heatwole's office before classes began and suggested that since I wasn't hitting worth a lick, he should replace me in left field with a junior who had a much better batting average.

I don't remember the words of Heatwole exactly, but basically, he said: "You have been in this program for four years, and I am sticking with you."

A few games later, we were eliminated in the regional tournament at old Memorial Stadium in Harrisonburg by George Mason High, a school from Falls Church that had a solid left-handed pitcher named Bob Tuthill.

I recall striking out with runners on second and third base to end one inning in the shutout loss.

In two varsity seasons, I had about 70 at-bats with an average well below the Mendoza line. I would only play one season past high school, at Division III Eastern Mennonite University, but those four years under Heatwole, though I didn't realize it at the time, certainly aided my life and career as a baseball writer.

I learned so much about the game, and that was so helpful while covering professional baseball for several publications over the years.

But I had known of the legacy Heatwole was building at TA well before I played for him, while I was a student at Dayton Elementary, which in the 1970s was right across the street from the old baseball/football field at the high school.

Back then, senior graduation was on June 1, and it seemed that most years, on that day the TA baseball team was playing for a state title in some part of Virginia.

Baseball was so big that WSVA, the local radio station, would send announcers on the road to broadcast those state championship contests. I remember being in the stands at Memorial Stadium in Harrisonburg when Turner Ashby beat Glenvar of Salem for the state crown in 1974—with future big leaguer Knicely hitting a bases-loaded double to win the game in the last of the seventh inning.

Growing up on a farm a few miles outside of Dayton, I recognized the truck that Heatwole drove from his home in Bridgewater to check in on his father at the family homestead between Harrisonburg and Dayton.

Often, I would be out playing some form of baseball with my two younger brothers when Heatwole drove by—and wondered if that would gain me favor by the time I got to high school.

Another time, a Mennonite man, unannounced, stopped by our farm and gave my brothers and me a wooden bat he had made at a nearby shop. He didn't charge us a cent and just said he had seen us out playing ball all of the time, so he figured it would be a challenge to make a bat of his own and wanted it put to good use.

My brothers, Daryl and Dennis, and I were part of the Little League baseball program in Bridgewater—one that was a pipeline for the Turner Ashby program and would produce two Major Leaguers (Knicely and Brian Bocock), a slew of minor leaguers, and many Division I college standouts.

I was fortunate to make the all-star team in my last Little League season, but we lost by a run to nearby Grottoes in the first game of the tournament—in no small part to an error I made in left field that allowed at least one run to score. Senior League would follow and then four years as part of the program at Turner Ashby.

I was also fortunate to play one summer on Harrisonburg American Legion Post 27 for Heatwole and another season for Jack Hale, the former coach at Harrisonburg High.

This was before the days of travel baseball, so the notion of being teammates in the summer with players from archrival and nearby Harrisonburg took some getting used to!

Kids probably don't understand that today; but I have good memories of those Legion summers and the chance to play with former HHS standouts such as Doug Ehlers, Tony Carter, and

Randy Hill. We advanced to the state tournament both years in Colonial Heights.

About a decade later, in 1992, the all-star team at Bridgewater Little League would come within three outs of a regional title and trip to Williamsport, Pennsylvania, for the Little League World Series.

Nancy Jones, then a columnist for the Daily News-Record newspaper in Harrisonburg, wrote a column in 1992 about the history of the Bridgewater program.

In her column, Jones, one of my English teachers in high school, noted the Bridgewater program began in 1954 after Carl "Pidge" Rhodes recognized a void for young boys after he returned from a Little League regional tourney in Front Royal.

"Outside of getting married, starting this Little League is one of the highlights of my life," Jones quoted him as saying.

Carl Stotz, who in Williamsport began what became Little League Baseball, visited the Bridgewater program in the spring of 1991 and died the following year, Jones wrote.

Jones, a writer, historian, and teacher, died in 2017, and her personal writing collection is housed at nearby JMU. She saw firsthand the grip that baseball had on Turner Ashby – and the central Shenandoah Valley.

I may not be the only youngster who grew up in a die-hard baseball community in the state of Virginia. But I certainly consider myself lucky to have played for Heatwole at Turner Ashby— perhaps the best baseball program ever in Virginia.

Stats of Virginia Players

Virginia natives, all-time Major League leaders

Note: as of July 14, 2022; source https://www.baseball-reference.com

HOME RUNS

Player	Birthplace	Total
Willie Horton	Arno	325
Justin Upton	Norfolk	325
David Wright	Norfolk	242
Todd Hundley	Martinsville	202
Michael Cuddyer	Norfolk	197

STOLEN BASES

Player	Birthplace	Total
Tony Womack	Danville	363
B.J. Upton	Norfolk	300
Steve Brodie	Warrenton	289
Billy Nash	Richmond	269
Al Bumbry	Fredericksburg	254

ALL-TIME HIT LEADERS

Player	Birthplace	Total
Paul Hines	(place unknown)	2133
Willie Horton	Arno	1993
David Wright	Norfolk	1777
Justin Upton	Norfolk	1754
Steve Brodie	Warrenton	1728

ALL-TIME WIN LEADERS

Pitcher	Birthplace	Total
Eppa Rixey	Culpeper	266
Justin Verlander	Manakin-Sabot	244
Deacon Phillippe	Rural Retreat	189

SAVES

Pitcher	Birthplace	Total
Billy Wagner	Marion	422
Mike Williams	Radford	144
Al Holland	Roanoke	78

Major League Managers born in Virginia

Walter Cannady, Norfolk
Bob Clarke, Richmond
Mike Cubbage, Charlottesville
Mack Eggleston, Roanoke
Buster Haywood, Portsmouth
Pete Hill, Culpeper
Jim Lemon, Covington
Billy Nash, Richmond
Branch Russell, South Boston
Pat Sullivan, Lewisburg
Jud Wilson, Remington

Note: Lewisburg was in Virginia when Sullivan was born there in 1854; Hill and Wilson, from the Negro Leagues, are in the Baseball Hall of Fame.

Virginia state high school baseball champions, 2022

Class 1 - Rappahannock defeated Rappahannock County 1-0
Class 2 - Appomattox defeated John Battle 4-2
Class 3 - Liberty Christian defeated Abingdon 6-5
Class 4 - Hanover defeated James Wood 11-0
Class 5 - Douglas Freeman defeated Glen Allen 4-0
Class 6 - Freedom South Riding defeated Herndon 2-1

Virginia Minor League Affiliates, 2022, And Parent Club

Triple-A Norfolk, Orioles
Double-A Richmond, Giants
Single-A Fredericksburg, Nationals
Single-A Salem, Red Sox
Single-A Lynchburg, Guardians

A complete roster of all players from the State of Virginia can be found at https://www.baseball-reference.com/bio/VA_born.shtml

Valley Baseball League

Valley Baseball League final standings for 2022

North
Woodstock	27-15
Strasburg	22-20
Purcellville	19-21
New Market	19-22
Front Royal	16-26
Winchester	14-27

South
Charlottesville	26-16
Waynesboro	26-16
Harrisonburg	25-17
Covington	19-23
Staunton	16-26

Note: Charlottesville beat Woodstock in the championship series in 2022.

Rockingham County Baseball

Rockingham County Baseball League, Final Standings 2022

Stuarts Draft Diamondbacks	15-9
Clover Hill Bucks	13-11
New Market Shockers	12-12
Bridgewater Reds	12-12
Grottoes Cardinals	11-13
Montezuma Braves	11-13
Broadway Bruins	10-14

Note: Bridgewater beat Stuarts Draft 4-3 in the best of seven title series, with Reds pitcher Chris Huffman throwing a shutout in a 2-0 win in the deciding game August 22. Huffman pitched at Fort Defiance High, at JMU and reached the Triple-A level with San Diego. Another key pitcher for the Reds was workhorse Derek Shifflett, another JMU product

Photo Credits

Photos used with the following permissions:

Page 2 – courtesy of the University of Richmond

Page 6 – courtesy of JMU

Page 12 – courtesy of Richmond Flying Squirrels

Page 14 – courtesy of Richmond Athletics

Page 20 – courtesy of Richmond Free Press

Page 23 - courtesy of Virginia Tech Athletics

Page 30 – courtesy of South Carolina Athletics

Page 31 – courtesy of Wikimedia Commons

Page 34 – courtesy of JMU

Page 39 – courtesy of Norfolk Tides

Page 46 – courtesy of JMU

Page 50 – By David Driver

Page 54 – courtesy of Chris Marinak

Page 57 – courtesy of Gallaudet Athletics

Page 65 – courtesy of Minnesota Twins

Page 68 – courtesy of Southern Maryland Blue Crabs

Page 74 – courtesy of Virginia Athletics

Page 85 – courtesy Virginia Athletics

Page 89 – courtesy of Longwood Athletics

Page 94 – courtesy of David Schaurer

Page 101 – courtesy of Bowie Baysox

Page 105 – courtesy of Lynchburg Hillcats

Page 107 – courtesy of the city of Culpeper

Page 121 – courtesy of Shenandoah University

Page 123 – courtesy of Willie Horton

Page 127 – courtesy of Ferrum

Page 131 – courtesy of Emory & Henry

Page 136 – courtesy of Virginia Tech

Page 134 – courtesy of Bowie Baysox

Page 143 – courtesy of Ian Ostlund

Page 145 – courtesy of Salem Red Sox

Page 148 – courtesy of Salem Red Sox

Page 154 – courtesy of Billy Sample

Page 156 – courtesy of JMU

Page 160 – courtesy of VMI athletics

Page 167 – courtesy of the Pittsburgh Pirates

Page 169 – courtesy of the Durham Bulls

Page 173 – courtesy of EMU

Page 178 – courtesy of Barbara Chittum Hutchens

Page 181 – courtesy of Doug Harris

Page 183 – courtesy of Tampa Bay Rays

Page 188 – courtesy of Steve Nagy/JMU

Page 191 – courtesy of the Minnesota Twins

Page 196 – courtesy of Joy R. Absalon

Page 203 – courtesy of Harrisonburg Turks

Page 209 – photo by David Driver

Page 212 – courtesy of Curt Dudley

Page 217 – courtesy of Samantha Gjormand

Page 222 – courtesy of Daryl Irvine

Page 231 – baseballreference.com

Page 233 – courtesy of New Market Shockers/Nolan Potts

Page 248 – courtesy of EMU

Page 251 – courtesy of findagrave.com

Page 259 – courtesy of Dana Allison

Page 266 – baseballreference.com

Page 268 – Photo by David Driver

Page 274 – baseballreference.com

Page 277 – baseballreference.com

Page 283 – courtesy of George Mason Athletics

Page 287 – courtesy of Samantha Gjormand/College of Charleston

Page 289 - JMU

Page 292 – courtesy of Virginia athletics

Page 298 – courtesy of Brian McNichol

Page 300 – courtesy of Kansas City Royals/Jin Wong

Page 302 – courtesy of the Baltimore Orioles

Page 304 – courtesy of Fredericksburg Nationals

Page 306 – courtesy of GWU

Page 312 – courtesy of Lynchburg College/Travis Beazley

Page 316 – courtesy of ODU athletics

Page 325 – by David Driver grave of Paul Hines at Mt. Olivet Cemetery in Washington, D.C.

Acknowledgments

There are many people to thank and hopefully, we won't forget anyone.

Russell Nemec did a wonderful job with the front and back cover of this book and Russ Eanes, who did the inside design, was a huge help with his decades of experience in the publishing world.

Among the first people we shared the idea of this project with were John Leonard and Curt Dudley over lunch in Harrisonburg. Leonard has followed and written about the Valley Baseball League for years while Dudley was in his 40th season as the voice of the Harrisonburg Turks in 2022 and is a long-time presence in Athletics Communication at JMU. They were both very helpful in the weeks that followed with tracking down information and photos.

Thanks as well to those from the five teams from Virginia that were minor-league affiliates of Major League teams in 2022. That includes John Stanley, the Director of Communications with Triple-A Norfolk; Trey Wilson, the long-time radio voice of Double-A Richmond; General Manager Allen Lawrence and Stephen Langdon with Single-A Salem; radio voices and media relations folks Joey Zanaboni and Eric Bach of Single-A Fredericksburg; and Jason Prill, the radio broadcaster and Media Relations Assistant with Single-A Lynchburg.

Out of state folks in the minors who were very helpful include radio guys Adam Pohl, who grew up in Arlington, and Matt Sabados of the Double-A Bowie Baysox in Maryland.

Kyle Brostowitz and Melissa Strozza, veterans in Communications with the Washington Nationals, were very helpful as was Todd Olszewski, a long-time photographer with the Baltimore Orioles; and Steve Grande, the Senior Manager in Communications with the Houston Astros.

A huge thank you to Sports Information/Athletic Department personnel from nearly every college and university in the state.

A special thanks to Michael Skovan and Brian Cox of Virginia Tech for their help during the historic Blacksburg Super Regional in June of 2022. Being able to include that in our book, with a photo on the back cover, was vital.

Thanks as well to Christian Howe at JMU; Steve Kolbe at George Mason; Scott Fitzgerald at Virginia; Alex Kerstetter at Longwood; Bridgette Robles and Bob Black at the University of Richmond; Matt Wurzburger at ODU; John Moyer at William & Mary; Andy Lohman at VCU; Scott Musa at Shenandoah; Clint Often at Mary Washington; Mark Robertson at Lynchburg; Will Wallace at Washington and Lee; Justin McIlwee at EMU; Jacob Brown, a former pitcher at Gloucester High and EMU who is now the Director of Athletic Communications at Marymount University in Arlington; and Jimmy McCumber, formerly of Bridgewater and now at Marymount.

Out-of-state help was also provided by Sam Atkinson of Gallaudet University; Matt Gilpin at the University of Maryland; Julian Coltre at George Washington; and Joe Browning at North Carolina Wilmington; and Nairem Moran of St. Mary's College of Maryland.

The job of Sports Information Director/Assistant has become incredibly challenging in the past few years and we appreciate those who had more work thrown their way during our book project.

Dave Facinoli, the guru of sportswriters in Northern Virginia, was very helpful on the current and past history on high school baseball in that region.

Thanks as well to Greg Madia, my (David) former colleague at the Daily News-Record in Harrisonburg, who is now at The Daily

Progress in Charlottesville and does a great job covering University of Virginia athletics, including baseball

Phil Kushin, a veteran copy editor, provided moral and word-smith support along the way. And thanks to former Liberty University pitcher David Schauer for his photo and memories of Al Worthington, his former coach with the Flames in Lynchburg.

Thanks as well to Randy Atkins, the former commissioner of the Rockingham County Baseball League, and to the skippers in the league such as Tim Nicely (Grottoes), Kevin Chandler (Clover Hill), and Nolan Potts, with New Market.

Bruce Alger, the face of the New Market Rebels and part of the Valley Baseball League for decades, was a huge help over the years. Sadly, he passed away after the 2021 season. Thanks as well to Bob Wease, the long-time skipper/general manager of the Harrisonburg Turks. Appreciation as well to my (David) former EMU coach, Roland Landis, who taught us more about life than baseball.

Thank you to those players, coaches, scouts, managers, and administrators who are featured in these pages. Many of them were very helpful in providing photos for the project as well as making sure we had our information correct. Any mistakes rest solely with us.

Last but not least, a huge thanks to our wives – who are used to being Baseball Widows – for putting up with yet another reason for us to head to a game, be it high school, college, the minors or majors.

About the Authors

David Driver was born in Harrisonburg, Virginia and played baseball at Turner Ashby High, Harrisonburg American Legion Post 27, one year at Eastern Mennonite University and for Clover Hill in the Rockingham County Baseball League. He graduated from EMU in 1985 with a degree in English and a minor in Journalism. From 2013 to 2019 he covered the Washington Nationals for several publications and he currently contributes to Federal Baseball for coverage of the Nationals. A former sports editor of papers in Arlington and Harrisonburg, as well as Laurel and Baltimore in Maryland, he now works part-time in Communications for MVP International, a leader in youth sports overseas travel that was founded in Northern Virginia. He can be reached at www.dayton-david.com and @DaytonVaDriver.

Lacy Lusk has been the Washington Nationals correspondent for Baseball America since the franchise moved to D.C. before the 2005 season. He has covered baseball in Virginia for more than 30 years, dating to his time at the University of Virginia as the baseball beat writer and sports editor of the Cavalier Daily. He's a 1988 graduate of Monacan High School in Chesterfield County, Va., and a 1992 UVa graduate. The first professional team he covered was the 1993 Martinsville (Va.) Phillies, whose Opening Day starter was future UVa baseball coach Brian O'Connor and whose third baseman was now-Hall of Fame candidate Scott Rolen. He was the minor league editor and a reporter at Baseball America from 1997 to 2001 and also has written about baseball for the Washington Post, Washington Times, Charlottesville Daily Progress, Martinsville Bulletin, and Culpeper Star-Exponent.

Authors David Driver (left) and Lacy Lusk at a University of Virginia baseball game in Charlottesville early in the 2022 season.

Made in the USA
Las Vegas, NV
25 February 2023

68161200R00203